MW01026473

THIRTYSOMETHING
Stories

THIRTYSOMETHING

Stories

by the writers of
*Thirty*something

POCKET BOOKS

New York   London   Toronto   Sydney   Tokyo   Singapore

An *Original* Publication of POCKET BOOKS

POCKET BOOKS, a division of Simon & Schuster
1230 Avenue of the Americas, New York, NY 10020

Copyright © 1991 by MGM/UA Television Production Group, a division of
MGM-Pathe Communications Co. All Rights Reserved.

First two photos for "Michael Writes a Story" copyright © Bonnie Colodzin/ABC/TV
First photo for "Mr. Right" copyright © Craig Sjodin
Second photo for "Mr. Right" copyright © Frank Carroll
First and last photos for "Strangers" copyright © Bob Coburn
Last photo for "I'm Nobody! Who Are You?" copyright © Robert Nese
All other photos: copyright © MGM/UA Television Production Group, a division of
     MGM-Pathe Communications Co.

Grateful acknowledgment is made for permission to reprint an excerpt from "All I Want" by Joni Mitchell.
Copyright © 1971, 1975. JONI MITCHELL PUBLISHING CORP.
All Rights Reserved. Used by Permission.

All rights reserved, including the right to reproduce
this book or portions thereof in any form whatsoever.
For information address Pocket Books, 1230 Avenue of
the Americas, New York, NY 10020

Library of Congress Cataloging-in-Publication Data
Thirtysomething stories / by the writers of Thirtysomething.
     p.   cm.
   ISBN 0-671-73577-2
   1. Thirtysomething (Television program) 2. Television plays,
American. I. Thirtysomething (Television program) II. Title:
Thirtysomething stories.
PN1992.77.A1T47   1991
791.45'72—dc20   90-24596
                                                   CIP

First Pocket Books trade paperback printing March 1991

10   9   8   7   6   5   4   3   2   1

POCKET and colophon are registered trademarks of
Simon & Schuster.

Printed in the U.S.A.

FOR
*Tim Busfield, David Clennon,
Polly Draper, Mel Harris, Peter
Horton, Patricia Kalember, Melanie
Mayron, Ken Olin, Corey Parker,
and Patty Wettig*

ACKNOWLEDGMENTS

The authors of this book thank:

Athos Demetriou, for guidance and encouragement; Wendy Weil, for graciously taking up the agent's baton; Leslie Wells, our editor at Pocket Books, for her belief that our scripts deserved a post-electronic life; Jeanne Newman, for guiding us through the legal forest; The Warner Brothers photo lab; our cinematographers—Dan Lerner, Robert Primes, Jerry Hartleben, Ernest Holzman, and Kenneth Zunder—for making us look good week after week; our film editors—Steve Rosenblum, Victor duBois, Joanna Cappuccilli, Marty Nicholson, Kevin Casey, Susanne Malles—for their tireless separation of wheat from chaff; and Phil Gorth, of Pacific Video and Pacific Film Laboratory, for locating, with an archeologist's zeal, the pieces of film that yielded the pictures for this book.

Special thanks to:

Mary Helfrich, who has managed our script department (and sometimes our lives) with wit, warmth, and generosity of spirit . . .

David Gerber, Lynn Loring, and Mark Pedowitz, for their gift of MGM/UA's share of this book's advance to the American Foundation for AIDS Research . . .

And, finally, Scott Winant and Ellen Pressman—for everything.

CONTENTS

THIRTYSOMETHING
Stories

THIRTYSOMETHING

BY

MARSHALL HERSKOVITZ

AND

EDWARD ZWICK

The only thing less fun than writing is writing about writing, so after four years we're not about to write one more word than we have to about *thirtysomething*. Instead, here's what we wrote back then, when we had to write *something*, if only to convince others we knew what we were doing. It was called "Something about Thirtysomething," and it went like this . . .

"This is a show about life on earth as we know it. At least a small slice of it. It's about a group of people, all of a certain age, who know enough about life to be totally confused by it. It's about growing up—no matter how old you are.

"Which means owning up to certain realities. Swallowing a pill or two. Not necessarily the compromise of principles, but rather the recognition that many of our notions of the future were idealizations and can't be lived in the world.

"It's what we like to call . . . the Dialectic. That, in modern life, everything seems in opposition to itself. You want to have a baby but you want to have a job. You want to be free but you want to settle down. You don't want a lot of responsibilities, but you want to make a living. And it cuts deeper than the questions of life-style: you want to be honest but you don't want to be hurtful; you want to be accommodating but you want what you want; you want to be grateful but you're also in pain.

"And it's a show about creating your own family. All these people live apart from where they grew up, and so they're trying to fashion a new sense of home—one made up of friends, where holidays, job triumphs, birthdays, illnesses, and gossip all take on a kind of bittersweet significance. Though each episode will be a complete story, it's the deeper currents among these friends that will be revealed over time.

"Which is to say we're interested in the stuff of real life. Small moments examined closely, showing the way people really talk, and dream, and even fantasize. Those seemingly random events that somehow add up to deep emotion. The kind of show that people might look at and say, 'That's my life, I said that last night.'

"And since everyone knows this is the first generation ever to have children, or buy houses, or try to have careers, it naturally assumes that everyone else will be interested in its noble endeavors. The truth is we know there's nothing inherently noble or even particularly interesting about people in their thirties. It just happens to be the territory we know best. And it's just the fact that we *aren't* the first to attempt any of the things we're stumbling through that leads us to hope that twentysomethings and fiftysomethings will identify with it as well. It's about people. Not ages . . ."

Okay. So who the hell were these people going to be, anyway? Four years ago we had some ideas on that, as well . . .

Michael Steadman

You voted for him for eleventh-grade class president. He lost. He didn't realize he was good-looking until he was twenty-seven, and by then it was too late to go back to high school and run again. He always wanted to be a writer but somehow ended up in advertising. Now, along with his friend Elliot, he has started his own agency, much to their mutual terror. He wants to be a good husband and a good father and a good friend, and sometimes the weight of these good intentions makes him depressed. Lately he finds his responsibilities are outweighing his dreams. Still, he's made all those choices happily and without regret. So go figure. He should stop thinking so much and relax and enjoy it.

Hope Murdoch Steadman

Hope is married to Michael. And he to her. And they to Jane, their nine-month-old daughter. Hope used to be what they called an overachiever; she went to Princeton and had what was starting to be a successful career in publishing. But now that her career has switched—temporarily at least—to mothering Jane, nothing seems so sure. She loves the time she spends with the baby, so why is she embarrassed to admit it to her friends? In truth, she loves most things about her life right now—except not sleeping—so what does she do about all the ambition that used to fuel her life . . . ? Right about now, her fondest dream is a substantive conversation with anyone over seventeen inches high.

Elliot Weston

Elliot is Michael's partner. They complement each other perfectly: Michael doesn't want to grow up, whereas Elliot doesn't want to grow up. They used to work, unhappily, at the same high-powered ad agency, where they discovered they had a great deal in common. Both were subject to existential anxiety attacks which could only be alleviated by long afternoons hiding out in the darkroom drinking beer and listening to the Phillies games. Elliot's always been the funny one, the life of the party, but lately finds fewer parties and less things funny. His marriage is under strain, and he's overwhelmed at times by feelings he never had to deal with before.

Nancy Krieger Weston

Nancy, too, is overwhelmed with unbidden feelings. There are two children now, and all the hard work that entails, and a history of fighting and trying and loving and withholding that goes back to when she and Elliot were more or less babies themselves—just out of Rhode Island School of Design, with long hair and Indian print skirts and the naïve belief that everything would be simple and easy for the rest of their lives. She was an artist then, and a good one, who slowly lost confidence in her ability, and then the kids came along and there just wasn't time to worry about it. Until recently, when Brittany started nursery school—and Nancy looked at her life, and her marriage, and asked, "Where am I?"

Gary Shepherd

Michael's oldest friend and best man at his wedding; he's that professor who was so important to you in your sophomore year that you switched majors from computer science to classics. A passionate teacher whose love is the epic—*Beowulf, The Iliad*—he'd be more comfortable on the deck of a Viking longship than in the rented duplex his assistant professor's salary affords. The thing about Gary is, well . . . women. He's very principled: never sleeps with undergraduates—more than three times a year, and, really, never during finals. He wants to be one of his classical heroes—strong, upright, disciplined—but finds that less mature aspects of his character are, unfortunately, more attractive to women. Thus giving him little inducement to ever grow up.

Melissa Steadman

Melissa is Michael's cousin. She's trying to make a go of it as a commercial photographer, but mostly finds herself doing weddings, bar mitzvahs, and boudoir photography. She's been groping her way through singlehood, slowly lowering her expectations; right now she'd be willing to settle for nothing more than a man, a baby, the perfect home, a brilliant career, and eternal youth. Her life is a roller coaster of emotions, and she feels compelled to take all her friends along for the ride.

Ellyn Warren

Driven, critical, vulnerable, she's always finding herself apologizing for things she never said, but thought, and everyone knew she was thinking anyway. Her career keeps advancing, and so does her ambivalence. Nothing's ever simple with her. She and Hope have been best friends since the age of eight. Now, after all these years, they are having a hard time reconciling the different paths their lives are taking. They'll probably work it out, though. After all, they didn't speak for two years after Hope went to the prom with Joey Jacobs, whom Ellyn always loved but never had the guts to speak to.

So that's who they were. Michael and Elliot hadn't lost their business so Miles Drentell didn't need to exist. Elliot and Nancy hadn't split up, so they didn't need to get back together. And so on. But people change, so *they've* changed. These days Hope is crusading, Gary's a father, and Nancy's sick. Next week is next week.

And whatever next week's stories are, they'll likely be written by those whose work is collected in this book. They are, at once, our employees, our peers, our scourges, and our wives, not necessarily in that order. After all this time, we've come to feel like hosts at a party that refuses to end. As it's worn on, secrets have been spilled, and confidences shared, and we all have to be at work in the morning. But there's still some wine left, and a little cold pizza, and you can sleep on the couch if you want to . . .

MARSHALL HERSKOVITZ
and EDWARD ZWICK

ACT ONE

A BLACK SCREEN (PRESENT)

We hear two people giggling, trying to be quiet.

WOMAN *(V.O.):* There's not enough time—

MAN *(V.O.):* Shhh, there is time—

WOMAN *(V.O.):* Wait—I heard her—

MAN *(V.O.):* You did not hear her.

WOMAN *(V.O.):* Shhh!

Silence. They're listening. Then:

WOMAN *(V.O.):* You're right, I didn't hear her . . .

Sound of a zipper. He starts to laugh appreciatively.

A RESTAURANT (PAST)

where we now can see these two people—though what we're seeing took place several years ago. He's Michael Steadman, twenty-nine here, Jewish, intense, funny. She's Hope Murdoch, twenty-eight, Episcopalian, intense, funny. This is their first date, intense, funny.

MICHAEL: . . . ask what the other person does, that takes three minutes.

HOPE: Then who do we both know and where do you live, that's another four.

MICHAEL: Which exhausts all possible human conversation and the salad hasn't even come yet . . . Which means what? Two hours later, take her home, should I kiss her, maybe I should've already kissed her—

HOPE: Will he kiss me am I too fat?

MICHAEL: An hour later—(*stops*) A week later, a month later I don't know, *sometime* later they, they . . .

HOPE: Do the terrible deed.

MICHAEL (*nods*): Then they move in, she wants to get married, he's afraid to commit, they get married.

HOPE: A year later they're having affairs.

MICHAEL: And their friends, who set them up in the first place—

HOPE: Tell them they knew it would never work.

MICHAEL: Which is why I never do this.

HOPE: Me neither . . .

They eye each other—embarrassed, interested, skeptical.

MICHAEL: So . . . how do you know Ellyn?

BLACK SCREEN (PRESENT)

The two people are moving to the bed.

MICHAEL (*V.O.*) (*bumps himself*): Oowwwww. I'm turning on the light.

HOPE (*V.O.*): No—you'll wake her.

MICHAEL (*V.O.*): Then close the door—

HOPE (*V.O.*): Then how would we hear her? (*bumps herself*) Oowwwww.

He starts to laugh.

A NEIGHBORHOOD BAR (PAST)

Hope and Ellyn sip drinks as various men cruise them.

HOPE: Ellyn, I don't know. He's really funny, he makes me laugh—

ELLYN: That's worth *something* . . .

HOPE: And it's true, he is this basically very nice person.

ELLYN: But . . .

HOPE: How did we get so old and set in our ways? Last night the argument was about where you sit in a movie theater. He says right-brained people sit on the left, so now I'm not creative . . . I haven't said anything to *him* about his polyester shirts. Am I allowed to have a relationship with somebody who wears polyester shirts?

ELLYN: They're not even blends? Can we get down to the real issue here?

HOPE: I don't know, sex is . . . actually sex is pretty not too bad . . .

ELLYN: So he's really funny, he's really nice, he's great in bed, and he wears polyester shirts. You're right. Forget it.

BLACK SCREEN (PRESENT)

Things are continuing.

MICHAEL *(V.O.):* What's that?

HOPE *(V.O.):* It's my foot, what did you think it was?

MICHAEL *(V.O.):* I thought it was an animal. Like a squirrel or a turtle or something.

HOPE *(V.O.):* You are so seriously deranged. Oowwwww. What are you doing?

MICHAEL *(V.O.):* It seems weird that I can't feel anything when I touch it. I've been around this foot so long it feels like it should be mine.

HOPE *(V.O.) (after a pause):* I can feel it . . .

OUTSIDE A COUNTRY CHAPEL (PAST)

Michael is urgently prodding Gary. Both wear dark suits.

MICHAEL: You have to go through with it, everybody's in there waiting for you!

GARY: You don't realize what a step this is for me. I've never even *attended* a wedding before.

MICHAEL: If you wimp out now, you'll regret it for the rest of your life.

GARY: But maybe this is wrong, maybe we're all making a terrible mistake. It's not too late to stop it!

Michael pulls him up the steps.

MICHAEL: Now we're going in there and taking up our positions just like we did in rehearsal. I'll be right there next to you— And when the rabbi and the minister ask you—

He opens the door revealing a chapel full of people, waiting. And Hope, resplendent in a wedding dress.

MICHAEL: —all you do is hand me the ring. You can do it, Gar, that's why you're my best man.

Michael touches Hope's arm in passing and starts down the aisle.

BLACK SCREEN (PRESENT)

Things have gotten a little more serious here in the dark. The sound of kissing.

HOPE *(V.O.):* . . . Ohhh. I really miss you. Don't you kind of like this in the dark? *(silence)* Mike? Are you okay?

MICHAEL *(V.O.):* I love you.

A long silence.

HOPE *(V.O.):* We're so lucky.

A BABY STORE (PAST)

A demented-looking salesman is in the middle of his spiel.

SALESMAN: You wanna talk construction? How about aircraft aluminum, how about—feel the rubber in these tires—

The object of his pitch: a baby stroller, Aprica's newest model. We wouldn't be surprised to find a twelve-cylinder engine under the canopy. Michael stares in disbelief.

MICHAEL: **Three hundred and sixty-four dollars . . . for a stroller?** *(looks around)* **Hope?**

An extremely pregnant Hope, bent double over the high chairs, is doing Lamaze breathing.

HOPE: **Hee-hee-hee-hee—**

BLACK SCREEN (PRESENT)

The sound of heavy breathing, not unlike that of the cut before. Things here are nearing their proper conclusion.

HOPE *(V.O.):* **I really . . . like . . . this—**

MICHAEL *(V.O.):* **Honey, oh God—**

HOPE *(V.O.):* **Wait.** *(he doesn't)* **Waitwaitwait—STOP.**

MICHAEL *(V.O.):* **Why are you stopping?** *(silence, then:)* **Oh, no . . .**

Now we hear it. In another room, a baby is starting to cry.

MICHAEL *(V.O.):* **It's not bad yet—she'll go back to sleep.**

The crying turns into a wail. We hear a dual sigh. A light goes on and we see them now: Michael and Hope, in the present tense. His eyes are closed in frustration. She starts to get up.

HOPE *(kisses his head):* **How silly we be.**

A NICE KITCHEN

It was nice, but now it's a total wreck. And past the undone dishes and yesterday's food and spilled dog kibble and unraveled paper towels—we see the reason for the wreck: Jane Steadman, aged six months . . .

She's sitting in her high chair, watching what could be a Ping-Pong game, but what is in actuality her parents simply trying to get through the morning. Hope is attempting to feed her while talking on the phone; Michael is making his breakfast.

HOPE *(into the phone)*: He did not say that . . . Melissa!

MICHAEL: I thought we had Raisin Bran . . .

HOPE *(into the phone)*: You call him right back—*(to Michael)* Honey, if you're looking for Raisin Bran I'm afraid I didn't get to the store. *(to the baby)* Julesetta, please eat this—

MICHAEL *(real grief, to the baby)*: No Raisin Bran, Ninsky, what am I going to do?

HOPE *(into the phone)*: Are you kidding, I can't eat *any* cereal . . . Because I'm so fat.

MICHAEL: You're not fat.

HOPE *(into the phone)*: I keep promising Michael I'll go to the gym, but it's so hard.

MICHAEL: Will you stop it with the gym—*(looking in refrigerator)* I thought we had milk . . .

HOPE: Mayjy, spitting out the food helps no one, really, trust me on that point. *(into the phone)* He says he doesn't but he does.

MICHAEL: I don't think you're fat!

HOPE: But you think I could lose some weight?

MICHAEL *(looking in the cabinet)*: I refuse to get in trouble for things that I'm not thinking but may or may not have worried that I might think at some earlier time and felt guilty about and therefore might show on my face even though I DON'T THINK YOU'RE FAT.

HOPE *(into the phone)*: He thinks I'm fat.

Michael has taken a large can of formula, opened it, and is now pouring it into a bowl of Raisin Bran.

MICHAEL: Do I get like small if I drink this?

A SMALL AD AGENCY

inhabiting a downtown loft-type space. Employees wander from their half-height cubicles to the doorway of an office where a phone conversation is taking place.

MICHAEL *(V.O.):* All right, you know what, just forget it . . . No, just forget it . . . Because it's sleazy, Mr. Teller, hasn't that occurred to you . . . ?

IN MICHAEL'S OFFICE

Michael is pacing while he talks. His partner, Elliot, is sitting on the couch, making agonized faces. The employees in the doorway make no attempt to conceal their avid interest.

MICHAEL: No, no, no, their campaign isn't sleazy, I love their campaign, I wish I had done their campaign, but I didn't do their campaign, therefore if I steal their campaign it's *sleazy*—*(listens again)* It doesn't matter what their sales were afterwards, am I speaking English here? Plagiarism, theft, taking things that aren't yours . . . ?

Elliot, meanwhile, pulls a pillow over his head and begins to hum in order not to hear what is about to transpire.

MICHAEL: Well, you know what? That's right. And one of the privileges of being "a bunch of amateurs," is we still have the illusion of doing our own work and having a little integrity which I now see any further association with your business—or in fact you personally—would make me sick to my stomach and throw up!

Michael hangs up and notices his gaping co-workers.

MICHAEL: What? We're not allowed to have principles around here? There're other accounts out there . . . C'mon, let's get back to work. Jeannine, shut the door on your way out . . .

He waits until they have gone, then takes the phone cord, wraps it around his neck, and falls across his desk.

MICHAEL: Aaaahhhggghhh . . .

Elliot picks up the phone dangling from Michael's neck.

ELLIOT: Mr. Teller? Hi, Mike's partner, Elliot. Uh, Mike's had an unfortunate accident and he's dead, and I just wanted to tell you how much I like the idea of stealing a Clio Award–winning campaign and especially how much I like the idea of two hundred thousand dollars because without that two hundred thousand dollars our company is going out of business and my partner forgot that and that's why he's dead.

MICHAEL: Why didn't you stop me . . . ? This is your fault. I'm going to lose my house, my wife is going to leave me, my kid will be expelled from day care.

ELLIOT: *Your* kid?

MICHAEL: I can't take this, I never respond well to pressure, that's why we left Bernstein-Fox in the first place.

ELLIOT: I thought it was because you don't respond well to authority.

MICHAEL: That too. *(jumps up suddenly)* I CAN'T TAKE THIS! I'M TOO YOUNG TO RUN A BUSINESS. YOU HAVE TO BE GROWN UP TO RUN A BUSINESS. *(lies back down)* I got two hours and forty-five minutes of sleep last night.

ELLIOT *(looks at him)*: You'll get used to it.

MICHAEL: Do you get used to, like, having no REM periods, like North Korean brainwashing camps where they wake you up as soon as you start to dream?

ELLIOT: She doesn't sleep through the night yet?

MICHAEL: I go in there sometimes, literally I am going to strangle her, and there she is, "Hi, Daddy, look at this smile I have for you! Aren't I cute? Don't you feel guilty for thinking those bad thoughts about me?"

ELLIOT: Wait'll it's two kids.

MICHAEL: Did I just make the dumbest mistake of our lives . . . ?

ELLIOT: Yes.

MICHAEL: What would you have done?

ELLIOT *(thinks)*: The same thing.

A DEPARTMENT STORE

Gumby placemats or Snoopy placemats: that is Hope's question as she unconsciously rocks the baby on her hip, oblivious to the shoppers around her.

HOPE: Is he waving at you? Is Gumby nice, is he waving at you, Buber? Look at Snoopy, he's a doggy, do you see the doggy, look at the doggy, honey. Do you want doggy or Gumby, Mommy wants doggy because Gumby is weird, Mommy didn't like things like Gumby when she was little because clay wasn't supposed to move.

She looks up. A salesman is staring at her.

A RESTAURANT

Crowded and loud with people hurrying through lunch. Hope is trying to deposit her paraphernalia while she apologizes to Ellyn.

HOPE: I was right across the street, I don't know what happened, I was early, and then I saw these incredibly cute socks and all of—

ELLYN: Hope. Sit.

Hope is trying. After the diaper bag, the Snugli. Then the bottle out of the diaper bag. Then the baby in the stroller. Now the baby is crying in the stroller.

WAITRESS: Can I get you something to drink?

HOPE: Uh, not right now. Thanks.

People are looking as Hope picks up the baby and tries to simulate a normal person looking at a menu, but can't hold the menu if she's going to give a bottle to the baby, which is the only thing that will make the baby stop crying . . .

ELLYN: I am so tired. We're in the office 'til ten every night now. Look at these bags under my eyes.

Hope stares at her, dumbfounded: *Ellyn* is tired . . . ?

ELLYN: You know how many people are under me, are you ready for weirdness? Twenty-seven.

HOPE: You're kidding me.

ELLYN: All of a sudden Gannon thinks I'm God's gift to city services.

Hope has to stand up to try to get the baby to stop crying.

HOPE: How's your stomach been?

ELLYN *(laughs):* Terrible. Really, it's total stress. Total stress. She's okay? *(Hope nods)* She's so cute. I told him I'm quitting in six months. I cannot take this kind of . . . politics, maneuvering, it's all maneuvering.

HOPE: You should quit.

ELLYN: I am gonna quit.

HOPE: There are so many other things you can do. *(to the baby)* What is it, Nanie? Why don't you take the bottle? *(to Ellyn)* We're trying preweaning, we're trying the concept of maybe, sometimes, drinking from a bottle instead of Mommy.

Ellyn watches Hope struggle with the baby for a moment.

ELLYN: You know what I've been thinking about lately? I'd like to open some kind of store, like a bicycle store, something like that. I imagine that would be a quieter existence.

Hope gives up; she sits down and unbuttons her blouse.

HOPE: I think it would end up being the bicycle rat race.

ELLYN: You think it's me.

HOPE: I think you don't know how to take it easy.

Amazingly, the baby is still crying.

HOPE: I don't know what's going on here. Buber, are you okay? Please stop crying . . . *(to Ellyn)* It's so embarrassing.

Ellen shakes her head, dismisses the notion.

ELLYN: Maybe if I take a year off, and try to make myself more available to life . . .

Hope puts her head down, covers her eyes for a moment.

HOPE: I'm really sorry, I'm gonna have to take her home. I don't know what this is.

ELLYN (*indicates the other patrons*): You know it's none of their business if the baby's crying . . .

HOPE: It's not them! Something's bothering her, I can't just ignore it.

ELLYN: Okay . . . We can try again next week or something. Maybe you can even get a sitter.

HOPE: I'm sorry, really. I've been so looking forward to this, to being a grown-up for one hour . . . I'll call you tomorrow, sweetie. God, I really miss you.

ELLYN: I miss you too. Go, it's okay, I'll take care of this.

Hope, all her equipment gathered, pushes off. Leaving Ellyn, who sits for a moment trying to concentrate on the menu, but is finally too annoyed to continue.

OUTSIDE THE FRONT DOOR

of the house, as Michael staggers up with a load of work and dry cleaning. He nearly trips over the stroller that's been left at the door. As he pushes it to the side, he notices the baby's blanket left in the stroller. He picks it up and smells it. Then goes inside.

INSIDE THE HOUSE

Michael staggers in to find Hope sitting with Gary.

MICHAEL: Uh-oh, look who's here. What are you doing here?

GARY: I'm making a play for your wife, what does it look like I'm doing?

MICHAEL: Making a play for my wife.

GARY: I am making a play for your wife.

MICHAEL: Take my wife.

GARY: I am taking your wife.

Michael kisses Hope.

HOPE: Who's dealing with dinner because I'm not dealing with it.

MICHAEL: Are you staying for dinner?

GARY: Are you?

MICHAEL: Where's Jazooki?

HOPE: Asleep.

MICHAEL: Is she supposed to be asleep now?

HOPE: If you wake her up, I will slit your throat.

MICHAEL: But won't she be awake later?

HOPE: Then we'll deal with it later.

GARY: Listen to you people, this is disgusting, should she be asleep, should she be awake? What is she, a show dog? Lighten up here.

MICHAEL: What do you know?

GARY: I was a baby once.

HOPE: Once?

They laugh, somehow because *she* said it.

GARY: Hey, I'm not wimped out like you people. There's gotta be more to life than getting a baby to sleep. What are you, joined at the hip?

HOPE: Just the breast, Gar.

GARY: Ooh, don't say that word.

Melissa bursts into the living room. Her life, were it read, would satisfy the most ardent admirer of soap operas . . .

MELISSA *(to Hope):* Thank God you're here.

MICHAEL: I feel the same way.

MELISSA: You won't believe this. I have to get something to eat first.

MICHAEL: Hello, Melissa . . .

MELISSA: I hate you, you're a man.

GARY: Have you checked recently, I wouldn't be too sure.

IN THE KITCHEN

Melissa is rummaging through the refrigerator. Hope catches up.

HOPE: What happened?

MELISSA: He went to New York last weekend? His mother was sick? Guess who he slept with?

GARY: His mother.

MELISSA: Darlene MacKinnon.

HOPE *(mouth opening):* You introduced him to Darlene MacKinnon.

MELISSA: I introduced him to Darlene MacKinnon because he desperately needed background on the redevelopment plan for Brooklyn Heights. Can you believe he then slept with her? *(picks up tile sample)* Oh, is this the new tile? It's nice.

HOPE: It doesn't matter who he slept with, he shouldn't have been sleeping with anybody.

MELISSA: It matters to me who he slept with—I was doing him a favor, let him pick up his own floozies.

HOPE: Melissa, he's supposed to be in love with you, it doesn't matter *who* he sleeps with, he shouldn't be doing it at all.

MELISSA: Will you let me be mad at what I want to be mad at. I'm not up to being mad at him for sleeping with anybody. I want to exhaust being mad at him for sleeping with Darlene MacKinnon. The bitch.

HOPE: I thought you liked her.

No answer is necessary. Gary enters the kitchen and puts a playful arm around Melissa's throat.

GARY: Know what you need? A change of venue. Let's go backpacking.

MELISSA: What a great idea . . .

GARY: We'll go backpacking, you'll forget about this sleaze-bag, you'll see the error of your ways . . .

HOPE: I can't believe he's even saying the word backpack.

GARY: It wasn't so bad.

MICHAEL: No worse than the Donner party.

MELISSA: Wait a minute, it wasn't so bad. So Gary and I argued a little.

MICHAEL: You tried to stab him with a tent pole—

MELISSA: He deserved it, he was breaking up with me.

GARY: You were breaking up with me.

MELISSA: But we're past that now, aren't we, adorableness?

GARY: Absolutely, honey-lips.

MELISSA: I think this is a great idea. Look at you guys, you're so tired, you need a break, come on, we'll all go backpacking.

HOPE: I don't think we can take the baby backpacking, can we?

GARY: Who said anything about the baby? Just the four of us, like before, only fun.

MICHAEL: Who would we leave her with?

HOPE: It's not like I can leave her with my parents—even if they weren't two thousand miles away . . .

GARY: So find a baby-sitter. She's not gonna be traumatized.

HOPE: We will.

MICHAEL: Guys, I don't know . . .

GARY: Come on, this is your chance for fun and adventure, rekindle that romance you once knew. Don't be wimps.

HOPE: Stop it, I hate that word. We have responsibilities, that's all. How's that for a word?

Because they really are friends, Gary backs off.

GARY: Re— re— resp— respo—

Everyone laughs.

THE BABY'S ROOM—THAT NIGHT

Hope is leaning over the crib as Michael comes to stand next to her. The baby is a sleeping angel.

HOPE *(almost painful)*: **She's so pretty.**

MICHAEL: **I know.** *(they watch)* **What if she grows up ugly?**

HOPE: **I think about that too.**

MICHAEL: **'Course you're not ugly, that helps.** *(she kisses him)* **What if she grows up poor?**

HOPE: **Will you stop worrying?**

MICHAEL: **You don't know what I did today. The bank is foreclosing in the morning, start packing, I blew off the Teller account.**

HOPE: **Good. Teller's a yutz. I can always go back to work.**

MICHAEL *(stern)*: **You will not go back to work until you want to go back to work. I make plenty of money, when I'm not going bankrupt.**

The baby moans in her sleep. Michael and Hope back out in terror of waking her up.

IN THE BEDROOM

Michael falls on the bed.

MICHAEL: **I am so tired. So completely, overwhelmingly, utterly, totally, unbelievably . . . ucchhh . . .** *(imitating his mother)* **Miiiikke . . . Did you do your homework, Mike? Is your business going bankrupt? Your brother's business isn't going bankrupt.**

HOPE: **Stop.**

She puts her forehead against the wall as she starts to unbutton her blouse.

MICHAEL: **What is it?** *(Hope shrugs)* **Why don't you talk to her about it?**

HOPE: **How can I talk to her about it?**

MICHAEL: **She's been your friend for forty-seven years, just tell** her, "Ellyn, I'm upset that you haven't noticed I've had a child for six months."

Michael watches as the blouse comes off.

HOPE: Ellyn and I don't deal with each other that way.

MICHAEL: Ellyn and you don't deal with each other.

HOPE: Thank you.

MICHAEL: I'm sorry.

She is taking off her pants. He is no longer tired. He puts his hand on her back.

MICHAEL: Let's go backpacking.

HOPE: Michael—

MICHAEL: We're allowed to have a life, aren't we . . . ? There's nothing wrong with spending a few nights away from your kid after six months.

She goes to get a nightgown. He watches as she pulls it over her head.

HOPE: What am I going to do, interview baby-sitters, how do you interview baby-sitters? "Good morning, do you know how to handle a genius, are you totally kind and wonderful and have there been any child molesters in your family for the last twelve generations?"

MICHAEL: Seems to hit the main points . . .

She is getting into bed.

HOPE: Bed. Oh, bed. How could anything feel as good as this?

MICHAEL (*quasi-casual*): So, you're tired . . . ?

She has curled up around her pillow. With her eyes closed:

HOPE: You're not tired.

MICHAEL: No, I'm kind of keyed up, I don't know. Don't worry about it.

She uses her last ounce of energy to move six inches to kiss his shoulder.

HOPE *(mumbling):* I'll think about baby-sitters tomorrow, if I think about baby-sitters today I'll go crazy. After all, tomorrow is another day.

She's asleep. He's not.

ACT TWO

ELLIOT AND NANCY'S HOUSE

Everyone is eating chicken and salad. Hope is trying to have a conversation with Nancy. She's lovely, a year or two older than Hope, and has the beatific look of someone on Thorazine. This is an illusion, however—she's merely exhausted and *wishes* she was on Thorazine. Why . . . ? She has two kids. Brittany, the eighteen-month-old, is in her high chair, food all over her face. Ethan, an intense four-year-old, is next to her, attacking her with Masters of the Universe figures. Janey sits in a Sassy Seat, observing the tumult.

NANCY: I know. I enrolled Ethan in nursery school when he was one and they laughed at—(*grabs his hand*) Ethan . . . Ethan . . . Not so rough around your sister.

HOPE: You're kidding me.

NANCY: If you're talking about preschool, you should have done it *in utero*. (*grabs him again*) Ethan, are we going to have to have another talk about this . . . ?

HOPE: What is this epidemic of kids lately . . . ? And then I think, what are we getting them into, anyway? Don't you just wonder what they're going to face, how the world's going to be totally different, are they going to hate us?

MICHAEL: That covers third-quarter overhead, I don't know what we do then . . .

ELLIOT: Go back to Teller and beg his forgiveness . . .

MICHAEL: Not . . . in . . . a . . . million years. I'd get on my knees at a bank first.

ELLIOT: I know a guy at Penn Savings, like this total freak in high school, I have pictures of him dancing naked at Woodstock, we could blackmail him.

MICHAEL: I was supposed to go to Woodstock but I got tonsillitis and my girlfriend decided to go anyway because we were so free and of course she met this other guy and eventually married him, but they're divorced now so I feel better.

Ethan knocks Brittany's milk cup out of her hands. It goes flying onto the dinner table, spewing milk in several directions, flooding Hope's plate. Nancy doesn't miss a beat, just starts cleaning it up.

NANCY: Did he spill your milk, honey? Mommy'll get you more. (*to Elliot*) Honey, can you take him for a while?

ELLIOT: Young man, what did I tell you about bothering your sister?

Nancy leaves the table with Brittany, Elliot leaves the table with Ethan. Hope and Michael are left alone together.

HOPE: Oh, hi . . . Still here? I thought you two had retired to the drawing room for brandy and cigars.

MICHAEL: We're just talking man stuff here, don't you worry your pretty little head about it.

Ethan careens back into the room. He dumps disgusting goop all over Michael.

ETHAN: I dropped you in the pit. Now you're slimed to the bone.

IN THE LIVING ROOM—A BIT LATER

Music is playing, the adults are sitting, an almost convincing simulation of adult life—except that Ethan and Brittany are tearing up the room and screaming at the top of their lungs.

ELLIOT: . . . this money for CDs, but can you believe this signal-to-noise, listen to this, can you hear a hiss? I defy you to hear any hiss at all.

THE CAR—LATER

As Hope and Michael settle into their seats, Jane sleeps in the back. They sit there frozen in shock.

HOPE: What did you say, I have no ears left, I can't hear you.

MICHAEL: Sticky. Houses with kids are always . . . sticky.

HOPE: Nancy didn't finish one sentence the entire night.

MICHAEL: Is our house sticky?

HOPE: What are we going to do?

MICHAEL: Exploit the downtrodden working class. Get help. Hire . . . a . . . baby-sitter.

THE GREEN-AND-PURPLE SPIKED HAIRCUT

of a heavy-metal groupie, now lounging on Hope's sofa.

GROUPIE: —like once with my baby brother, I like dropped him, it was sort of the second story but but not that high—and like he was okay you know, 'cause babies' bones are so soft, did you know that?

Hope sits across from her, openmouthed, trying to restrain herself from chasing this alien out of the house with a broom.

HOPE'S BEDROOM—LATER

Ellyn, in a business suit, picks up clothes and toys. The doorbell rings O.C.

ELLYN: You can't just leave them standing out there.

HOPE: Yes, I can, then they'll go away.

We discover Hope, curled up in the corner, her arms over her head. Ellyn comes to kneel beside her, absentmindedly brushing off a fuzzball of dog hair that clings to her wool skirt.

ELLYN: Hopey, these people can find other jobs, if you start being guilted out about each one you'll be a basket case.

HOPE: Too late. *(on Ellyn's look)* Do you remember what *we* used to do, do you remember what you fed little Joey Jacobs to make him sick so his parents would come home so you could go see The Who?

ELLYN: A little castor oil is not dangerous.

HOPE *(suddenly remembering):* Oh, God, Linda Gimpel . . . I used to tell her that Dracula was coming to get her and she'd cower under the covers from seven o'clock on so I could make out with Barry Duffy . . . *(gasps)* In her parents' bedroom.

ELLYN: You made out with Barry Duffy . . . ?

HOPE: —and don't you see? We were *good*. These young people today, they have no values, they're all on drugs . . .

ELLYN: . . . and listening to that degenerate rock and roll.

They look at each other and start to smile. The doorbell rings again. Hope shakes her head in resignation.

HOPE: I'll get it.

A FOUR-HUNDRED-POUND WOMAN

out of a Fellini movie, sitting on Hope's couch . . .

JUMP CUT: A CHAIN-SMOKING SCHIZOPHRENIC

black hair, tangled and matted, sitting on Hope's couch . . .

JUMP CUT: A FIFTY-YEAR-OLD NAZI NANNY

blond hair in pigtails, holding the baby upside down while demonstrating a more efficient burping technique . . .

JUMP CUT: A FRESH-FACED, LOVELY COED

Pepsodent smile, caring eyes, great tits.

COED: . . . three younger brothers, and of course my baby sister, she's five now and so *cute*—which is why I guess pediatric nursing is still my dream: I just love kids.

AT THE DOOR—A LITTLE LATER

Hope smiles as the co-ed leaves. Then:

HOPE *(to Ellyn):* Absolutely not. No way.

ELLYN *(stupefied):* With her background, with those credentials?

HOPE: With that body?

AN OUTDOOR PLAZA

where Elliot and Michael have grabbed a hot dog and are walking back to work. There are beautiful women everywhere.

MICHAEL: . . . have to do *something*—why don't *we* advertise ourselves. Yeah, we could—

He trails off as a leggy secretary passes by.

MICHAEL: —because . . . Look, we gotta be aggressive or we're going to be in the toilet. We have to—

Again, he loses his train of thought, as two young women in workout leotards brush by them.

MICHAEL: —be really aggressive if we . . . *(stops himself, incredulous) What* is going on here . . . ?

ELLIOT: Bunch of australopithecines out on the savannah. The ones who win out are the ones who can spot a great-looking australopithecine rear end at four hundred yards. And the australopithecine girls are really into it, they're thinking, any guy that can see me from four hundred yards and beat up all these other apes must be a hell of a hunter-gatherer, so I think I'll wave my rear end a little, catch his attention. Two million years later, what do you got? A bunch of guys in ties and jackets supposed to be working, and what are they doing, what are you doing?

Michael is staring at yet another woman.

MICHAEL: Looking at women on the street.

ELLIOT: Exactly. That's called evolution.

MICHAEL: What I don't understand is, what are we supposed to do about it? I mean, it's just there, right, and we're supposed to suffer? Ignore it? Have an operation?

ELLIOT: I don't know.

MICHAEL: You think some people . . . *do* anything about it . . . ?

ELLIOT: Naahhh.

MICHAEL: Would you ever do it? *(on Elliot's look)* The real question is, would you ever tell me?

ELLIOT: Would you?

MICHAEL: I would tell you—I'd have to tell somebody.

ELLIOT: That's the truth.

MICHAEL: So?

ELLIOT: So what?

MICHAEL: *Have* you?

ELLIOT: Have *you?*

MICHAEL: *NO!* HAVE YOU?

Elliot doesn't answer. Michael stops in his tracks.

MICHAEL: Wait a minute. Excuse me? Wait a minute. *(looks at him)* Wait a minute. EXCUSE ME?

ELLIOT: Never mind.

MICHAEL: When? *(pause)* I don't believe this. *(pause)* With who? Everything. Right now.

ELLIOT: It was nothing, it was last year—*(he stops)* Never mind, I really don't, I really can't talk about this.

MICHAEL: It was last year what—? Oh, God, it was last year in the office, oh, God, it was Cheryl Eastman.

ELLIOT: I really don't want to talk about this.

MICHAEL: You slept with Cheryl Eastman. You slept with Cheryl Eastman? Where? At the office.

ELLIOT: No. It was someplace else. Really, it was no big thing.

MICHAEL: How many times?

ELLIOT *(long pause):* Six.

MICHAEL: Six occasions or six acts?

ELLIOT: Occasions.

In shock, Michael sits down on a bench.

MICHAEL: You had an affair. I don't believe it.

ELLIOT: Is that what an affair is? I thought I was just having a protracted nightmare.

He sits down next to Michael. They look at each other and, in spite of themselves, start to smile.

ELLIOT: Do you know how hard it's been not to talk about this? I don't know, I just, I didn't know how to begin telling you.

MICHAEL *(shaking his head):* And it was probably great, too.

ELLIOT: I'm telling you it was not great. The first time we did it was the most humiliating night of my life and after that it settled into being merely horrible. *(thinks about it)* Okay, the second time was pretty great, but after that it was horrible.

MICHAEL: Does Nancy know?

ELLIOT: I don't even know. It's like, our lives were so busy and she had, I don't know, started to lose interest in sex, and I guess I was mad, or having two kids was too hard, but it's like once I did this—before this I couldn't even buy a present for her without ending up blabbing what it was. I could not keep a secret from her. And all of a sudden, I'm lying, I'm making up things, and the worst thing is, it's totally easy, like some psychopath was lying around inside me just waiting for this chance to jump out.

Michael looks at his friend, who seems at this moment like some shell-shocked veteran, just returned from a hideous and violent war.

MICHAEL: So you'd recommend this to all your friends as a worthwhile experience . . .

ELLIOT: The problem is, once you do it, now it's real, it's this *thing* that's with you, and you can't tell her about it, and what you get . . . is this . . . abyss . . . between you, and you have no idea how you're going to ever cross it.

HOPE AND MICHAEL'S DRIVEWAY

Michael drives up, turns off the car, and sits for a moment.

IN THE KITCHEN

Hope is feeding the baby. We witness a few moments of real connection, real laughter, between mother and daughter. Finally:

MICHAEL *(V.O.):* June, I'm home.

HOPE: In here, Ward.

Michael walks in and kisses both of them.

HOPE: We're painting faces again.

MICHAEL: Hi, Nanie, hi, Banie, hi, Lanie. You look disgusting.

HOPE *(singsong):* How was work?

MICHAEL: I never talk about work at home.

HOPE: How was work?

MICHAEL: Work is wonderful, work is thrilling, I'm completely fulfilled and well paid.

He walks out with the mail. The baby yells for more food. Or bangs the table. Or waves the spoon. Or does something, we hope.

HOPE: Who asked you?

THE MOST DELICIOUS MOMENT OF THE DAY

Michael settles into his favorite chair and devotionally holds before him two catalogs, among his life's greatest pleasures: The Sharper Image and the L. L. Bean catalogs . . . As he prepares to plunge into the latest forty-eight-function automatic telephone:

HOPE *(V.O.)*: **Honey, do you think you could give her a bath?**

JANE SPLASHING IN THE BATHTUB

while Michael laughs. There are those moments in having a kid that are so pure and joyous that it's hard to tell who's having more fun, the child or the grown-up child.

MICHAEL: **And then I splash you, and Oh, No! you splash me!—TIDAL WAVE, AAaaaahhhhh—**

Hope appears, drawn by the laughter.

HOPE *(hands him a towel)*: **Who's taking the bath?**

He gives her a look most parents share, a kind of conspiratorial shock at the beauty and wonderfulness of their offspring.

HOPE *(shaking her head)*: **All day . . .**

MICHAEL *(quietly)*: **I'm like reeling . . .**

HOPE: **Do all kids radiate light, or is it just her . . .**

These feelings are too strong, too overwhelming to even talk about. She shakes her head and starts out.

MICHAEL: **Vait. Vait. So, sit . . . I not getting chance to talk vit you.**

She perches on the toilet.

MICHAEL: **Baby-sitters . . . ?**

Hope slumps against the tile.

HOPE: **Can't we talk about it later?**

MICHAEL: **That bad . . . ?**

HOPE: **We're never going to have a baby-sitter, we're never going to leave the house, we're never going to have a life—until she's thirty and then she can baby-sit for us.**

She gets up and walks out of the bathroom. Michael doesn't quite know what to say. Jane gurgles and splashes.

THE HALLWAY—LATER

Michael tiptoes out of the baby's room and ever so gently closes the door—leaving it open just a crack.

IN THE KITCHEN

It looks like a grenade has exploded. Michael opens the refrigerator; it's bare of all save baby food, formula, and black lettuce.

IN THE LIVING ROOM

he finds Hope, passed out on the sofa. Not knowing quite what to do, he stands there for a moment looking at her.

MICHAEL: Honey, are you hungry? Honey?

Groggily, Hope half opens her eyes.

HOPE (*mumbles*): . . . just need to rest for a minute.

MICHAEL: Never mind.

A long beat. The vibrations reach Hope and rouse her unwillingly.

HOPE: Sorry I didn't get to the market. There's frozen stuff, I think.

MICHAEL (*a long pause*): Any idea where I could find it? It's a little bit, I don't know what, never mind . . .

He gets up to walk away. Now she knows something's really wrong.

HOPE: I didn't have a chance to clean up, I'm sorry. *You* can clean up, too.

MICHAEL: I just put her to bed, I gave her a bath, I come home from work, what, you think I don't do anything all day . . . ?

HOPE: Well, what do you think *I* do all day? I cleaned up three times today, I just haven't cleaned up since five o'clock so it's a mess in there.

MICHAEL: Never mind. Sorry. Go to sleep.

He starts to walk away, but doesn't get far.

MICHAEL: What, you met all these baby-sitters and none of them were any good?

HOPE: Exactly.

MICHAEL: How many?

HOPE *(grudgingly):* Seven.

MICHAEL: And, what, they were too old, or were they weird, or what?

HOPE: You want to interview them, you stay home all day and interview them, you stay home with her all day and try to figure out what she needs every five minutes. If we get somebody really old, does that mean she's not gonna walk her around enough, or just put her down and let her cry, and if she doesn't speak English, I don't know, maybe she'll know what to do in an emergency but maybe she won't. If she's really young, does, is she really responsible, and when the baby chokes, what—who's she gonna call? And today when she's crying for an hour and *I* don't know what to do and I finally got her to stop, you think somebody else is gonna be able to . . .

By now, the tears are flowing freely. Michael is stunned by her intensity. He's realizing, perhaps for the first time, just how strung out she really is.

MICHAEL *(moved):* She cried for an hour . . . ? *(going to her)* What do you think it was?

HOPE *(swallowing):* I don't know. Nothing. I gave her orange juice, maybe it upset her stomach. There was no more apple juice because I'm a terrible mother and didn't get to the store.

MICHAEL: Oh, honey . . . Why don't you just go to bed now. I'll clean up. If you get hungry later, I'll get you something.

Reluctantly, grudgingly, but finally with real intensity, she hugs him.

HOPE: I don't know why, I just get so upset about this stuff.

MICHAEL (*gently*): **Shhh . . . We'll find a baby-sitter.**

She kisses him, gets up, and starts toward the bedroom.

HOPE: **I just need to sleep a little.**

Left alone on the sofa, Michael watches her go, more than a little unnerved by what just happened.

ACT THREE

THE KITCHEN—MORNING

Michael is watching *Sesame Street*. The baby isn't; she's on the floor putting blocks in her mouth. Hope looks up from the paper and smiles at her husband.

HOPE: **I hope you're enjoying that.**

MICHAEL: **I have a crush on Maria.**

The phone rings. Michael answers it.

MICHAEL: **Hello . . . I told you never to call me here . . . When? . . . All right, I can't wait.** (*covers the mouthpiece*) **Gary wants to buy equipment today.**

HOPE: **Already . . . ?**

MICHAEL: You have to spend a lot of money before you go backpacking, it's the law.

HOPE: We don't even have a baby-sitter yet.

MICHAEL: We will . . . *(looks at her)* Honey, what's the matter, do you really not want to do this . . . ?

HOPE *(trapped now):* Go ahead.

MICHAEL *(into the phone):* You're on. We'll spend lots of money, we'll buy knives.

HOPE: You have enough knives.

MICHAEL: A man never has enough knives.

IN THE LIVING ROOM

Michael gets his stuff together.

HOPE: Have lots of fun in the real world . . .

MICHAEL: I'm not in the real world, I'm in an office.

HOPE: Where people eat solid food.

MICHAEL: You want to go in my place? I'll stay home with the baby.

HOPE: I should.

MICHAEL: Will you stop it?

HOPE: I just worry.

MICHAEL: And I told you not to worry.

HOPE: I had to take another thousand out of savings this week and now you want to buy equipment . . .

He suppresses his own fear and holds her reassuringly.

MICHAEL: I make enough money. I just don't always make it when we need it.

He kisses her and the baby and goes. The phone rings. Hope answers it.

HOPE: Hello—

INTERCUT—IT'S ELLYN

ELLYN: I've been thinking all night and I've made a decision.

HOPE: Okay . . .

ELLYN: You need to go back to work.

HOPE: Oh, God. Thank you for making my morning.

ELLYN: Really. I've never seen you like you were yesterday. You're really suffering and you need to find a way out of it.

HOPE: Ellyn, I am not suffering. I'm having a perfectly delightful life taking care of my child. And Michael is doing his best to support us.

ELLYN: I'm not talking about supporting you, I'm talking about you. When's the last time you did *anything* for yourself, when's the last time you went to a movie, or went shopping even?

HOPE: Shopping. There's a concept . . .

ELLYN: I mean you looked terrible yesterday. You did. I think you have to set some new priorities. Call Shilliday, it can't hurt. Ask him if you can go back even part time. For you.

HOPE: Shilliday is out of the question. He was furious enough when I got pregnant. "This job takes total dedication."

ELLYN: Then sue the jerk. That's illegal.

HOPE: Goodbye, Ellyn.

ELLYN: I'm saying all this because I love you, you know that, goodbye . . .

JUMP CUT: HOPE falling on the bed, face down. Defeated. She lies there for a moment, then picks up her head.

JUMP CUT: HOPE in her closet as she violently pushes hangers around. She finds a dress and pulls it out.

JUMP CUT: HOPE in front of a mirror as she tries to put it on. It's too tight. She tries a different dress, and another, peering at herself from different angles. She really looks fine, but doesn't think so herself. Finally, she finds a pose that seems right—defiant, slightly pouty. It's not a mother's pose; it's tougher than that. The baby starts to cry.

A SPORTING GOODS STORE

Michael and Gary look at sleeping bags.

GARY: Here we go: minus ten degrees.

MICHAEL: Are you kidding, we'd roast in that thing.

GARY: I forgot, you carry a supplemental female heating system.

MICHAEL: Oh, right, and you've never made it with anybody backpacking . . . *(Gary shrugs mysteriously)* What . . . ?

GARY: You mean did I ever take a woman with me, or did I ever *meet* a woman on the trail and end up sleeping with her?

MICHAEL: I never even thought of that. Forget it, I don't want to know.

GARY: It was great—she was with these two other girls who were stopping because they were out of shape. She was, like, on the American ski team, I mean she was . . . healthy. That's the thing, you know, healthy women, they really get into it. Plus, their bodies are totally flexible. So we were together a couple of days, but then she was gonna meet these guys to go hang-gliding off the side of the mountain, so I figured sex is one thing, death is another . . . *(looks at a parka)* So how is it after she has a baby? I hear, you know, there are some anatomical changes . . .

MICHAEL *(shakes his head):* Same as ever.

GARY: At least she's beautiful. I think she'll lose the weight.

He walks off, leaving Michael to stare after him.

A PILE OF CAMPING EQUIPMENT

forms in Michael and Hope's front hall. In a series of jump cuts, it grows and grows. Sleeping bags. Canteens. Parkas. A tent . . .

AT THE FRONT DOOR—LATER

as Nancy hands over a bag full of baby clothes to Hope.

HOPE: . . . that's really sweet.

NANCY: I had to hide them from Brittany. The only time she pays any attention to her clothes is when I try to give them away.

Michael comes through the living room.

MICHAEL: It's disrespectful to give someone's clothes away, you should be ashamed of yourself.

NANCY: I hear you're going camping.

HOPE: Some year.

NANCY: Under the stars, no kids . . . Sounds so romantic it's obscene, if you ask me.

MICHAEL (grabbing Hope): It is, isn't it?

HOPE: Rocks under your sleeping bag, bears attacking you in the middle of the night.

MICHAEL: No kid to get up and feed . . .

That shuts her up.

NANCY (on her way out): I want to hear every illicit detail.

HOPE: Thanks again for the clothes.

Nancy leaves; Hope closes the door, looks at the clothes.

HOPE: Wasn't that nice?

MICHAEL: Are they sticky?

HOPE: Stop it.

Hope starts going through the clothes.

MICHAEL: That was weird.

HOPE: What?

MICHAEL: She really seemed interested in whether we were having sex.

HOPE: Why is that weird?

MICHAEL: I don't know. I guess I don't think of her as being very interested, that's all.

HOPE: When are you going to understand that everybody's interested?

MICHAEL: Some people are more interested than other people.

HOPE: Can we please not hear about how women are biologically programmed to be less interested in sex?

MICHAEL: No, no, even among women, some of them are more interested than others.

HOPE: And Nancy's not interested?

Michael has idiotically set a trap for himself, then walked directly into it.

MICHAEL: I don't know if she's interested.

HOPE: You just said she's not interested.

MICHAEL: I said I *think* she's not interested.

HOPE (*looks at him*): What did Elliot tell you about Nancy?

MICHAEL: Elliot didn't tell me anything about Nancy. I can't have my own opinions?

HOPE: Why do you have that look on your face?

MICHAEL: I don't have a look on my face.

HOPE: He told you something about Nancy.

MICHAEL: He told me nothing about Nancy.

HOPE: You told him something about me—

MICHAEL: Will you stop this.

HOPE: Michael, you are the worst liar in the world, there is something you're obviously not telling me and I think you should tell me.

Michael starts humming in order to shut her up.

HOPE: Okay . . . Nancy's not interested in sex . . . (*nope*) Nancy's frigid. (*nope again*) *Elliot* is frigid.

MICHAEL: Impotent.

HOPE: Elliot is impotent?!

MICHAEL: No, no, no. You said Elliot—men are impotent, *women* are frigid, you said Elliot was frigid.

HOPE: Elliot's not impotent—

MICHAEL: Never mind, okay, just never mind, I don't know why you always have to do this.

He tries to turn away. All of a sudden, Hope gets it.

HOPE: Oh, God. He had an affair. Oh, no. Did he really?

MICHAEL: Can we just forget this?

HOPE: He had an affair and Nancy doesn't know, and oh, God . . . Was it one affair? Just tell me if it was one. *(Michael is silent)* Michael, this is really upsetting, please tell me if he's a total jerk or if this is just something that happened, which would make him only somewhat of a jerk. Damn.

She sits down.

MICHAEL: It was one thing, and apparently it was pretty awful.

HOPE: Good. Serves him right.

MICHAEL: Hope.

HOPE: This is not what I needed to hear today. Why did you tell me this?

Michael can only shake his head: why did you *tell* me . . . ?

MICHAEL *(finally): I* didn't have an affair.

HOPE: Are you sure?

He thinks about it. She sprawls out on top of him.

IN THE KITCHEN

Melissa is happily feeding the baby.

MELISSA: —and here . . . comes . . . the airplane! *(to Michael and Hope)* What a good baby. Is every baby this good? I want this baby. Can I have her?

Michael and Hope sit there, exhausted, smiling.

MELISSA: I know, I know . . . How am I ever going to have a baby? I'm dating babies.

MICHAEL AND HOPE'S BEDROOM

Michael, Hope, and Melissa are snuggling, having put the baby down for the forty-third time. Michael is surrounded with papers and sketches from work. From the house next door, we hear throbbing rock and roll.

HOPE: Are you crazy, I love your body.

MELISSA: It's totally out of proportion.

MICHAEL: Let me see . . .

They both lunge for him, wrinkling his papers in the process.

MICHAEL: Hey, hey, I'm working here.

HOPE: Just wait 'til you have one, you'll learn about proportion. And stretch marks. And gravity.

MICHAEL: Would you tell her how great she looks?

MELISSA: I tell her every day. I tell her how great her kid looks, I tell her how great her life looks . . . *(listening)* Oooh, I love this song. Let's go next door and crash this party.

MICHAEL: They're eighteen.

MELISSA: Young meat.

HOPE *(laughs):* That's no joke, the older brother is really cute.

MELISSA: Get him over here. *(yells)* Hey, kid, you want to meet a horny thirty-two-year-old . . . ? *(back to them)* Can't you ask him to baby-sit or something . . . ?

Michael and Hope laugh.

HOPE: He's an illiterate zombie.

MELISSA *(sinks down on the bed):* At least he isn't married. So, who *is* going to stay over when we go backpacking?

HOPE *(stretches):* Oh, God . . . Do you remember when we were eighteen . . . ? How can they be eighteen, *we're* eighteen.

MICHAEL: Who *is* going to stay over?

MELISSA: I actually lied about my age last week. I told some guy I was born in 'fifty-six. I don't know *anybody* who was born in 'fifty-six.

Michael, meanwhile, gives Hope a significant look.

MICHAEL: Who?

HOPE *(mouthing):* Not now.

Michael moves closer. Melissa mistakes his intentions completely and laughs.

MELISSA *(getting up):* You guys are disgusting, can't you wait till I'm out the door. Goodbye.

HOPE: Don't go, Melissa.

MICHAEL: Go, Melissa.

As Melissa starts out, Hope jumps up, escaping Michael's grasp.

HOPE: I'll walk you to the door.

THE MIDDLE OF THE NIGHT

Next door, the music still throbs. Michael and Hope lie there, absolutely still. Hope rolls over and sees that Michael is also awake.

HOPE: Twelve . . . Twenty . . . Four. She will wake up in one hour and thirty-six minutes.

He doesn't say anything.

HOPE: You okay? *(no response)* You're still mad. *(no response)* I told you I would start looking for a sitter again on Monday. Can't we just drop this?

MICHAEL *(re the music):* I'm calling the police.

HOPE: It's Friday night. They're allowed to have a party on Friday night.

MICHAEL: You led me to believe you were working on this and you weren't, I mean, what am I supposed to think?

HOPE: You *assumed* I was working on it—

MICHAEL: Oh, come on—

HOPE: You could've asked me, you could've tried to help.

MICHAEL: You want me to look for a sitter, I'll look for a sitter, but watch out, 'cause I'll find one—

HOPE: I don't want to find a sitter . . . ?

MICHAEL: You don't want to go.

HOPE: What does that mean?

Next door, drunken screams accompany a new song.

MICHAEL: I'm going over there.

HOPE: You're not going over there. They're kids. We were kids, too. Remember?

MICHAEL: I just think you don't want to go.

HOPE: I don't know what I want. You don't think I want to be alone with you? I wouldn't mind a few nights by myself either. I just don't know if I'm ready to leave her.

MICHAEL: We're talking about two nights.

HOPE: It's not two nights, it's a whole attitude. I have to be so available to her all day, every minute, and I don't know how you turn that off, I don't know if I'm supposed to turn that off, maybe that's what being a good mother is. Ellyn thinks I'm too good a mother, you think I'm going to end up like Nancy—everybody's a critic. I only know that Jane's happy, and why aren't I allowed to be proud of that?

MICHAEL: Okay, so we won't go.

HOPE *(after a long pause)*: Is that terrible? Do you hate me?

MICHAEL: I don't hate you. If you're not ready to go, we won't go.

They lie there for a moment.

HOPE: Just tell me I haven't become my mother.

The music pounds. Michael bolts up and storms out of the room. He runs down the steps, still in his underwear, until he reaches the front door and opens it, screaming.

MICHAEL: TURN OFF THE MUSIC, HEY, TURN OFF THE MUSIC . . . ! *(laughter V.O.)* HEY, YOU LITTLE TWERP, YOU WANT ME TO COME OVER THERE AND BEAT YOUR FACE IN . . . ? TURN OFF THE *DAMNED MUSIC*—

AT THE TOP OF THE STEPS

Hope slumps down, crying, watching her husband below.

ACT FOUR

IN HOPE AND MICHAEL'S LIVING ROOM

Gary and Melissa look directly at us.

GARY: Really?

MELISSA: It's okay . . .

GARY: No, it's okay . . . You guys do what you have to do.

MELISSA: I mean, this is a tough time . . .

Hope and Michael stand there abjectly, opposite them.

HOPE: It's not like we don't want to go.

MICHAEL *(swallowing it):* It's just . . . I don't think it can work right now.

GARY: Guys, it's *okay.* People have kids, priorities change, old friends don't mean anything anymore, Elliot and Nancy'll drop by, you'll all change some diapers . . . *(pats their shoulders)* I understand.

MICHAEL: Gary—

MELISSA *(clipped):* Well, I have to go . . .

HOPE: Look, are people mad here?

GARY *(really not mad):* I'm not mad, I never liked you people anyway.

HOPE: Melissa?

MELISSA: I'll call you when we're back, okay?

She hurries out. Gary, Michael, and Hope raise eyebrows at each other.

GARY: What's twelve years of friendship anyway?

He goes. Hope closes the door in dismay. Michael pulls out a samurai sword and commits seppuku.

SPORTING GOODS STORE

Michael returns the sleeping bags.

MICHAEL: No, no, they're fine, we just, we hadn't realized we had these other sleeping bags and, uh, they really weren't as good, I mean these have these great Velcro here and—

SALESMAN *(tolerant):* All I need is your receipt . . .

WOMAN: What temperature do those go down to?

Michael turns to find a lovely, athletic girl caressing the smooth nylon of the bag.

MICHAEL: I think they, uh, I think they go down to minus ten.

WOMAN: Really? I need a warm bag, I get so cold when I sleep.

MICHAEL: Yeah, me too.

She smiles at him and turns to the salesman.

WOMAN: Do you have these in that burgundy color I saw back there?

She's no longer aware of Michael's presence, but he continues to watch her as she heads back with the salesman . . .

OUTSIDE THE STORE

Michael is just leaving as she hurries out, carrying a large bag.

WOMAN: I bought the kind that zip together, just in case you wanted to come with me . . .

She is so beautiful. Ever so slowly, he reaches out to touch her face.

SMASH CUT BACK TO:

REALITY

Michael still standing there at the cash register, watching her disappear forever into the back of the store.

A PARK

Kids, large and small, swarm around. Mothers, old and older, try to relax while maintaining radar contact. Hope sits there watching the older kids careen; a vision of the future.

ELLYN *(V.O.):* Feels strange to be in a park without tear gas.

Hope looks up to see Ellyn, dressed, as always, in one of her suits.

HOPE: Janey, look who came to see us. How'd you find us?

ELLYN: I really, I wanted to see you, because . . . something weird is going on and I'm . . . upset about it . . .

HOPE: Ellyn . . .

ELLYN *(laughs nervously):* It's not terrible, I don't know, it just occurs to me we haven't spoken in six days . . .

HOPE: I've been thinking about that, too. Oh, Ellyn, my life . . . everything is such chaos . . .

ELLYN: And you don't . . . feel like you're ready to do anything about it . . . ?

Hope looks at her old friend.

HOPE: Okay, I don't really get this, did you come here to yell at me—

ELLYN: I'm not yelling at you, I'm asking you. I called you and gave you what I thought was a good way to change the—

HOPE: What *you* thought—

ELLYN: —situation you're in and then you don't call me for six days.

There's no turning back now.

HOPE: Ellyn, you don't understand the situation I'm in now. I don't sleep at night, my husband is mad at me . . . And there I am, caring for this . . . creature who's . . . *of* me. With this . . . connection I've never felt before, with anyone. I love her. She's the greatest thing that's ever happened to me, she . . . changed my whole life. I don't know how to separate from that and I don't know if I want to. And I don't think you want to understand that.

ELLYN: I can understand that.

HOPE: Lynnie, you don't even look at her. You don't ask about her, you hardly acknowledge her existence.

Ellyn looks as if she's been struck. She's really hurt.

ELLYN (*long pause*): Okay. What was . . . I saw you two days after she was born, and a week after, and ten days after, and I don't believe this.

HOPE: You saw me. You didn't see her.

ELLYN: What the hell was the present I bought her?

HOPE: Ellyn, you bought her a book of Arthur Rackham fairy stories, it was beautiful, I loved it—but she won't read it till she's ten, look, I don't want to criticize your present, it was a wonderful present, I'm just saying—please don't get defensive—she's in my life now. You can't look the other way or pretend she's not there. She's a part of me. If you want to have a relationship with me, she just comes along—I can't change that.

Ellyn looks away, eyes tearing up.

ELLYN: I'm a part of your life too. I have prior claim. You can't just turn away from . . . people who care about you— *(shakes her head)* This is like in high school when you would get a boyfriend and then, oh, where's Hope.

HOPE *(gets it now)*: Lynnie, I'm sorry. I'm really sorry.

ELLYN *(crying now)*: I'm not exactly ignorant of the looks.

HOPE: What looks?

ELLYN: Poor Ellyn can't find a man, poor Ellyn is too committed to her career which is a load of bull.

HOPE: I never say that stuff.

ELLYN: Can we just be honest after all these years. You think it.

They sit in silence.

HOPE: What, we're not supposed to be friends anymore? I can't accept that.

ELLYN: Who's saying that? Can't I be upset, can't we both be upset?

HOPE *(starts to smile)*: You know I can't deal with conflict of any kind.

ELLYN: I know. *(sighs)* Maybe we're just going our separate ways.

HOPE: That sounds awful.

ELLYN: Can't we go separate ways and still be friends? Can't we just respect what the other person is doing?

HOPE: I respect you so much. Do you respect me?

ELLYN: Don't you understand? I do respect you, I'm jealous of you.

HOPE: But I'm jealous of you—

ELLYN: Oh, God . . .

Two grown women hugging on a park bench amidst screaming children . . .

ELLIOT AND MICHAEL'S OFFICE

Elliot's prostrate on the sofa, Michael's slumped in his chair. They stare at one another for a moment, very bummed out. Finally, Michael produces a bottle of Bushmills from a drawer, takes a swig, caps it, and tosses the bottle to Elliot.

ELLIOT: By the time we get through with the campaign, nobody'll be able to tell it was a rip-off.

MICHAEL *(kicks the telephone)*: He didn't have to be so damn patronizing about my apology: "I know you kids got principles, that's what I like about ya', you wanna do your thing . . ." I HATE THIS. What are we doing here? Why did we start this company?

ELLIOT: To do our thing. *(on Michael's look)* We won't always have to deal with sleazeballs like Teller. We'll deal with higher-class sleazeballs. We'll come back to fight another day, but right now we have two wives, three kids, four cars, two mortgages, a payroll. And that's life, pal. You be de breadwinner now.

MICHAEL: Is *that* what I am . . .

THE LIVING ROOM

Michael enters the house. It's dark. Light spills from the baby's room. He walks into the hallway and looks in on Hope, who is rocking Janey to sleep. Michael stands in the shadows for a moment watching them, and then moves quietly away.

THE LIVING ROOM—LATER

Hope finds Michael sitting alone, staring into the shadows.

HOPE: I didn't hear you come in.

Michael just shrugs. She looks at him with concern.

HOPE: There's food. I got to the store . . . *(he nods, silence)* You want to be alone.

MICHAEL: I don't know what I want, Hope.

She comes over to him. His look of desperation scares her.

HOPE: Michael . . . ?

MICHAEL (*finally*): I spent every day this week . . . trying to figure out . . . how we could keep from going under, the business from going under.

She sits down, realizing all this money talk has been serious.

MICHAEL: And I couldn't. So I . . . crawled back to Teller today. I sold out.

HOPE (*touches him*): Honey . . . Why didn't you tell me?

MICHAEL: I tried to tell you—

HOPE: You made jokes about it—

MICHAEL: Because you don't want to hear it and I don't blame you. I'm supposed to deal with this stuff. I earn the money now.

HOPE: Michael, I keep telling you—I don't expect that of you. You're doing this incredibly brave thing and I don't want you to have to compromise.

MICHAEL: But you going back to work is a compromise too. You love her, you don't want to go back to work now. (*throws up his hands*) This is all just not . . . according to plan.

HOPE: Whose plan? Our lives are so full now and we have a wonderful baby who we love so much and who needs us.

Michael puts his hand over his face.

MICHAEL (*finally*): Then why do I feel so terrible . . . ? God, I hate people who talk like this. I know we're lucky. I've just been so angry and I don't know, embarrassed, because I feel like a two-year-old and you're not paying enough attention to me, or rubbing my head at night, or cooking or taking care of me like you used to. And I see you being this incredible mother to Jane and I know that's one of the reasons I married you in the first place and I feel unbelievably guilty for even having any of these feelings, on top of which I've got nobody to talk to about them because you've always been my best friend and I've always—(*he is choking up*)—told you everything, only now I can't because they're all about you and I'm afraid you'll hear it and just explode, or kill me.

HOPE *(gently)*: You can tell me.

MICHAEL: No, I can't. It's too . . . hurtful.

She waits, but he almost can't go on.

MICHAEL: I don't want to be this . . . tortured couple, I don't want to be Elliot and Nancy. I don't want to be attracted to other women.

HOPE: Are you attracted to other women . . . ?

MICHAEL *(long pause)*: Yes. *(sighs)* Not really.

Now she sighs.

MICHAEL: I'm sorry, I admit it, I really liked our life. I liked the fact that you were . . . beautiful and you were exciting and you had a dirty mind, and . . . you were there for me.

She shakes her head ruefully, not about to explode at all.

HOPE: Don't you think I want to be thin and interested in sex every night and exactly the way I was before . . . ? *(his silence means yes)* I do. But I might need some help, that's all, you might have to remind me sometimes. And it'll never be perfect, can you accept that?

He is nodding, so relieved to hear her say these words.

HOPE: But Michael, we have to learn how to talk about all this or else it's gonna get us.

MICHAEL: People have had babies before, why is this so hard . . . ?

HOPE: We expect too much. Because we've always gotten . . . too much. *(gently)* I think all our parents had a meeting in nineteen forty-six. "Let's all have lots of kids and give them everything they want so they can grow up and be totally messed up and unable to cope with real life."

Michael slowly slides off the sofa until his head is resting on her knee. She rubs his head.

THERAPY

BY

SUSAN SHILLIDAY

When Ed and Marshall got the pickup for this series with the title everyone at the network loathed, they looked at each other in despair, realizing that the episodes were not going to be so obliging as to write themselves. And since they had no coherent explanation of what the show was supposed to be, they turned to their wives (i.e., Ed to Liberty and Marshall to me), to whom they were not required to be coherent, and said, "Start writing."

Now I thought I was very clever. One thread of the show, Ed and Marshall knew, would be the troubled marriage of Elliot and Nancy. I realized that this storyline *actually resembled a plot,* unlike everything else these *soi-disant* executive producers were thinking about. Therefore, I reasoned, Elliot and Nancy would be easier to write about than those nebulous other characters.

"Separation" was the first episode I wrote. "Separation" was the first anything I wrote. Something happens in it: Elliot walks out. Unfortunately, after it was written, Ed and Marshall realized that we had avoided exposing the reasons for the breakup of the marriage. It's easy to say, "A marriage breaks up." It's hard to say why. Another episode was clearly necessary. So there I was, assigned to the task of asking "Why," with *no resemblance to a plot whatsoever,* for an episode that would actually precede "Separation" in both fictional and airtime.

This kind of episode, that would delve into the smallest, most intimate details, the most incredibly boring and utterly fascinating corners of a marriage, was exactly the kind of show that Ed and Marshall had hoped they would be able to do on *thirtysomething.* It was natural to turn to the device of counseling sessions as a way of hacking through the tangled undergrowth of a marriage. It was plausible, even probable, that Nancy and Elliot, given the specific imaginary world they inhabit, would turn to conjoint therapy in a crisis.

57

The danger in using therapy sessions in drama is that you talk about conflict instead of showing it. That is the history of the various drafts of "Therapy." The first draft had Nancy and Elliot telling the therapist about their problems rather than experiencing them. Patty Wettig and Tim Busfield, after reading the first draft, were incredibly perceptive in pointing out this problem. The challenge was to show Nancy's and Elliot's behavior—the withholding, the judging, the dismissiveness—not only in the scenes outside of the therapist's office but within that dark little cave as well; not to say, "We had a fight," but to see the fight unfold and bloom again in front of the therapist and in front of the audience.

It meant imagining a complex subterranean relationship, and also devising a structure on which to hang four acts' worth of that relationship. In the end we took a bit of inspiration from Odets' *The Country Girl.* Let's be honest—it was the movie we remembered. In the first half, Grace Kelly looks like the worst bitch who ever lived. Only in the second half do we discover that most of what she supposedly did to Bing Crosby, *he* actually did to her. This notion of peeling back layers of truth was the key to our structure.

Early on, we revealed that Elliot's complaints about Nancy's withholding and controlling were well founded. She, in fact, realizes it herself. It's only when she makes sincere attempts to change that we realize that Elliot's anger now has a life of its own, independent of Nancy's behavior. Their miserable dynamic became so real to me that I frequently found myself simply transcribing what I could hear them snarling at each other in my head—for a writer, a felicitous state of mild schizophrenia.

In the final drafts, Marshall, as the director, became more involved in working on the script, especially in refining the therapy sessions themselves, making them more pointed, more unguarded, more brutal. I would like to take this opportunity to forgive my husband for stealing my thunder on this, my first-ever-to-be-broadcast episode of television, by taking on the role of triple-hyphenate: producer-director-actor. That was him, playing the therapist.

Then there's the subplot. I hate that word, "subplot." It reminds me of the days when Ed and Marshall worked on *Family:* a wonderful show, but the subplot was always something inane, like "Buddy cleans her room." Then there's "B-story," which suggests that scripts can be broken down into algebraic formulas, an attitude that is in fact widespread in television writing. The story of Ellyn's tattoo and the gossip about it was inane and algebraic, but the juicy adolescent sexuality and silliness of it made the wasteland of the marriage seem all the sadder. And if there was ever an episode that needed some comic relief, this was it. The funny thing is that, unbeknownst to me, Polly Draper really does have—oops, I don't think I'm supposed to tell anyone about that.

Two more things about "Therapy." My favorite line is Elliot's: "I don't know if I love Nancy any more . . . And no matter what she does, I can't seem to forgive her for that." Long after writing that I was reading *Middlemarch,* which I hadn't picked up since high school, and I found this: "In marriage, the certainty, 'She will never love me much,' is easier to bear than the fear, 'I shall love her no more.'" I found myself glowing with pride that I had come up with the same idea that George Eliot had—however much more beautifully and economically expressed by her.

Incidentally, "Therapy" has another line that's a favorite of mine. Michael asks what went wrong with the marriage, and Elliot answers, in part: "What happened? Mountains wore down, ice ages came and went." I wish I'd written that, but as it happens, it was Marshall's contribution. Did I say I'd forgiven him? Maybe not.

Thing Two. During the first season of *thirtysomething,* the Museum of Broadcasting held a panel discussion about the show at the Los Angeles County Museum. A sold-out audience of hardcore fans had been promised that a new episode, not yet broadcast, would be shown. But inevitably there were technical problems, and the new show wasn't ready in time. Marshall and Ed decided to screen "Therapy"—which of course most of the audience had already seen. The announcement was made. The audience groaned. I slid down in my seat in the auditorium, very much wishing to be dead. I felt hot. I felt cold. Boulders were grinding together just behind my eyes. I would have to sit there while the bored, disappointed audience waded through the interminable crisis of the Weston marriage.

But a shocking thing happened. The audience got into it. They *laughed*. I had never written for the stage, never witnessed an audience responding to my writing, certainly never thought of myself as *funny*. And I had certainly never thought of "Therapy" as funny. I became completely intoxicated. For a moment I almost understood the psychology of actors—only for a moment. Audience approbation was a drug. A drug with certain side effects. On the way home Marshall had to pull over to the curb so I could throw up at the corner of Wilshire and Santa Monica. So much for the glamour of Hollywood.

SUSAN SHILLIDAY

ACT ONE

There is a babble of voices as we FADE IN on

MICHAEL AND ELLIOT'S OFFICE

Michael, Elliot, Hope, Nancy, and various employees are standing, sitting, and milling around a table on which sit the remains of Elliot's birthday cake. Jane and Brittany are sitting in Sassy Seats at their respective fathers' desks, happily mashing cake into their faces, hands, and hair. Everyone else is more or less using a fork.

ELLIOT: So when I was eleven, no it must have been twelve, my father took me to see *Goldfinger* for my birthday—

He picks up a Phillies cap and hurls it à la Oddjob.

ELLIOT: —and then he figured I knew all I needed to know about sex.

MICHAEL *(appreciatively):* Right. Pussy Galore.

61

NANCY: My mother gave me a book. She told me to read it and ask her if I had any questions. So I read it and asked her if she could take it back and get me *National Velvet* instead.

MICHAEL: Nobody ever told me anything. I had to figure it out all by myself.

HOPE: And a very nice job you did of it, too.

MICHAEL: It's all in who you work with.

NANCY: You two, it's revolting, I don't know if I can take all this cuteness from people who have been married for five years.

ELLIOT: Couldn't we have a little conflict here, a little hostility, something memorable for my birthday celebration?

NANCY *(laughing, not angry):* The last time Elliot said anything that sweet to me was when Nixon resigned.

MICHAEL: Come on . . .

NANCY: Seriously. We don't relate that way anymore—*(quieter)* That's why—

The phone rings and Michael and Janine both reach for it. He beats her.

MICHAEL *(enjoying himself):* Michael and Elliot's Company, two hucksters, no waiting . . . The . . . the three-hole binders only come in blue or . . . One moment please. Janine?

JANINE *(to Hope and Nancy):* 'Bye . . .

Janine heads for her desk. The rest of the staff take this as a sign that the party's over and follow her out. Nancy has paused.

HOPE *(to Nancy):* That's why what?

Nancy glances at the employees who are leaving the room.

NANCY: Just an idea.

MICHAEL: What?

Elliot gives her a look, but she decides to go on.

NANCY: What do you guys think about marriage counseling?

ELLIOT *(exasperated):* Yeah, all four of us, we could get a special group rate.

HOPE *(ignoring him):* I don't know. Probably every marriage could use an outside agitator.

NANCY *(trying to convince herself):* I think it would be fun. Really get into it, figure out the dynamic of our relationship.

HOPE: Alice Hampton and her husband went to a marriage counselor—

ELLIOT: And look what happened to her.

NANCY: What?

MICHAEL: She's the channel for a four-hundred-year-old Albanian sheep farmer. I kid you not. And his sheep.

NANCY: Come on, you guys—

Hope gives Michael a look. They both know that this is no joke.

MICHAEL: No, it sounds good. How do you find a marriage counselor, the Yellow Pages?

ELLIOT: Maybe we could get a lube job thrown in.

MICHAEL: Maybe Gary knows someone at Haverford.

HOPE: How about Melissa? Maybe her therapist—

ELLIOT: Please, this is embarrassing enough without involving the entire known world . . .

THE OFFICE—LATER

Michael is alone now, idly leafing through stacks of papers as he talks to Melissa on the phone. We cut back and forth between them.

MICHAEL: Yeah . . . Bring, I don't know, bagels. Cream cheese. No onion. Yecchh—

He has just discovered a paper plate filled with smashed birthday cake under a loose-leaf binder.

MELISSA: Michael?

MICHAEL: People around here are such slobs. Elliot's birthday cake. All over my desk.

He scrapes up some icing with his finger and eats it.

MICHAEL: So meanwhile, Elliot and Nancy are really in trouble, I think. They want to see a marriage counselor.

MELISSA (*interested*): Really?

MICHAEL: Yeah. Nancy might call you to ask if you know anybody, so act surprised.

MELISSA: I know nothing. What's wrong?

MICHAEL: I don't know exactly. They fight a lot.

INT. GARY'S OFFICE AT SCHOOL—DAY

Gary glances through a stack of blue books as *he* now talks to Melissa on the phone. As we cut between the two of them:

GARY: What about the kids?

MELISSA: I said a marriage counselor, not a divorce lawyer.

GARY: What's with people these days? Can't anyone fight the good fight, solve their own problems anymore?

MELISSA: How can you say that to me?

GARY: You're different. Your problems are . . . epic.

MELISSA: Gee, that's the nicest thing you've ever said to me.

INT. MICHAEL AND ELLIOT'S OFFICE—DAY

Later that afternoon. Elliot hangs up the phone and turns to face Michael, who has just come in.

ELLIOT: That was Gary.

MICHAEL (*confused*): For you?

ELLIOT: He said he has this buddy, Fred Nicolson, who does marriage counseling.

MICHAEL (*quickly, turning away*): That's terrific—

ELLIOT: Oh, Michael—

Michael stops.

ELLIOT: Why not try a billboard on Broad Street? "Elliot and Nancy: Marriage on the Rocks? Watch This Space."

MICHAEL (*embarrassed*): I only talked to Melissa.

ELLIOT: And she only talked to Gary.

MICHAEL: You mad?

ELLIOT *(thinks, shrugs; what's the point?):* Nah . . .

MICHAEL: Anyway, it's a therapist, and that's what you wanted, right?

ELLIOT: What Nancy wanted.

MICHAEL: What do *you* want?

There is a pause. Elliot makes a rueful face.

ELLIOT: Courtside season tickets for the Sixers . . .

INT. DR. NICOLSON'S WAITING ROOM—NIGHT

Nancy and Elliot, clearly nervous, sit in the tiny, nondescript waiting room. Dr. Nicolson enters.

NICOLSON: Hi, I'm Fred Nicolson.

ELLIOT: Hi, Elliot Weston—

He gestures toward Nancy, uncertain about therapeutic etiquette: should he introduce her?

NANCY: Nancy Weston . . .

They all shake hands and exchange awkward hellos; Nicolson leads them into his office. Behind him, Nancy and Elliot exchange exaggeratedly panicked looks and gestures. Because the doctor, to their horror, is just like them: he is their age, he is dressed like them, he looks like them, he talks like them.

INT. NICOLSON'S OFFICE

Nicolson gestures them to seats in his pleasant, ordinary office. There are lots of books, some plants (one or two are dying), nonintimidating posters and prints, and framed photos of his wife and two preschool age children.

ELLIOT *(laughing nervously):* I thought you'd be older.

NICOLSON: Gary Shepherd and I were in grade school together, actually. I used to beat him up at recess.

They all laugh. Then there is a deadly silence.

ELLIOT: Well . . .

He looks at Nancy, resenting her for having gotten him into this insane situation. Nancy lifts her hands in an "I don't know" gesture.

NICOLSON: How can I . . . help you?

NANCY: We've never done anything like this before. Tell us what to do.

NICOLSON: Why don't you tell me a little about yourselves.

NANCY: Okay.

She takes a deep breath.

NANCY: We have two kids, Ethan, he's six, and Brittany, she's three, and we've been married, God, about twelve years . . .

ELLIOT: It was a one-night stand that got out of control.

Nancy laughs in embarrassment.

NANCY: Elliot is head of an advertising company he started, and I don't work, I take care of the kids.

NICOLSON (*quietly*): That's work.

NANCY: You know what I mean . . .

We dissolve to a series of out-of-sequence remarks:

ELLIOT: . . . Pretty good, really, I mean Nancy is an unbelievable mother, she has such patience and so much love for them—

NANCY (*interrupting him*): Is this what we're supposed to be talking about?

ELLIOT: Better? I don't know . . . What's supposed to be better? (*indicates Nancy*) You're the one who thinks things are bad.

NANCY: I don't think things are *bad.*

ELLIOT: Actually, this is her idea of fun. After this we're going to see *Cries and Whispers.*

NANCY: —oh, fine, Nancy's compulsive about money, but you don't even think, I mean, no one's asked what *this* costs, how do we know we can afford this?

ELLIOT: I'm sure we can't . . .

NANCY: When's the last time you even looked at a bank statement?

ELLIOT: I don't need to—my wife is compulsive about money.

ELLIOT *(laughing)*: Sex? Whoa. *(long pause)* . . . sex? Sex is . . . I'm trying to remember what sex is like . . . No, sex is fine. It's sex.

NANCY: Why don't you tell him?

ELLIOT: Tell him what?

NANCY: Tell him what you . . . tell him the truth, tell him—

She can't believe the blank look on Elliot's face, the innocent tone. She turns to Nicolson.

NANCY: Elliot's very unsatisfied with our sex life.

ELLIOT: Nancy . . .

NANCY: Go ahead, tell him, we're here, you might as well take advantage of it, you never miss an opportunity to tell *me* about it, tell him. *(to Nicolson)* Elliot thinks I'm not sexy enough, he thinks I don't care about sex anymore, he thinks I don't care about his needs.

NICOLSON *(to Elliot)*: Is that what you think?

ELLIOT: If she says it, it must be true.

NANCY: Oh, stop it—

ELLIOT: Stop what, you've got it all figured out—

Nancy is furious now, but also deeply embarrassed.

NANCY: Damn you. I am trying to save *our* marriage, I am trying to find out why you have to make *our* life miserable, day in, day out, with your insults and your irresponsibility and your . . . disinterest, and I have a right to expect you to at least—

ELLIOT *(seething, finally)*: You don't want to know what I think, you don't want to—*(turns to Nicolson)* Want to know why we're here? This is why we're here. Right there.

NANCY: What?

ELLIOT: Because you don't care what I think, you don't know what I think, you don't want me to think—you won't be happy till there's just Nancy . . . and the way Nancy wants *everything* to be.

We see both of them sitting there, at an impasse.

Elliot seems tired now. His shoulders sag.

ELLIOT: The future, I don't know, what's the future of anything? We could have a nuclear war. Or we could just go on.

NANCY *(to Elliot):* We can't just go on.

Elliot shrugs.

NICOLSON: Do you want to set up a regular time to go over some of these things?

ELLIOT *(rueful smile):* You think there's hope for us?

NANCY *(desperate):* What about in between? I mean we go home and, but we don't talk about things like this, I mean what happens if . . . I don't know what I'm saying.

NICOLSON *(gently):* I think you're saying you're angry. And that's scary. But I'm pretty sure it's not as destructive as you're afraid it will be. For either of you.

NANCY: But what's scary, I mean, it feels like maybe that's *all* there is, just anger.

NICOLSON: I think if there was only anger—you two wouldn't be here.

Nancy glances at Elliot, but he's looking away. A pause . . .

NICOLSON: Is this a good time for you every week?

INT. STEADMAN HOUSE—LIVING ROOM—NIGHT

Michael, Hope, and Ellyn are on the floor playing Scrabble.

ELLYN: Hope. Ho—ope . . .

MICHAEL: She has nothing.

Hope has been staring at the board intently. Finally, she makes her move.

HOPE: X, E, N, O, N. Triple letter score on the X.

ELLYN: Where else?

MICHAEL: You didn't get that.

HOPE: Thirty, one, two three four plus eight, forty-two, please Michael, and make sure you add it up right.

MICHAEL: She doesn't trust me.

HOPE: I know you too well.

While Michael studies the board Hope and Ellyn chat.

ELLYN: So they're seeing the marriage counselor tonight . . .

HOPE: They're probably home by now.

ELLYN: Why do I even bother trying to have a relationship?

HOPE: Stop. You really like him.

ELLYN: I think I like him. I do like him. Do you think I like him?

Michael puts out his letters.

MICHAEL: Well, it's not a lot of points, but it's artistic. T, A, T, T, O, O. With a double word score, plus "trot" and "amend."

Michael looks up: Ellyn is blushing and Hope is giggling.

MICHAEL: What?

HOPE: Nothing.

MICHAEL: What!

ELLYN: Nothing!

MICHAEL: You're lying.

HOPE: I'm not lying, I'm observing a discreet silence.

MICHAEL: Oh so you both know something here that you're keeping from me—I hate secrets, come on, give—

Still giggling, Hope glances at Ellyn.

HOPE: Unh-unh . . .

MICHAEL: I'm begging.

He is.

ELLYN: Hope, don't you dare . . .

But she is laughing as she says it.

HOPE: It *is* just Michael . . .

ELLYN: It's the deepest, darkest, most profound secret of my life!

HOPE: How old were we, fifteen?

Ellyn is stretched out on the floor with her face buried in her hands.

ELLYN: It was my sixteenth birthday. Please.

HOPE: We were in tenth grade. We went to this Donovan concert, and we were right up front, and Ellyn here was in love, I mean completely—

ELLYN: I was wearing my pink satin pants suit with the Nehru jacket, God it was gorgeous—

HOPE: And Donovan handed her a flower.

ELLYN: A rose. He gave me a rose. It was unbelievable. I still have it.

HOPE: In more ways than one. So the next day . . .

ELLYN *(yells):* Hope, we were sixteen.

Michael begins to get it.

MICHAEL: Oh my God, this is great. Where is it?

HOPE: Where the sun don't shine.

Hope leans over and pokes Ellyn's butt.

HOPE: It says "Mellow Yellow." And a picture of a rose.

MICHAEL: This is the most wonderful thing I have ever heard.

ELLYN: Michael Steadman, if you ever, ever tell anyone, may your dog get rabies and your wife get . . . fleas. Really. Never.

MICHAEL: Okay, I promise, but I mean other people must've, I mean, Woodman must've—

ELLYN: No he hasn't—

MICHAEL: You mean after all this time he hasn't seen your, I mean, you don't, what about when you do it from—*(he starts to laugh)* Do you, like, keep the lights off?

ELLYN: I hate you. I completely hate you. He doesn't think of me that way. I'll tell him when I'm ready.

HOPE: Ellyn, you are bizarre—

MICHAEL: "E-lec-tri-cal banana, bound to be the very next phase . . ." *(Ellyn kicks him)* I promise! I promise.

Trying to keep a straight face, Michael settles back to the game board.

HOPE *(with sudden decision):* I can't take the suspense. I'm calling Nancy.

MICHAEL: Hope, leave them alone.

HOPE: I worry about them, I won't be obvious.

MICHAEL: Yeah, right.

HOPE *(getting up):* Nancy was going to give me the name of a children's haircutter.

MICHAEL: Hope, Jane won't need a haircut for two years.

HOPE: I want to be prepared.

Ellyn is laying out her letters on the board.

ELLYN: They'll tell you about it when they're ready, Hope, you can't just call and ask. There.

Michael looks at her word.

MICHAEL: Ellyn, there's no E in groovy.

INT. WESTON HOUSE—NIGHT

Elliot and Nancy enter and greet the baby-sitter, Carla.

NANCY: Kids go to bed okay?

CARLA: Sure, after we sang the Tin Man song twenty times . . .

Nancy and Elliot laugh. The phone rings. Nancy reaches for it.

NANCY: Honey, can you pay—? Hello— Hi, Hope, no, we just walked in the door . . .

As Nancy talks Elliot rummages for money, trying to figure out what they owe the sitter.

NANCY: Yeah, it's right here. *(checks her address book)* Five-five-five eight-nine-six-seven . . . Sure. Ask for Michelle . . .

We now cut back and forth between the Westons and the Steadmans; Michael and Ellyn kibitz on the Steadman end.

HOPE: So, you were out?

MICHAEL: Oh, very subtle.

Nancy turns away from Carla and Elliot.

NANCY: Yeah, we had our first uhh—

HOPE: Oh, god, I'm sorry, I didn't mean—

Michael and Ellyn roll their eyes, etc.

NANCY *(laughing):* It's okay.

HOPE: Did you like him? Are you going back?

ELLYN: Leave her alone, you ghoul.

MICHAEL: Ask if they talked about sex.

NANCY: Yeah, next week.

HOPE: Are you glad?

NANCY: Yes. Definitely. I'll call you tomorrow, okay . . . Right, 'bye.

Nancy hangs up and turns back to Carla with a bright smile.

CARLA: Was it a good movie?

ELLIOT: Real good.

NANCY: Yeah, it was. Can you sit again next week, same time? We really need a regular night out . . .

CARLA: Sure. See you then.

Carla goes. Nancy sits. There is a loud silence.

ACT TWO

EXT. BASKETBALL COURT—DAY

Michael, Gary, and Elliot are playing a bizarre form of one-on-one-on-one. Michael decisively bodychecks Gary.

GARY: See him fouling me?

Michael steals the ball, then moves in for the lay-up.

MICHAEL: Foul? I don't see any blood.

Elliot is out of breath.

ELLIOT: When did I get too old for this game?

GARY: You should exercise more.

ELLIOT: In a gym, with cute girls, not out here where it's cold.

GARY: So how's my old pal Freddy Nicolson?

ELLIOT: I hear he used to beat you up at recess.

GARY: *He* beat *me* up? That's an amusing twist . . .

ELLIOT *(guarded):* He seems okay.

MICHAEL: How can you trust someone Gary learned subtraction with? I mean, this guy could just be me, or Gary, or anybody.

ELLIOT: He probably *is* just anybody.

MICHAEL: When did we become the authorities? Do you realize there are judges now our age? *Judges* . . . Hope's obstetrician looked like she should have been joining a sorority.

GARY: She probably was. Delivering Jane was her pledge assignment.

MICHAEL: No, really, I find this whole development very upsetting. Aren't we still the kids?

ELLIOT: We'll always be the kids. It's our tragic flaw.

GARY: Sixteen. That's what I'd like to be again . . . to do it *right* this time.

Michael suddenly laughs.

GARY: What?

MICHAEL: I'll tell you one person who's changed since she was sixteen . . .

GARY: Who? What?

MICHAEL: Her sixteenth birthday . . . She got a tattoo, that says "Mellow Yellow," on her ass.

GARY: Who?

MICHAEL: Guess.

GARY *(in disbelief):* Not Hope.

MICHAEL: Of course not.

GARY: It's certainly not Melissa. Helen Miller?

MICHAEL: You know she hasn't spoken to me for eight years.

GARY: So who?

MICHAEL: Ellyn.

GARY: You are kidding. Silk-suit-and-briefcase Ellyn?

Michael nods.

GARY: I love it. I wonder if she'd let me see it . . .

MICHAEL: Shepherd—you're dead if you say one word. I promised I wouldn't tell.

GARY: Okay, okay, you can trust me . . . But exactly where—

ELLIOT: Can we go eat now?

INT. DR. NICOLSON'S OFFICE

Elliot and Nancy are sitting in the same chairs.

ELLIOT: Okay. Okay. I feel like she's *on* me all the time, like I can never do anything right . . .

We go with them to a scene from the recent past.

INT. WESTON HOUSE—KITCHEN—NIGHT

The kids are rampaging and Nancy is trying to get dinner when Elliot returns home. He comes up behind her, gives her a hug that interferes with what she is doing, and kisses her neck.

NANCY: Hi—Elliot—

She doesn't stop what she's doing. He disengages and turns quickly to the kids.

ELLIOT: Hi, bunny rabbit, hey, Ethan . . .

NANCY: Ellie, could you get Ethan's peanut butter and jelly before I kill him, please?

Elliot gets out bread, jelly, and peanut butter.

ELLIOT (*to Ethan*): Kid, it's a big, exciting world out there, a world of hot dogs, and hamburgers and scrambled eggs and fried chicken, and someday maybe you'll get tired of PB and J and move on out into that world . . .

Elliot has reached the spreading-jelly-on-bread stage.

ETHAN (*watching Elliot*): I hate that, it has seeds.

Nancy looks over at Elliot, reaches for the jellied bread and tosses it in the garbage.

NANCY (*more amused than annoyed*): How could you not know by now that he only likes grape?

She gets out the grape jelly and begins a new sandwich.

ELLIOT: I forgot, I'll do it—

NANCY: No, no, go ahead, sit down.

Elliot walks quickly out of the kitchen.

BACK TO DR. NICOLSON'S OFFICE

where Nancy is truly surprised.

NANCY: I wasn't *yelling* at you—

ELLIOT: You took the bread right out of my hand.

Nancy looks down. She did, indeed, do that. And now there is
another story to share with Dr. Nicolson, so we go to

THE WESTONS' LIVING ROOM

Elliot sits on the couch, looking at the mail. Nancy comes in from
putting the kids to bed. At first, their voices from the session are
heard over the scene . . .

ELLIOT *(V.O.):* And I don't know, the whole issue of money,
    she's like on the warpath—

NANCY *(V.O.):* Elliot—

And now, as Nancy calls to Ethan, we are in the scene itself.

NANCY: Then leave the closet door open, I don't care. I told
    you there is no abominable snowman in there.

An offscreen Ethan corrects her.

ETHAN: Yeti.

NANCY *(closing her eyes):* Yeti . . .

Nancy collapses on the sofa, then looks through the stack of mail. A
manila envelope catches her attention.

NANCY: What's this?

ELLIOT *(glances up):* I joined Michael's health club so I can get in
    shape.

NANCY: Elliot—this costs three hundred and eighty-five dol-
    lars a year!

ELLIOT: It was a special deal.

NANCY: We can't afford this!

ELLIOT: Nancy, you've been bugging me to start exercising ever since I had those tests. So I finally got around to it.

NANCY: Writing out a check for three hundred and eighty-five dollars isn't what I call exercise.

Elliot throws down the catalog he's been trying to read.

NANCY: Why didn't you discuss it with me?

ELLIOT: What, I need your permission to lift weights?

NANCY: You know we're on a tight budget—

ELLIOT: I make good money—

NANCY: And it all goes out, every month, just for essentials. Damn it, Elliot—

Elliot takes a deep breath, trying to collect himself.

ELLIOT: Nancy. I am sorry. You're right. I should have told you about it, it just slipped my mind. Okay?

NANCY: Okay. *(pause)* So can you still cancel the membership?

ELLIOT *(furious)*: Why should I cancel the membership, I need the exercise! This is insane!

Elliot storms out. Over the image of Nancy sitting alone on the couch we hear Nancy and Elliot in Nicolson's office.

NANCY *(V.O.)*: I just thought, these days, you don't give up a job that pays well to start a company that could fail and ruin us, and Michael and Elliot had no track record—

And we're back now in

DR. NICOLSON'S OFFICE

as the story goes on in the present.

ELLIOT: We had won two awards and had been promised three separate accounts—

NANCY: They were local awards.

ELLIOT *(hurt)*: Sorry. They forgot my Clio this year. What have *you* won lately?

NANCY: I just meant it was a risky thing, setting up on your own.

ELLIOT: And you didn't have any faith in me.

NANCY: I was worried about the mortgage, and the kids—

ELLIOT: And you didn't have any faith in me.

NANCY: Faith has nothing to do with it, you're doing someth—

ELLIOT: Faith has nothing to do with it!? Nancy! *(turns to Nicolson)* Am I crazy here? Am I crazy? I'm taking this chance on something I dreamed about and she doesn't trust me at all—

NANCY: I'm out buying second-hand clothes for the kids at garage sales—

ELLIOT: Because you enjoy being cheap.

NANCY: And you have to have whatever you want, whenever you want it—

They are at an impasse.

NICOLSON: What's interesting is, for every accusation there's a counteraccusation, and each one seems plausible in its own way. I guess it could go on that way forever.

ELLIOT: Meaning . . . what?

NICOLSON: It could go on that way forever, and . . . neither of you would be any closer to getting what you want from each other.

INT. MICHAEL AND ELLIOT'S OFFICE—DAY

Elliot tacks up drawings, each showing a different perspective on a happy consumer about to bite into a piece of fried chicken.

MICHAEL: I mean, do you yell at each other over there, or what?

ELLIOT: Sometimes. Sometimes we yell, sometimes we just schmooze.

MICHAEL: Do you think it's helping?

Elliot now puts pushpins in the eyes and nostrils of the happy consumer.

ELLIOT: Did you ever actually try this junk? I wouldn't feed it to my cat, and I hate cats.

MICHAEL: Is it helping Nancy?

ELLIOT *(sits down):* Who knows? It takes some of the pressure off, I guess. *(pause)* It's like I'm always trying to get something from her and I don't know what it is.

MICHAEL: Sex . . .

Elliot thinks about this for a moment, then shrugs.

ELLIOT: Why not? Naahh, I mean, after you're married for twelve years, what's sex supposed to be like, anyway?

MICHAEL: You tell me.

ELLIOT: It *used* to be great. I mean, she was really, I used to feel sorry for other people 'cause they weren't us, I used to look in the mirror with her and think, how did this beautiful girl ever get fool enough to end up with me?

MICHAEL: So what happened? Anyway, she's not so beautiful, you're just ugly.

ELLIOT: What happened? Mountains wore down, ice ages came and went. I don't know, she lost interest in me. I didn't matter anymore. I think she just likes to see me squirm now . . .

MICHAEL: Have you told her about the, about the . . .

ELLIOT: The. Oh, Nance, by the way, I slept with Cheryl Eastman last year, you don't mind, do you?

They look at each other, and as they do we hear Nancy's voice, in therapy . . .

NANCY *(V.O.):* I want to be there for you, I really do—I don't know what it means anymore.

We now find ourselves back in

INT.—DR. NICOLSON'S OFFICE

ELLIOT: More excitement, more experimenting, like it used to be . . . I wish, I don't know . . . Like I heard this thing about Ellyn—*(starts to laugh)* She has this tattoo, on her ass—

NANCY *(laughing incredulously):* You're kidding! Ellyn?

ELLIOT: And it just sounded so . . . obscene . . . it's great . . .

NANCY: Ellyn?

ELLIOT: I mean, like last night.

NANCY: Last night I was exhausted, I knew Brittany was going to wake up, she's been having nightmares, you were grabbing me and insisting, and I—

ELLIOT: I wasn't insisting, I just wanted—

NANCY: You push me and push me and where does it end? It's one thing one night, and the next night you want me to use . . . or wear something, fine, whatever it is, you never even ask me what I want, everything is Elliot, Elliot . . . Where does it end?

NICOLSON *(to Nancy):* What *do* you want?

Nancy is thrown by Nicolson's question.

NANCY: To be left alone sometimes.

NICOLSON: Is that all you want, sexually?

NANCY: No, God, I want things, but what's the use of even asking? Elliot's not—I mean I'm so tired at the end of the day I don't even remember that I'm a sexual person.

ELLIOT: And whose fault is that?

NANCY: It's not about fault! Elliot, we have two kids, I spend my day talking about Rainbow Brite and Transformers and whether Brittany will drink her milk! Couldn't you help me to switch gears a little bit, would that be so hard? I mean, excuse me if the women in porno tapes don't need any help, but real people are different—

ELLIOT: You wouldn't even watch it with me—

NANCY: Because it was a huge turnoff, because it made my flesh crawl, those weren't real women, they're robots—

ELLIOT: Why? Because they don't mind making men happy?

NANCY: And if you had any sexual or emotional maturity you'd understand the difference— What?

His look, right now, is deadly.

NANCY: What?

Elliot is silent.

NICOLSON: What?

ELLIOT: What can I say? It's clear I'm a bad person, what's the point of even going on?

NANCY: I never said that.

ELLIOT: I'm a pervert, that's what you're saying, go ahead—

Silence.

NICOLSON: Do you think she's saying that?

ELLIOT (*after a long pause*): It doesn't matter what she's saying . . . To his embarrassment, tears are starting to well. He stops and looks away. Because what she's saying is she doesn't want me—

NANCY: I'm not saying that—

ELLIOT: She says it every day, I come in the door and she's not glad to see me, just "take the kids" or later if I try to . . . touch you it's what does Elliot want—don't *you* want me, I don't mean anything, you don't trust me, you fight me, you fight me, you just fight me—

NANCY: Ellie, I don't fight you, I—

ELLIOT: You're doing it now, you're doing it right now, can't you just stop for one minute? (*closes his eyes*) I just can't feel that everything I do . . . is . . . evil . . .

The room is very quiet. She is amazed at his vulnerability.

NANCY: Oh, Ellie. That's all I want, too . . .

ACT THREE

EXT. PLAYGROUND—DAY

Hope's eyes are closed as she lies on the ground, feeling the bright early winter sun on her face. Jane plays happily in the sand while Nancy watches Brittany climb on a jungle gym. Melissa joins them, hung about with cameras and camera bags.

HOPE: I was almost asleep . . . the sun feels so good.

Melissa hands Hope a bag of pretzels and joins Jane in the sandbox.

MELISSA: Carbohydrates and sodium. Have some.

HOPE: I thought you had to work this afternoon.

MELISSA: I do. Some guy who got divorced last month wants portraits of his kids. Three o'clock at the Liberty Bell.

Hope looks around to see where Nancy is. She lowers her voice.

HOPE: Let's hope it's not Elliot next month.

MELISSA: Tell all.

HOPE: What do I know? She doesn't tell me anything.

MELISSA: Do you ask her? Gary said that Michael said they fight all the time—

HOPE: They don't fi—

Hope sees Nancy approaching.

HOPE: Nancy—

Hope gives Melissa a quick look of embarrassed complicity as Nancy sits down.

MELISSA: So how are you, have a pretzel . . .

NANCY: Thank you, fine—Brittie, that's Janie's, don't grab. *(notices the cameras)* Is this work or play?

MELISSA: I've got a half hour before I have to be anywhere. Thought I'd stop by and see what real life is like.

Hope holds Jane's pretzel in her teeth as she tries to brush sand off Jane's mouth and hands. Real life? Nancy and Melissa laugh.

MELISSA: How's Elliot?

NANCY *(slightly guarded)*: He's fine.

MELISSA: How's counseling going?

HOPE: Melissa!

But Nancy is laughing.

MELISSA *(to Hope)*: All right, sorry, they scheduled my three sessions a week for the rest of my life the day I was born, I don't know what privacy is anymore.

HOPE: Nancy, I don't want you to think that I was saying anything bad—

NANCY: It's okay, we haven't exactly kept our problems to ourselves lately.

MELISSA: So is this person helping?

NANCY: Nicolson. Yeah, I think he really is. I mean it's not that so much has changed, but I think at least we're understanding better what we do to each other.

MELISSA: Like what do you do to each other?

Hope can't believe Melissa's directness. But Nancy's not offended.

NANCY: Well . . . It's hard to think . . . I mean, Elliot's an angry person . . .

HOPE: He is?

NANCY: All the time. You didn't know that? I think he saves it for me . . . And *he* says I'm really controlling—

HOPE: I never thought of you as controlling . . .

NANCY: Neither did I, but I don't—there are all these things that go on . . . this is really silly—

MELISSA: What?

NANCY: Well, like, when I do the laundry, I just noticed the other day, I always leave his clean clothes stacked on the bed. I mean, I've lived with this man for twelve years, I know where he keeps his jock straps, but it's as though I need to make some point of not doing that for him . . .

MELISSA: And he complains about that?

NANCY: Oh, no, no, it's not like that . . . I'm just . . . I'm just thinking . . .

INT. WESTON HOUSE—LIVING ROOM—NIGHT

Elliot comes in to an unnaturally quiet house. We even hear adult music playing, a Lyle Mays tape instead of "Big Bird Learns to Count." He stops short, then:

ELLIOT: Nancy?

NANCY (*offscreen*): Be there in a minute.

ELLIOT: Where are the kids?

NANCY (*offscreen*): Carla took them for hamburgers . . .

Elliot goes into the living room; a fire is lit and a bottle of champagne is chilling in a child's plastic sand bucket. Nancy comes in and gives Elliot a big kiss. She looks very pretty.

ELLIOT: What is this, I've walked into a Doris Day movie?

NANCY: I was thinking more Noël Coward. You know, put up

our feet, "Darling, how was your day?" "Can I get you a martini?" . . . That kind of thing.

ELLIOT: Sounds great.

Elliot takes off his shoes and stretches out on the couch while Nancy wrestles with the champagne bottle.

ELLIOT: You look nice.

NANCY *(turns and smiles):* Thanks.

ELLIOT: Aren't we supposed to be at Michael's?

NANCY: The game doesn't start till eight.

She brings him a glass of champagne.

NANCY: So. How *was* your day?

ELLIOT: I'm exhausted. Janine couldn't find the contracts for the Starlight Dairy account. Michael finally dug them out. She had them filed under M for milk.

NANCY: Not really.

ELLIOT: I swear to God.

A pause. It's Elliot's turn to think of something to talk about.

ELLIOT: It's a shame we have to go out. We could just watch the game here.

NANCY *(a little tentative, but trying):* Carla could handle the kids, I guess. Do you think they'd leave us alone?

ELLIOT: Probably not.

Another pause—then Nancy stretches out on top of Elliot.

NANCY: Still, I'm not sure this is an opportunity we can afford to waste.

Elliot puts one noncommittal arm around her and reaches with the other for his glass of champagne. He tries to take a sip but can't with Nancy on top of him.

ELLIOT: Nance—I can't—

NANCY: Sorry.

They both laugh. Then—silence. They sit there. Nancy waits for Elliot to make a move. Elliot waits for the interest or inspiration to make one. He can smell her hair . . . She can feel his beard against her forehead . . .

Elliot gets up.

ELLIOT: I'm starving. Are there any pretzels?

Nancy, angry and hurt, sips her champagne.

INT. STEADMAN HOUSE—KITCHEN—NIGHT

Melissa enters, holding a bag of groceries.

HOPE: Shhh . . . I just got her down.

MELISSA: "Down?" What is she, a German shepherd? Down, Jane, down.

Melissa points at Michael, who is slicing ham.

MELISSA (*accusingly*): Does your mother know about this?

MICHAEL: Just think of it as pastrami, Meliss.

MELISSA: Who else is coming over?

MICHAEL: We've rounded up the usual suspects.

Hope grabs more snacks and goes out to the living room. Elliot and Nancy enter now; he's got a bowl of salad, she's got a bottle of

NANCY: Champagne?

Melissa gets out a few ill-assorted cups and glasses.

MELISSA: These are classy guests. Just coming from cocktails with Noël Coward?

NANCY: No, Doris Day.

Melissa is confused, but lets it pass. Now Gary walks into the kitchen, followed by Hope.

GARY: Hey, where's *my* champagne?

HOPE: Why does everyone hang out in kitchens?

MICHAEL (*to Gary*): You're too late. Where's the beer?

Gary turns so Michael can remove two six-packs from the rucksack on his back.

GARY: Where's the dip?

MELISSA: Is Ellyn bringing Woodman?

HOPE: I think so. So everyone has to act civilized.

MICHAEL: I can handle it, I can handle it.

The doorbell rings. Everybody herds into the living room; Michael and Gary bring up the rear.

GARY: I was just thinking about Ellyn 'cause I read in "Dear Abby" about removing tattoos and . . .

Michael punches Gary's arm.

MICHAEL: Shut up, Shepherd.

INT. STEADMAN HOUSE—LIVING ROOM—NIGHT

Half-time; everyone is stretched out, surrounded by dirty plates, beer cans, and decimated bowls of snacks. Ellyn and Steve Woodman are together on the couch. Nancy has to climb over their legs as she heads for the kitchen.

NANCY: Excuse me—

GARY (chanting mindlessly): Beat L.A. . . . Beat L.A. . . . Beat L.A. . . .

STEVE (to Hope): So you're the one to come to for references on Ellyn, huh?

HOPE: I have found Ellyn to be completely responsible in carrying out all the duties which she is assigned. She is also a highly motivated self-starter and I recommend her without any reservations.

ELLYN: Hope, you are such a feeb . . .

HOPE: I am uniquely qualified to discuss you. Who else would put up with you for twenty-five years without even being related to you?

ELLYN: Remember in ninth grade we convinced Howard Pittler we were twin sisters who had been separated and adopted at birth?

STEVE: A kid with a name like Howard Pittler would believe anything.

ELLYN (to Hope): I hear he changed his name after he was indicted.

ELLIOT: A name like that has to be surgically removed.

MELISSA: That reminds me, Ellyn, I read in "Dear Abby" the other day—

Michael virtually lunges at her to get her attention.

MICHAEL (much too loudly): Melissa!

MELISSA: What?

MICHAEL: Help me in the kitchen . . .

MELISSA: I'm comfortable here . . .

He practically picks her up in his rush to hustle her into the kitchen. She realizes her near *faux pas* on the way. They pass Nancy walking back into the living room from the kitchen.

NANCY: Oh, Ellyn, by the way, I read in "Dear Abby" this week that tattoos can be removed, did you see that?

There is an agonized (and amused) silence. Nancy and Steve speak at the same time, but Steve is invisible right now.

NANCY: What—did I say something?

STEVE: What?

He starts to laugh.

STEVE: Oh, so that's why . . . Ellyn—

Ellyn is furious and near tears. She walks out of the room.

HOPE (to Michael): You *knew* not to do that, why did you do that?

Hope follows Ellyn out of the room. Michael feels awful, but he is also inclined to laugh.

MICHAEL: I only told Gary. (to Gary) Why do you have such a big mouth?

STEVE: Would someone please tell me—

GARY: I only told Melissa . . .

MELISSA: *I* didn't tell anyone . . .

STEVE: What is going on—

Nancy is near tears and feeling terrible.

NANCY: I heard it from Elliot, I had no idea it was a secret, I feel so bad . . .

ELLIOT: I heard it from them—

He points at Gary and Michael.

ELLIOT: I didn't know it was a secret either.

STEVE: Would someone clue me in here as to what's going on?

GARY: Just establishing the utter breakdown of our communal moral fiber . . .

Michael, meanwhile, is talking to a teary Nancy.

NANCY: I didn't know it was a secret.

MICHAEL: Nancy, it's my fault, really. It's my fault.

ELLIOT: Nancy . . .

Gary reaches over and turns up the volume of the TV.

TV ANNOUNCER: Drives down the lane . . . It's two on three, *blows* the lay-up . . .

INT. STEADMAN HOUSE—DINING ROOM—NIGHT

ELLYN: What is *wrong* with Michael, anyway? Why would he do that to me?

HOPE: I'm sure he didn't mean to hurt you, he just didn't think . . .

ELLYN: I specifically asked him not to tell anyone, and then he goes and . . .

Michael enters. Ellyn punches him in the stomach and walks out.

HOPE: Ells, it wasn't malicious, I guess he just thought it was funny—why am I defending him? There was no excuse. Oh, we all have such mouths on us . . .

EXT. WESTON HOUSE—NIGHT

As Nancy and Elliot walk up to their front door . . .

ELLIOT: Calm down about this thing, you didn't do anything wrong.

There is exasperation in his voice, as he has been saying this, and variations on this, for the last half hour.

NANCY: Oh, it just makes me cringe, I can't stop thinking about it. Why do I *always*—

ELLIOT: Oh, Nancy, don't start with the "always," you don't "always" anything.

NANCY: Yeah, but out of everybody there, I'm the one who blows it.

ELLIOT: You didn't blow anything. Would you stop obsessing?

Nancy gives him a quick look. He agrees that she blew it. He goes inside, and she follows. Carla turns to greet them.

CARLA: Hi, too bad the Sixers lost, huh?

INT. WESTON HOUSE—ELLIOT AND NANCY'S BEDROOM—NIGHT

Nancy and Elliot go through the ritualized motions of getting ready for bed. She kicks off her boots, sits on the bed, and laughs ruefully.

NANCY: What a night . . .

She looks over to Elliot, takes a deep breath—then reaches out her hand to him.

NANCY: Ellie, I want to be here with you. I won't obsess anymore.

He joins her on the bed. Nancy snuggles up to him.

NANCY: Before we went to Michael's, did I do something wrong?

ELLIOT: No, I was just tired, half of me was still worrying about Starlight Dairy and lowfat banana yogurt.

NANCY: Woodman's cute, isn't he?

ELLIOT: **How could he not know about the tattoo? I thought they've been going out for a while . . .**

Elliot has been running his hand over her hips and legs. She hooks her leg over his.

NANCY: **Maybe she always turns the lights off.**

ELLIOT: **That'd be boring . . .**

NANCY (*the romance of it*): **I think it'd be fun once in a while.**

They start to kiss.

NANCY: **You still tired?**

Elliot's hand is still running along her leg. He grimaces in mock horror.

ELLIOT: **Panty hose . . .**

An old fake battle between them. Nancy laughs as she wiggles out of her panty hose.

NANCY: **I have to wear *something* under my boots . . .**

ELLIOT: **No you don't . . .**

NANCY (*unbuttoning his shirt*): **You probably want me to wear stockings and a garter belt with a short skirt.**

He shrugs: it's not a bad idea.

NANCY: **Only Elliot . . .**

They lie next to each other, touching and looking. He is back to stroking her leg, now that the offending panty hose are gone.

It takes a few moments to realize things aren't going to work. Without removing his hand, and without any heat in his voice—in fact, with studied innocence—Elliot asks:

ELLIOT: **Don't you ever shave your legs anymore?**

Nancy can only stare for a moment. Immobilized. Then she gets up. She tries to speak, and can't.

ELLIOT: **What?**

In spite of her rage, or perhaps because of it, the most she can manage is a sad, regretful look. Then she walks into the bathroom. Elliot rolls onto his back and stares up at the ceiling.

ACT FOUR

INT. DR. NICOLSON'S OFFICE—NIGHT

Nicolson is smiling slightly, nodding, as Nancy tells the story.

NANCY: . . . I put on the clothes that he likes, I get out a bottle of champagne . . .

NICOLSON: And . . .

NANCY *(shrugs):* You tell me.

ELLIOT *(defensive):* I was tired, what do you want from me? I mean, I come home—this is great: she's allowed to say she's tired any time she wants. I try to say it once and forget it. So much for the end of the double standard.

NICOLSON: Were you tired?

ELLIOT: I just said I was tired.

NICOLSON: Too tired to have sex?

ELLIOT: I don't get this . . .

NICOLSON: I'm just wondering what went through your mind

when you saw Nancy dressed that way and the champagne . . .

ELLIOT: I don't know, it was fine.

NICOLSON: Was it stimulating?

ELLIOT (*up against it*): I don't know if it was stimulating. I was
probably a little turned on, I don't know. Why don't you
ask her something?

NICOLSON: I'm just wondering, if you were turned on, why
you think you didn't do anything about it.

ELLIOT: If I did something about it every time I felt turned on
we would've gotten divorced a long time ago. She
would've said I was a pervert or something.

NANCY: That's not true—

ELLIOT: Oh, come on—

NANCY: No, why don't you try, why don't you come home for
once and act like you do at the office, for Michael and all
the cute girls there, instead of walking in like . . . it was
the last place in the world you wanted to be.

ELLIOT (*yelling*): Why don't you try? Why is it always me, why
am I always the bad guy?

NANCY: I did try! I tried last night! And I got humiliated and
insulted. Whatever it is, it's never enough for you—

ELLIOT: And I'm supposed to switch gears just like that, after
all you've put me through, all the cutting me down,
pushing me away, for years and years, do you think that
one night is enough to change all that?

NANCY: It went both ways, Elliot, we lost *each other*. You can't
go back and find out who was to blame, we were both to
blame—

They are silent, like two battleships waiting to unleash the final
broadside.

NANCY (*quietly, slowly*): We have . . . to start . . . somewhere.

Nicolson turns to Elliot. They look at each other.

NICOLSON: What *would* be enough?

Elliot doesn't answer.

INT. NATURAL HISTORY MUSEUM—DAY

A rainy Saturday; we should be able to smell the steam heat and wet wool. Elliot entertains Hope, Michael, Nancy, and the kids with an imitation of the allosaurus attacking the duckbill.

IN THE AFRICAN ROOM

Hope, Nancy, and the kids—the men are elsewhere—peer into a diorama of cheetahs. Ethan uses the guardrail as a jungle gym.

HOPE: It wasn't your fault, it was Michael's, if it was any-body's—

BRITTANY: How come they don't work anymore?

NANCY: They're stuffed, honey.

BRITTANY: Stuffed?

NANCY: Yeah, that means—

She pauses; how to explain this to a three-year-old?

NANCY: That means that Daddy will explain it later.

They move on to the next display.

NANCY: I swear, I still wake up at night just cringing—

HOPE: Don't take it so seriously, Ellyn will recover.

NANCY: But will Elliot?

HOPE: What's Elliot got to do with it?

NANCY: Oh, everything I do bugs him.

HOPE: I don't get it, I really don't.

She means the whole situation. Nancy glances at Ethan and Brittany, who have run ahead to another display.

NANCY: Ethan, watch her! (*to Hope*) Me either. I get this feeling that I'm just supposed to stand around and . . . wait . . . till he gets all the crap out, all the bad feelings, so he doesn't turn them against me anymore . . .

HOPE (*a lovely thought*): How long is that supposed to take . . . ?

NANCY: I feel better in a weird way. It's like, at least I don't think it's all my fault anymore.

ETHAN: It's fifteen minutes, can I have popcorn now?

EXT. NATURAL HISTORY MUSEUM—DAY

Michael and Elliot are leaning against the columns, watching people come up the steps through the rain.

ELLIOT: . . . and I *am* too hard on her, but it's like she never really listens to me. She fights me. Either I do everything her way, or I'm this irresponsible jerk.

MICHAEL: Really?

ELLIOT: She totally doesn't trust me with money.

MICHAEL *(gently):* Elliot, neither do I.

ELLIOT *(smiles):* Thank you for your support.

They are silent for a moment, surrendering to the irony of life.

ELLIOT: Are you supposed to *like* being married?

Michael pauses before answering.

MICHAEL: I like it. I groan and complain, but yeah . . . my life feels . . . complete, in a way it never did before.

ELLIOT: It's like we're just all raw edges now. When I'm with her I can't . . . *feel* . . . anything anymore. Like we're on opposite sides of a . . . window . . . I don't know.

MICHAEL: Did you talk about the affair yet?

Elliot is not looking at Michael. He shakes his head.

ELLIOT: Believe me, that would kill everything.

Michael says nothing very loudly.

ELLIOT: You're in love with Hope.

MICHAEL *(embarrassed):* Yeah, I am.

ELLIOT: The thing is, see, I don't know—*(he stops, but can't stop)* I don't know if I love Nancy anymore.

MICHAEL: Elliot, I'm sorry.

ELLIOT: And no matter what she does, I can't seem to forgive her for that.

INT. STEADMAN HOUSE—KITCHEN—DAY

Sunday brunch. Hope, Melissa, and Gary read *The New York Times*. And, yes, Gary is probably looking at the lingerie ads. Michael reads the sports section of the *Inquirer*. Peace reigns until there's a knock at the door, followed immediately by

ELLYN *(offscreen):* Hello?

HOPE *(calls out):* In here!

MELISSA *(the identity of the new arrival has not registered):* You guys should really keep your door locked.

Ellyn enters the kitchen with the light of battle in her eyes.

ELLYN: I'm glad you're all here so I only have to say this once.

GARY: You guys really should keep your door locked.

There are some feeble hellos from the other three.

ELLYN: I suffered through one of the most humiliating moments of my life just because you bunch of babies couldn't keep your mouths shut about what was none of your business anyway. I mean I really like this guy—

HOPE: Ellyn, it's not like you had a disease or something—

ELLYN: It doesn't matter *what* it was, it's not for any of you to judge what's important and what isn't and that includes you, Michael Steadman. It should have been enough that it was my secret.

MICHAEL: Ellyn, I am really deeply sorry, truly, I have learned my lesson.

ELLYN: Don't apologize, I'm not finished yelling at you.

MELISSA: Woodman seemed like a nice guy.

ELLYN: Yeah, well, he still is.

GARY: Was he revolted, or embarrassed or something?

ELLYN: No, not exactly embarrassed . . .

HOPE: Well, exactly what, then . . .

Ellyn is trying unsuccessfully to hide a grin.

ELLYN: He was sort of, you know, turned on . . .

Michael throws a bagel at her. There's another knock at the door and Hope goes to answer it.

ELLYN: Michael, there was cream cheese on that!

MELISSA *(thinking)*: Now how much did it really hurt . . .

MICHAEL: So I did you a favor and you come here to yell at me—

ELLYN: That's not the point and you know it.

MELISSA *(to no one in particular)*: She had hers done years ago, maybe it's painless now . . .

MICHAEL: Ellyn, we only talk about you because we like you.

ELLYN: Then like me a little less, okay?

MICHAEL: Okay.

Hope returns to the kitchen followed by Steve Woodman.

STEVE: Hi, everybody . . . El—did I give you enough time?

Everyone greets him as he puts his arm comfortably around Ellyn.

HOPE: Steve. De-caf or regular?

GARY: Ellyn—

ELLYN: Yes?

GARY: Could I see it sometime?

ELLYN: You slime-mold . . .

SUNDAY MORNING AT THE WESTONS

Nancy and Elliot are trying to read the paper, too, but Ethan and Brittany are rampaging. Elliot finally gives up.

ELLIOT: Okay, you guys, get your coats, we'll go out.

ETHAN AND BRITTANY: To the park, to the zoo, hot dogs, I want ice cream, yea, Daddy, Daddy, Daddy . . .

Nancy puts down her paper and laughs.

ELLIOT *(to Nancy)*: Do something nice for yourself. Relax.

He looks around the wreck of the living room.

ELLIOT: No cleaning up. I'll do it later.

NANCY: **Thanks, Ellie.**

As he herds the kids toward their coats, Nancy stretches out on the couch.

LATER—AT THE DINING ROOM TABLE

Nancy, totally absorbed, looks through a stack of the kids' drawings. She hears the front door open. Ethan runs past her to the kitchen, then Elliot enters, carrying a sleeping Brittany.

ELLIOT: **She passed out when Cinderella lost her shoe.**

Nancy gets up to take off Brittany's coat as Elliot holds her. Elliot then puts her down on the living room couch.

NANCY: **Maybe you should put her in her room . . .**

ELLIOT: **Yeah, but I love to watch her sleep.**

They stand together looking down at Brittany for a moment.

NANCY: **Thanks for giving me some time this afternoon.**

ELLIOT: **I haven't given you much of anything else lately.**

They are standing there, very close and suddenly aware of it. Nancy gets uncomfortable, and moves away slightly—but not too far.

Elliot watches her as she straightens things on the coffee table—her hands as they work, her hair as it swings back and forth, her neck as she stretches. He's *seeing* her, and she knows it.

They're four feet apart and, for a moment, he can do nothing. And when he starts to take the tiniest step, by coincidence she moves away to put something down.

But she stops, seeing his move, and waits, and, finally, he goes to her . . .

Their embrace is very gentle.

INT. NANCY AND ELLIOT'S BEDROOM—NIGHT

They have just made love. Nancy sleeps with one hand touching Elliot's shoulder. Elliot is restless. He looks at Nancy, strokes her hair back from her face, turns over, and turns out the light.

There is a pause.

Elliot sits up, turns the light on again, picks up a book, and tries to read.

THE
MIKE VAN DYKE
SHOW

BY

MARSHALL HERSKOVITZ

AND

EDWARD ZWICK

In "The Mike Van Dyke Show," we wanted something silly to say something serious. Our friend Gary once told us that our show was a sitcom without the laughs. And so we chose the sitcom, the most frivolous of TV forms, to tell the story of Michael Steadman's crisis of faith.

We also wanted to talk about TV itself—how its shopworn constructs had taught us, for better or worse, a way of seeing the world. How we, as writers, had somehow bought its portrayal of an emotional landscape absent of contradictions and ambivalences, where people always say exactly what they mean, where problems are nicely shaped and tidily resolved. And why, in trying to do a show whose self-conscious mandate was to only tell the "truth," were we always coming back to the familiar rhythms of "Hi, honey, I'm home . . ."?

So, okay, we had an idea. Now we had to find a subject . . .

In our first season, we'd been pretty happy about our Christmas show. Richard had managed to evoke many of our mixed feelings about mixed marriages. We were all proud of what had to have been the only consciously ambivalent holiday show on network television.

So we figured—fine. If it worked once . . .

Here was a chance to do something we had always wanted to do: to talk about a problem we had talked about before. And in talking about it again, to really say something about the nature of all problems—that you solve them, and they don't go away.

As for the plot . . .

We steal from ourselves. We turned to something that had happened a few years before. A car crash, a phone call, a seven-months-pregnant wife, and a mad dash to the hospital. And though this had all happened long before *thirtysomething,* it remained a particularly vivid moment of horror that we had shared, one that had hovered unspoken between us for years, finally

101

landing on the pages of this script. As we began to summon up the memories of those few scary days, we realized they'd had an unexpected reverberation in our lives: by trying to reconcile the lurking presence of catastrophe in the context of everyday things, we were forced to confront our own particular articles of faith.

We are both Jews—raised conservative, bar mitzvahed, the dutiful sons and grandsons of more or less true believers. We are also both married to non-Jews. As religion goes, we are skeptical when it suits us, ardent when we need to be, and mostly uninterested in the observance of anything more than the benchmark holidays. Imagine our surprise when we discovered how unprepared we were to deal with even the outside chance of calamity.

Okay. So we've got calamity, comedy, Christmas . . . and a deadline. Now we need an outline, right? We sit down together, fight over who holds the keyboard and who gets to pace. The phone rings, the computer goes down, there's a crisis on the set, and then it's time for lunch. After the same tuna sandwich we've eaten for the past three years, we have exhausted every conceivable distraction and finally get to work. The scene goes something like this:

INT. MARSHALL'S OFFICE—DAY

Ed and Marshall—two tense, bearded guys, looking nothing like Ken Olin and Tim Busfield—are pretending to work. Ed is at the keyboard.

ED: Okay. Act One, Two, Three and Four . . .

MARSHALL: Wait a minute, there's something wrong with the computer. It'll just take me a second to fix it . . .

TWO HOURS LATER—SAME OFFICE

Same two guys, only tenser.

MARSHALL: All better. Okay. "Obligatory Beats . . ."

ED (*rapid fire*): End of Act One—the car crashes. End of Act Two—she's not getting better. End of Act Three—she's *really* not getting better. End of Act Four—he puts on a yarmulke and everybody cries . . . Okay. F-seven. It's saved. Now write it . . .

MARSHALL: I don't feel well. Is there any chocolate?

ED: Shut up and work. Subplot. We need a subplot—

MARSHALL: Why does this need a subplot? It's going to be tough enough with the stupid sitcom . . .

Marshall goes into the bathroom. Ed looks through Marshall's mail.

ED *(calls out):* It needs a subplot because it needs a subplot! Also, the other actors will be happy, they'll have something to do . . .

MARSHALL *(V.O.):* Well, who else is there?

ED: Elliot and Nancy.

Offscreen—the sound of a flushing toilet. Marshall reappears.

MARSHALL: Any messages?

ED: Did you wash your hands?

MARSHALL *(ignoring him):* How can we use Elliot and Nancy? They're separated.

ED: That's why they're perfect. Christmas in a broken home. The kids. Who spends time with who—

MARSHALL: Whom.

ED: Fuck you.

MARSHALL: What does this have to do with faith?

ED: I don't know yet, we'll figure it out. What we've got to do is put in the sitcom beats.

MARSHALL: I don't know how to write sitcom beats. I don't feel well.

Now Ed goes into the bathroom.

ED *(offscreen):* What's our favorite sitcom?

MARSHALL: *The Honeymooners. Dick Van Dyke. Lucy* . . .

ED *(offscreen): Moonlighting* did *The Honeymooners.* This is a terrible idea . . .

Ed returns, excited now.

ED: Wait! No! *Dick Van Dyke*—it's perfect! A TV show written by writers about writers writing a TV show—

MARSHALL *(cutting him off):* —only this time, it's a show about Christmas. And Santa Claus. Belief in Santa Claus—

ED: Belief, period. And Santa Claus is Carl Reiner!

MARSHALL: We'll never get Carl Reiner.

ED: The point is—Santa Claus is God.

MARSHALL: He is?

ED: Work with me here . . .

And so it goes. Somewhere along the way we realize that a year has passed since Michael's father's death. Not only do we steal from our lives, we also steal from the continuing finite universe of our show. As the beats fall into place and an outline emerges, it just conveniently happens that the Christmas tree lot where Michael stops to pick up a tree is near a synagogue. Sometimes structure is merely a matter of allowing your characters to tell you what *they* want to say or do. While our outline read, "Michael Drives Ethan Home," we didn't know until we wrote the scene that Ethan would be curious about what it means to be a Jew. And as the sitcom plot played out, Michael ended up in the Santa Claus suit.

We wrote it. Rewrote it. And rewrote it again. Some people liked it. Some just said, "Huh?" And on the last rewrite, only days before shooting, we added what was to become our favorite moment—when the simplicities of the sitcom and the complications of *thirtysomething* become one and the same—as "Mike" Van Dyke walks from the world of black and white into a world of living color.

MARSHALL HERSKOVITZ
and EDWARD ZWICK

ACT ONE

INT. STEADMAN LIVING ROOM—NIGHT

Ellyn, Michael, and Hope are playing Trivial Pursuit.

ELLYN: *Orange!* Oh, no . . . !

HOPE: "Name the northernmost island in the world."

MICHAEL: Ha, ha, ha, ha . . .

ELLYN: In the world?

MICHAEL: She's not going to get it.

ELLYN: Wait, wait, wait, wait . . .

GARY *(V.O.):* She might get it, she's the product of an utterly useless liberal arts education.

And now we reveal Gary, nearby, standing on his head.

MICHAEL: How can she not know this? I know this.

HOPE: We know you know, Michael, you know everything.

Michael sings the *Jeopardy* time-limit theme and then:

MICHAEL: BUZZZZ.

ELLYN *(desperate):* Banff!

Gary falls over. He and Michael shake their heads in unison.

ELLYN: What?

MICHAEL AND GARY: Banff isn't an island.

HOPE *(hides the card):* Okay, then . . . The name of the island is—

MICHAEL AND GARY: Spitzbergen!

ELLYN *(dismissive):* I knew that . . .

He lands on purple . . . It's Gary's turn.

GARY: Aagghh, television!! Why do I always land on television? Can't our generation define itself any other way besides what tunes it remembers from old TV shows?

Hope picks the next card. She reads it and starts humming *The Dick Van Dyke Show* theme. Michael joins in.

HOPE: "Who played Buddy and Sallie on *The Dick Van Dyke Show?*"

ELLYN: Oh, God, remember the one about the walnuts! You know, with the aliens and finally he opened the closet and they all fell on top of him.

HOPE: *Ooh,* ooh—when they thought they brought the wrong baby home from the hospital—and then the father was Greg Morris.

Michael starts humming the theme from *Mission: Impossible.*

GARY: Gee, and to think I was wasting my time reading *Ivanhoe.*

MICHAEL: Roger Moore, 1958. Made in England.

ELLYN: You ever notice how mothers are always dead on TV shows? I mean, like, *My Three Sons, Bachelor Father, The Rifleman,* and that one with Brian Keith and the fat guy.

(lies down) I always used to wonder about that when my mother was yelling at me . . .

MICHAEL: I used to stay home from school and watch all these shows, and think—oh, my God, is this what life is supposed to be? I mean, one week, Chip starts his own business and makes all this money and the next week he's flunking out of school because he's chairman of the dance committee—only what happened to the business . . . ? I mean, didn't you worry about Uncle Bub? Wasn't he lonely sitting there in that kitchen all the time? And then he died and they brought in Uncle Charley and he had to live in the kitchen, too.

HOPE *(stretching)*: I love TV. Everything's always nice and everybody's always happy.

GARY: Julius and Ethel Rosenberg.

ALL: What?

GARY: They played Buddy and Sallie. *(on their look)* Didn't you see the episode where they're executed as Russian spies?

Ellyn throws the dice at him. Hope hits him with the box. Michael just laughs.

INT. MICHAEL AND HOPE'S BEDROOM—NEXT DAY

Janey unravels rolls of wrapping paper as Michael tries to dress.

MICHAEL: But is that going to be enough?

HOPE *(offscreen)*: Michael, it's a tricycle, that's a huge present.

MICHAEL: I know, but what if she doesn't like it, then there's no backup. What if we get her the entire F. A. O. Schwarz catalog just to be safe?

HOPE *(offscreen)*: *And* the presents my parents are sending, *and* the ridiculous clothes that Melissa will give her, *and* the things you've already bought her for Hanukkah. And anyway—

MICHAEL: I'm not changing the subject, I'm talking about Christmas.

HOPE *(offscreen):* No, you're talking about presents. I just want to know if we're talking about the same holiday here.

Michael prepares himself, then walks into the bathroom where, discreetly, we see Hope sitting on the toilet.

MICHAEL: Okay. We got a tree and a menorah.

HOPE: Correct.

MICHAEL: Are we talking lights on the outside of the house?

HOPE: Are we talking going to synagogue?

MICHAEL: All right: theology. You want to know if I accept December twenty-fifth as the birth of Jesus.

HOPE: Michael.

MICHAEL: Okay, I accept it. Now you want to know if I accept that a star led three wise men to a manger where a lady who claimed she hadn't had sex just had a baby— *(hmmmmm . . .)*—who was the son of God.

HOPE: And I'm supposed to accept that a tiny drop of oil lasted eight days and that six guys with bows and arrows defeated all the Roman legions.

MICHAEL: Syrians. Okay, look . . . I'll give you the star and the three wise men if you agree to no lights outside, presents on at least two nights of Hanukkah, and a fifty-percent reduction in medium-range ballistic missiles.

HOPE *(sighs):* Michael, I just want this all to be okay for you, because last year you were really sad and . . . obnoxious and because . . . well, because . . . And because—

MICHAEL: —it's Christmas.

HOPE: Right.

INT. STEADMAN HOUSE—KITCHEN—SOON AFTER

Hope and Michael elbow each other out of the way as they fight for counter space. She's trying to get to the soda crackers, he's making oatmeal for Janey, eating her banana while he stirs.

MICHAEL: It's totally simple, listen to me: I get classical tapes for Gary today at lunch, on the way home I stop and pick up the print for Melissa, and tomorrow at the airport I get one of those toy airplanes that fly back to you for Elliot, he loves those.

HOPE *(looks at him):* Which leaves Ellyn, Nancy, Ethan—

MICHAEL: I'll get him one too—

HOPE: Poor Ethan, Nancy says all he talks about is shooting down Santa Claus with his missile launcher.

MICHAEL: Little heat-seeking action, SAM-six, should do the trick.

HOPE: Not to mention Brittany, Linda, Carol—*(bends down suddenly)*—sweetie, don't eat the pit. Mommy'll throw the pit away. Do you want to throw the pit away? *(going right on)* Jim, Barton, your brother—

MICHAEL *(disbelief):* We don't have to get him anything—

HOPE *(ignoring him):* —your mother, my parents, oh my God, the Post Office, I'm gonna spend my entire lunch hour standing in line.

MICHAEL: You want me not to go.

HOPE: No, I want you to go. I just want you to be in two places at once. *(bends down again)* Oh, honey, did you spill that? Michael—

He's already getting the paper towels. They continue on the floor.

MICHAEL: Look, we pick out a charity, we make donations in everyone's name. It's quick, it's convenient, it's virtuous.

HOPE: Steve, David, and Marlene . . .

MICHAEL: AIDS Project, the homeless—*(points)* There's some left over there.

HOPE: Michael, it's Christmas, of course you make donations, but you *still* have to *buy presents.*

MICHAEL: But why?

HOPE: Explain to me again why they wait a year to put up your father's headstone?

MICHAEL: They want to make sure he's really dead.

HOPE: Okay, so you leave tomorrow and you're back Friday morning, which brings us to Christmas Eve, which means the food, the extra chairs, the tree . . .

Hope smells something . . .

HOPE: Oh, God—

The oatmeal is burning. Michael jumps up, knocking over Janey's Duplos. As the baby cries, Hope and Michael meet at the stove.

MICHAEL *(hugs her):* It's just life, where would we be if life were manageable?

Hope kisses him on the forehead, but can't linger.

HOPE: Janey, why are you always late for day care? Don't your parents know that socialization begins at preschool?

She carries Janey out, waving bye-bye to Daddy.

MICHAEL *(to himself):* It's just life.

While spooning out the burnt oatmeal, he reaches over and turns on the TV. Canned theme music introduces what sounds like an old sitcom. Michael isn't really paying attention. But as the camera moves in it angles to include theTV—and we see

The Mike Van Dyke Show

in glorious black and white, already in progress: a two-wall, simplified 1960ish version of the Steadman living room. Mike Van Dyke, in narrow-lapelled suit and snap-brim hat, enters to thunderous applause.

MICHAEL: Honey, I'm . . . *(trips on a tricycle)* . . . home.

CANNED LAUGHTER

HOPE *(offscreen):* Hi, darling. Oh, by the way—

As Michael starts to get up from the floor, he notices that a large child's fingerpainting is stuck to his pants.

In walks Hope Tyler Moore, resplendent in ponytail, toreador stretch pants, and Capezios.

HOPE *(continuing):* —you have to take a look at what—*(grimaces)* —little Janey painted today.

MORE CANNED LAUGHTER

MICHAEL *(pulling it unstuck):* Beautiful.

They kiss sweetly. As they hug, a list unrolls from Hope's hands.

MICHAEL: What's that?

HOPE: Just the presents we still have to buy.

MICHAEL *(taking off his coat):* Oh, honey, I am so glad to be home. Do you know what Thorndike did today, you don't want to know, I don't want to know but I have to know . . . All you have to know is I am *so glad* to be in my own home, alone with my very own wife—

HOPE: Darling, that's so nice, but—

MICHAEL: —ready to spend the entire night doing absolutely—

HOPE: —but darling . . .

MICHAEL: —nothing. Recharging my batteries, shutting out the world, not speaking to another living soul until tomorrow.

ELLIOT *(offscreen): Mikey . . . !*

Elliot Paris, wearing a Santa cap, enters to thunderous applause and laughter. Behind him is his mousy wife, Nancy, and their two bratty children.

ELLIOT: Ho, Ho, Ho, big fella! How's the ad game?

MICHAEL *(looks at Hope):* Elliot, how are you doing, *what* are you doing—*(sotto voce)*—here.

ELLIOT: Just a small flood in the kitchen. Old Nance put too much soap in the dishwasher again.

NANCY: If he had washed the dishes any time in the last two years he'd know the dishwasher is broken—

ELLIOT: You want to air our dirty dishes in public?

ETHAN: Real funny, dad.

MORE LAUGHTER

MICHAEL: Hello, Nancy. Hi, kids.

The kids glower at him.

ELLIOT: You know why we're here, Mikey-boy?

MICHAEL: You want me to wash the dishes?

ELLIOT: Better than that—the opportunity of a lifetime.

Elliot puts a Santa cap on Michael's head.

ELLIOT: You were right, Hope. He'll be perfect.

MICHAEL: What?

HOPE: Darling, it *is* only one afternoon. And it's for charity.

MICHAEL: *What* is for charity?

On his look we cut back to:

MICHAEL, IN THE KITCHEN

staring at the television—on which a weatherman is giving the forecast for the tristate area.

INT. MICHAEL AND ELLIOT'S OFFICE—NEXT DAY

Elliot is working away, trying to balance a ruler on his nose. He looks up to discover Michael, staring at him.

ELLIOT: What?

Michael says nothing.

ELLIOT: So the guy walks in and says: "Don't give me *Cherry* Soda, I'm not into *Berry* soda, let me have the *very* soda that I really need: Layton's Natural Gentle-Working Fast-Acting Mineral Tonic."

MICHAEL: A rap song to sell laxative?

ELLIOT (*utterly without anger*): What the hell do *you* want then? I'm sick of this, I'm sick of carrying this company, I'm sick of you sitting there passing judgment on every idea I have, inhibiting my creativity.

MICHAEL: We could show before and after pictures.

ELLIOT: I know why *I'm* not working. Why are *you* not working?

MICHAEL: I'm working. Just badly. Tomorrow I see my father's headstone.

ELLIOT: That should be fun.

MICHAEL: I don't know if I want to be buried.

ELLIOT: Putrefaction is part of the life-cycle. Replenishing the soil, so plants can grow, animals can eat, people can eat animals and get clogged arteries and die so they can replenish the soil some more.

MICHAEL: Wanna know what I'm buying you for Christmas?

ELLIOT: "I don't believe in Christmas. I'm shooting down Santa's reindeer with a machine gun."

MICHAEL *(rueful smile):* I thought it was a missile launcher.

ELLIOT: He changes his weapons daily. He's into ordnance.

MICHAEL: What are you going to do about it?

ELLIOT: Tell Santa to take out insurance. What can I do? It's his first Christmas since we broke up—who can blame him?

MICHAEL: Is there anything we can do?

ELLIOT: Tell his parents to get their crap together.

Now Michael gets an idea.

MICHAEL: Wait a minute, here we go: Two really old guys, only it's the future, right, they're wearing weird clothes, and people float by, and one says—*(Yiddish accent)* "You goin' to Mars today?" And the other says: "Go to Mars, I can't even go to the toilet!" *(no response)* It's great!

ELLIOT *(deadpan):* This is the future . . . ?

MICHAEL: Right.

ELLIOT: But people still have accents like that?

MICHAEL: Forget it.

ELLIOT: Won't people not have accents like that then? I mean, don't you have to come from the old country to—

MICHAEL: Elliot, it's a commercial in the present. It's supposed to be funny *now*—never mind.

The phone rings. Michael picks it up.

MICHAEL: What? . . . What? Put them on.

We watch his face fall and then turn white as he listens.

MICHAEL: Yes . . . When? . . . What do you mean? Is she— What hospital?

Elliot is getting it now, starting to stand up.

MICHAEL: What do you mean you can't tell me if she's okay? . . . All right, okay . . . okay.

He hangs up, trembling.

MICHAEL: Hope was in an accident with Janey and she's at the hospital.

His voice is starting to crack.

MICHAEL: They took them to the hospital and they won't tell me anything oh my God Janey oh God.

ELLIOT (getting their stuff together): Which hospital, come on, I'll drive, did they say which hospital? Come on, Mike, we'll just go—

Michael lets Elliot lead him out.

IN ELLIOT'S CAR—

As they drive.

ELLIOT: Listen to me, you don't know anything, you just have to wait until we get there. (no response) Michael—I just know everything's okay, I don't know why, I just know it.

Michael is silent for a few moments, then:

MICHAEL (to the car up ahead): Stupid asshole, one lane or the other, MOVE IT!

Grimly, they drive on.

INT. THE HOSPITAL

Michael rushes to the front desk and is directed to the elevators. He shifts his weight from one foot to another until it arrives.

IN ANOTHER CORRIDOR

Michael is at the nurse's station.

MICHAEL: E . . . A . . . D . . M . . . A . . N.

NURSE *(nods)*: I'm going to have to page Dr. Richards.

MICHAEL *(choking up)*: Why do you have to page him? Why can't you tell me if she's okay? Is she alive—

NURSE: Sir, your wife is alive, please just take a seat, the doctor will be with you right away.

Michael nods and steps about two paces away from the nurse's station. Over the P.A. we hear them paging Dr. Richards.

DOWN THE HALL

he sees Janey, looking tiny and forlorn next to a policewoman. His eyes tearing, Michael runs to her and picks her up.

JANEY: Where Mommy? Where Mommy?

MICHAEL *(squeezing her)*: Daddy's here . . .

VOICE: Are you Mr. Steadman?

Michael turns to see a doctor standing above him.

HOSPITAL HALLWAY

Dr. Richards and Michael approach a private room.

DR. RICHARDS: . . . the contusions on her face look worse than they are, and there's no evidence of concussion—she's lucky really that she had her seat belt on.

MICHAEL: And . . . and . . . in terms of, of any internal . . . stuff—

DOCTOR RICHARDS: Well, we've scanned her and there's no fluid in the abdominal cavity. It's hard to tell with internal injuries, probably the best thing to do is keep her quiet for a few days and watch her.

They go into the hospital room. Michael kneels by Hope's bedside. She is looking at him, her face bruised and bandaged.

HOPE *(almost inaudible)*: I'm okay, believe it or not.

MICHAEL *(can barely speak)*: Are you okay?

HOPE: Where's Janey?

MICHAEL: She's outside, she's fine.

HOPE: I have to see her.

Michael looks to the doctor, who shrugs.

DR. RICHARDS: In a little while.

HOPE: Do I look horrible?

MICHAEL *(tries to laugh):* No, silly.

She looks at him, sees the terror he's been holding inside—and reaches for his face. They kiss.

HOPE *(dreamy):* I'm driving along and Janey was singing "Kumbaya" and then there was this car just, like, drifting across all four lanes of the expressway, like bouncing off other cars, and I just kept thinking, "This is so weird . . ."

His grip on her hand grows tighter; they just look at each other across the chasm of Fate.

ACT TWO

INT.—HOPE AND MICHAEL'S BEDROOM—NIGHT

Hope is lying in bed, watching Michael's frenetic activity with a certain degree of drugged-out amusement.

MICHAEL: Or I can just leave the tray here in case you're hungry later on, you want your bathrobe here or in the—

HOPE: Michael, I can get up to get my bathrobe.

MICHAEL (*drill sergeant*): You can't get up for any reason.

HOPE: Yes, sir.

MICHAEL (*looking at his watch*): And it's time for more drugs.

HOPE: I don't need drugs.

MICHAEL: Hey, babe, "Better Living Through Chemistry." Doctor says get high.

HOPE: I can't feel my toes, do I still have toes? Do you like my toes?

MICHAEL *(kisses them):* Now, tomorrow, tell me again, you were gonna order the turkey and then go into Germantown to get the hats for your father's golf clubs.

HOPE: They're not hats.

MICHAEL: And then . . . no, wait, I'll remember—oh, right, Christmas decorations. I'll be sure to get lots of ones with crosses and Nativities.

HOPE: You're going to Chicago.

MICHAEL: Honey, I can't go, how can I go?

HOPE: I can manage here. Ellyn offered to take off work. Honey, it's your father's headstone.

MICHAEL: Hope—I can go later. He's not going anywhere.

HOPE *(starting to laugh):* It hurts when I laugh . . .

MICHAEL: Don't laugh, you're not allowed to laugh.

They are both laughing now.

HOPE: Shut up and get me more drugs.

MICHAEL: You can take the girl out of the counterculture, but you can't take the counterculture out of the girl.

He gets out the tablet, gives her water, straightens the covers, generally acts like a Jewish Mother. Their faces are close together.

MICHAEL: Can I get you anything? Are you sure you're okay?

HOPE: The biggest danger here is I might get to like this.

INT.—KITCHEN—LATER THAT EVENING

The troops have mobilized. Ellyn is feeding Janey while Elliot does his best to prepare grown-up food.

ELLYN: Did they do, like, all kinds of incredibly painful tests on her?

ELLIOT: I don't know, I spent most of my time in the waiting room next to this guy with this really tiny bullet hole right in his forearm . . . It was really cool, it hardly bled at all . . .

ELLYN: Gross. Was Michael okay?

ELLIOT: Basically out of his mind, but okay.

ELLYN: Looking on the bright side isn't exactly his strong suit.

Janey knocks her food off the high chair.

ELLIOT: *Ooops.*

ELLYN: Don't worry, Janey, I'm signing an affidavit that you didn't spill that.

Michael enters, carrying the dinner tray.

ELLYN: How's she doing?

MICHAEL: Stoned.

ELLIOT: Ah, gee . . . *(puts his arm around him)* How're *you* doing?

MICHAEL: Not stoned, but generally okay.

ELLIOT: You hungry? Today's special is a tempting house salad with a floor wax vinaigrette.

The phone rings. They all roll their eyes.

MICHAEL: Who's left? *(answers it)* Hi, Gar. No . . . she's okay . . . No, we've got everything pretty much in hand. Elliot's trashing the kitchen.

ELLIOT: Janey did it.

MICHAEL: —no, she was on the expressway and some idiot lost control and bounced off the guardrail . . . Yeah, tell me about it. Sure, no, well maybe tomorrow would be better. Okay, yeah. I'll tell her. Thanks, man. *(hangs up)* If I have to tell this story one more time . . .

ELLIOT: Print up a detailed account. Be sure to include how I spent twenty dollars on cab fare from the hospital.

The phone rings again. Michael hangs his head, then picks it up.

MICHAEL *(perfect . . .):* Hi, Mom . . .

Ellyn and Elliot try not to laugh as Michael goes on.

MICHAEL: Oh, right, well, actually, um . . . Uh, before we talk about flight times— See . . . um . . . Hope had a small accident today. NO, NO, she's okay, she just has to stay in bed.

Nancy and Ethan enter through the kitchen door. She stops short upon seeing Elliot.

MICHAEL *(watching them):* No, we just have to watch her for a while. I mean, yeah, it was an accident—

ELLIOT: Hi, Nance. Everything's okay. *(to Ethan)* Hi, pal.

NANCY: She's okay?

ELLYN: She's fine, she's on painkillers.

NANCY: What kind?

MICHAEL *(still on the phone):* —the car's messed up, but thank God she's okay and Janey's okay . . . Yes, Janey was in the car.

NANCY *(hand to her throat):* Janey was in the car!?

MICHAEL: Mom, she wasn't hurt *at all.* They just want to make sure there's no internal injuries.

ETHAN: Is the car like all smashed up? Can I see it?

MICHAEL *(still on the phone):* . . . I hate to say it, but I really think you're right. I mean, she's in bed. I'll come next month, we'll have more time that way anyway.

ETHAN: Dad, are you coming for Christmas or not?

Elliot and Nancy look at each other.

ELLIOT: Sure, guy, I guess. Or, maybe you and I'll do our own Christmas thing . . .

Ethan turns and walks out of the room.

MICHAEL (still *on the phone):* Okay, I'll tell her.

NANCY *(furious):* I can't believe you just said that.

ELLIOT: What? You're the one who says not to lie to them.

NANCY: So you make another promise to him you won't keep?

Elliot turns away, equally furious.

MICHAEL: We love you too, Mom. 'Bye. *(hangs up)* Hi, Nance.

NANCY *(holding it together):* Hi, Michael. I'm just gonna go up-stairs and stick my head in, okay?

She hurries out. Elliot leans his head against the refrigerator. An awkward moment as Ellyn doesn't quite know how to respond to what just went down. She starts humming a jaunty up-tempo version of "Sleigh Ride."

THE KITCHEN—THAT NIGHT

As Michael enters the kitchen and turns off the overhead light, all that remains is the blue glow of the TV set. Exhausted, he picks up a stack of unattended bills and junk mail and tries to summon up the will to go through them.

The sound of the TV gradually comes up until we hear recognizable voices. It's—*The Mike Van Dyke Show!*

And we're in Michael and Elliot's office—or, rather, the early sixties version of it. Several men in various stages of portliness are standing in line in Santa Claus outfits.

MICHAEL: Elliot, we're on a deadline and you've got us auditioning Santas for Ethan's Christmas pageant. We're going bankrupt, I *know* we're going bankrupt . . .

ELLIOT: Mike, stop whining and complaining. Worst that'll happen is we'll go bankrupt.

He turns to the next waiting Santa.

ELLIOT: So . . . you're Santa Claus, eh?

SANTA #1 (*mile-a-minute spiel*): Absolutely been Santa for thirty years Gimbels Wannamakers Lit Brothers Strawbridges you name it I worked it kids love me and I turn 'em over thirty an hour.

Michael and Elliot exchange a look.

ELLIOT: Thanks. We'll get back to you.

Michael dials the phone—rotary dial, of course—while Elliot looks out at the rest of those auditioning. One Santa is so old and drunk that he can't get one leg into the trousers.

MICHAEL (*hanging up*): Where is Hope, she should've been home hours ago, there's a blizzard out there . . .

ELLIOT: Mike, stop worrying and agonizing, we've got *real* problems here. These Santas are terrible! Which means—

He holds up a large red false nose.

MICHAEL: What's that?

ELLIOT: Just wait, it'll look great.

MICHAEL: Oh, no—

Too late. Elliot has attached the nose to Michael's face.

MICHAEL *(nasal):* Elliot.

ELLIOT: It's beautiful, it's you . . .

MICHAEL *(trying to take it off): Elliot . . .*

ELLIOT: I smell chestnuts roasting on an open fire, I hear sleigh bells . . .

He does indeed, because we can also hear the faint tinkling of bells as a door opens offstage.

MICHAEL *(clawing at his face):* ELLIOT!

Now, a disheveled gentleman in a muddy union suit approaches Mike and Elliot.

GENTLEMAN: Excuse me, gentlemen—you haven't seen several reindeer pass this way, have you?

MICHAEL: Excuse me?

GENTLEMAN: What a mess! Someone's gonna hear about this!

He pokes at the waiting Santas, scrutinizing their suits. Michael and Elliot look at each other: who is this nutcase?

GENTLEMAN *(mumbling to himself):* Nope, too big, nope, too thin. If I don't hurry up, I'll miss Belgium and Liechtenstein. *(raising his voice)* You call this a suit? This wouldn't keep my elves warm! Try going to Spitzbergen in *this* suit!

MICHAEL: Excuse me, sir—are you all right?

GENTLEMAN: All right? I'm a mess. These television antennas are a menace, you can't find a decent rooftop anywhere. So I park on the street, I'm in a house not five minutes, and my sleigh is being towed away. I see a nice group of kids on the corner, I ask for help, and the next thing I know, they're stealing my clothes. *(sighs)* Goodwill to men, *indeed!*

He shakes his head and starts to walk away.

MICHAEL: Elliot, that man needs help.

ELLIOT: *I'll* say.

MICHAEL: No, really, he's a sick man. We can't let him go wandering the streets out there. It's Christmas Eve.

ELLIOT: Exactly, and we have one hour to get to Ethan's school and that doesn't leave any time to get involved with crazy men in their underwear.

MICHAEL: Don't worry, I'll just talk to him for a second.

He runs off, leaving Elliot shaking his head, as we go back to:

MICHAEL IN THE KITCHEN

He has fallen asleep. The TV's blue glow flickers across his face.

EXT. A TOWING YARD—DAY

Michael talks to an insurance adjuster, moving past rows of damaged cars, ending up at Hope's jeep, its front end smashed and mangled. Michael stares at it.

EXT. A PARKING LOT—DAY

Michael and Melissa linger in the car, not yet ready to face the cold.

MICHAEL: I don't know, it was just weird seeing it . . . I'd finally gotten to the point where I wasn't cringing every five minutes thinking about what could have happened.

MELISSA: But it didn't happen.

MICHAEL: Right. So—everything's great.

MELISSA: It *is* great.

MICHAEL: I know it's great. That's why we're here.

He thinks for a moment.

MICHAEL: I didn't go to my father's unveiling.

MELISSA: I'm sure they unveiled it without you. What is it, like a curtain they pull back?

MICHAEL: I don't know, I didn't go to my father's unveiling.

MELISSA *(looking around, then:)*: Do you believe in God?

MICHAEL: The problem is, if you *do* believe in God, where does that fit in with any rational way of looking at the universe? I mean, what is there left for Him to have done? We had a Big Bang, we have particle physics, He didn't make the world. I mean, if He's around, He's pretty minimalist. On the other hand, if you *don't* believe in God, not only are you saying that ten thousand years of human beings were complete idiots but also . . . it's just so . . . dreary.

MELISSA: You know—you could come with me later.

MICHAEL *(almost shivers)*: Synagogue . . . Serious business.

MELISSA: It's not serious, it's actually kind of fun.

MICHAEL: You're kidding, right?

MELISSA: No, I was surprised myself. Shelley Feinman roped me into one of these Friday night deals and I really kind of liked it. I mean it's not a Springsteen concert, but there's just this, I don't know, warm feeling.

MICHAEL: And single men.

MELISSA: And single men.

MICHAEL: Nerdy single men.

MELISSA: They're not nerdy, though I admit I assumed they'd be nerdy, too. Michael, it's not like Hebrew school anymore. I mean, real people are coming back and getting involved with this stuff. *(getting into it)* I mean, this guy Markowitz, the new rabbi, he's really smart.

MICHAEL: And cute? *(Melissa hits him)* Melissa, the last time I was in a synagogue, besides when Dad died, I think was in nineteen sixty-seven—when Nate the janitor caught me and Allen Moss slugging down the Manischewitz. It's like, I don't know—Hebrew school and all that, what did it have to do with Little League and the Beatles and getting girls to go to second? But that wasn't even it, it just sort of stopped making sense.

MELISSA *(not unkindly):* Maybe 'cause it's not about sense.

MICHAEL *(chews on that):* We really should get this done.

They get out of the car and start walking—and only then do we discover that they are in

A CHRISTMAS TREE LOT

MELISSA: So, what kind are *you* getting?

MICHAEL'S CAR

—a large Christmas tree tied to the top—pulls up outside a synagogue.

Inside the car, Michael and Melissa smile at one another.

MELISSA: Last chance. Rabbi Markowitz is really cool . . .

MICHAEL *(finally shakes his head):* Thanks.

She kisses him, gets out, and looks at the tree.

MELISSA: This is God's revenge for the time you planted the tree in Israel for Alfred E. Newman.

And he watches her as she crosses the street and walks into the imposing building.

INT. STEADMAN HOUSE—NIGHT

Michael is coming up the stairs when he hears Hope throwing up in the bathroom. He rushes to the bedroom; she emerges, wiping her face with a towel.

MICHAEL: Honey, honey—are you okay?

HOPE: I'm fine. I just felt dizzy.

She slips between the covers as he watches her in mute concern.

ACT THREE

INT. THE KITCHEN—THE NEXT MORNING

Hope and Michael are, once again, going about the business of living.

HOPE *(feeding Janey):* Did you dream of sugarplums and angels and kissing little boys under the mistletoe?

MICHAEL *(to Hope):* At least call him.

HOPE *(still to Janey):* Have you decided what you want Santa to bring you for Christmas?

MICHAEL *(pushing it):* You're going to pick up the phone and tell him what happened to you last night, and if you don't do it, I will—

HOPE: I got dizzy, Michael, I was in bed taking drugs for two days and I got up too fast. Please. I've lost enough time already—

MICHAEL: You don't think you're going out today . . .

HOPE: Michael, we're on the brink of disaster here. If I don't go out today, we won't be ready.

MICHAEL: Forget it. Forget the dinner and forget the presents.

HOPE *(stares at him):* And the first thing we have to do is go to the rent-a-car place.

MICHAEL: I'll get the stuff, I'll make the dinner.

HOPE: Honey, I can't do that, okay? I feel fine. I want to get out of here, I have to get out of here. This scared me too and I just want to . . . *(shakes her head)* Okay, I need the turkey and stuff for the stuffing, and—you can get the chairs from Elliot, right?—and flowers, I'll do that tomorrow. This could be like a really convincing simulation of Christmas dinner. Janey, Christmas dinner, it'll be so pretty, we'll have candles and holly and what I should really do is bake some bread—*(looks at him)* Honey?

MICHAEL *(finally):* I'll drop you off.

INT. MICHAEL AND ELLIOT'S OFFICE—LATER

Ethan is working on a paper airplane. Nearby is a beautiful drawing of a smoking F-16 about to crash.

ELLIOT: So it becomes this argument . . . Larry Slutsky's saying there's no Santa Claus and I'm saying there is, and he says, oh, yeah, what is he, like Superman, flying down people's chimneys—?

Michael is fast-forwarding through a videotape, paying no attention to Elliot.

ELLIOT: —what is he, invulnerable? So he ties together three cherry bombs and sets a trip wire inside my chimney—

MICHAEL: How late are stores open on Christmas Eve?

ELLIOT: Christmas Eve, my father goes to light a fire . . . blows a three-foot hole in the roof.

MICHAEL: Ethan, is your father telling the truth?

ELLIOT: Okay, it was two feet . . .

Elliot looks at Ethan's drawing of the smoking F-16.

ELLIOT: Ooooh, Eth, look at that, that really is *great* . . .

No response from Ethan.

ELLIOT: What happened, he get hit by antiaircraft fire?

Elliot emits a spray of appropriate noise, but still gets no response from Ethan.

ELLIOT: Hey, guy, you still want to be an artist when you grow up?

ETHAN: He got hit by a heat-seeking.

Ethan takes the paper airplane, dashing out on a strafing run.

MICHAEL: Larry Slutsky? You have a history of consorting with Jews, don't you?

ELLIOT: I admire the Jewish race, their warmth, their infinite patience in the face of adversity. Jews have played a key role in my personal development. Of course, they also killed our Lord, but I've forgiven them for that.

MICHAEL: What role in your personal development?

ELLIOT: I lost my virginity with Judy Saperstein.

MICHAEL: But you didn't marry her. You married someone of your own persuasion.

ELLIOT: I would've married her, but she dumped me for Gordon Birnbaum.

MICHAEL *(sighs):* And of course *they're* happy now, lighting candles on Friday night, not eating shellfish together . . .

ELLIOT: Actually, I heard they became sikhs and were last seen living in an ashram in upstate Oregon.

Ethan runs back in for a crash landing.

MICHAEL *(shaking his head):* I swear to you, I'm in this synagogue last night, and I might as well have heard voices: "Michael, why did you do it, why did you marry a shiksa?"

ELLIOT: Hope isn't Jewish?

MICHAEL: Thank you, Elliot.

ELLIOT: No, you're right. It's been such a comfort that Nancy and I are the same religion, kind of a beacon for our marriage. This holiday season especially.

ETHAN: Will you give me presents if you're not there for Christmas?

Elliot turns and approaches his son.

ELLIOT: Are you crazy? I would never give you presents. Presents?! Presents are for people who aren't . . . BEING TICKLED!!

He picks up Ethan, flips him upside down, and starts to tickle him. Ethan laughs, but he's also undaunted.

ETHAN: Are you coming? *Are you?*

ELLIOT: *I don't know.*

ETHAN: You have to.

ELLIOT: Your mom and I have to talk about it.

ETHAN: That's what you always say—

ELLIOT: Because it's true.

ETHAN: —and then you never do talk about it.

ELLIOT: We will talk about it, I promise.

ETHAN *(pulls away):* I want to go home.

ELLIOT: Pal, remember, I have to stay here 'til three. I can't take you now.

ETHAN: Then I'll go myself.

He walks out. Elliot follows. Which leaves—Michael, staring at the fast-forwarding videotape, which miraculously slows down and turns into

THE MIKE VAN DYKE SHOW

Mike is at home, applying a hot towel to his face. Melissa and Gary are there—she looks a lot like Rose Marie, and he looks a lot like Mel Cooley.

MELISSA: —you brought this man home and you don't know who he is or what's wrong with him?

MICHAEL: Melissa, he needed help. It's Christmas Eve and he's all alone.

GARY: The man's in his underwear.

MICHAEL: They stole his suit!

As Michael removes the towel we see that the false nose is still there. The doorbell rings.

MICHAEL: It's her! She's home. Thank heavens . . . *(runs to the door)* Honey—

But it's Nancy and Ethan.

NANCY: I didn't know you cared . . . Rudolph. What *is* that nose?

MICHAEL: Ask your husband. *(looks out the door)* And where's my wife? You didn't see her on the road, did you?

NANCY: I could barely see the front of my car. You mean she's not home yet?

MICHAEL *(throws up his hands):* What are we going to do? She's lost in the snow. I know it.

ELLIOT: Look on the bright side, Mike. She's probably out buying you a great present.

MICHAEL *(starting for the stairs):* Yeah, well, I think I'm calling the police anyway.

ELLIOT: And we'll go drink several cups of Christmas cheer.

NANCY: And if you get drunk you can walk home.

Elliot and Nancy head into the kitchen. Ethan enters—to applause, of course—and calls for his dad. Mike, screened from Ethan's view, watches as the old gentleman enters from the kitchen. He's in a full Santa suit now, and looks pretty impressive.

ETHAN: Mr. Steadman, you look really neat.

GENTLEMAN: Mr. Steadman? That's amusing. I'm not Mr. Steadman, I'm Mr. Kringle.

ETHAN *(amused)*: Okay.

GENTLEMAN: You don't believe me either.

ETHAN: There's no such thing as Santa.

GENTLEMAN *(laughs)*: Sometimes I think you're right . . .

ETHAN: Okay, if you're Santa, what do I want for Christmas?

GENTLEMAN: A Fanner-Fifty with Shootin' Shells and Greenie Stick'm Caps.

ETHAN *(amazed)*: My dad told you—*(realizes)* But I didn't tell my dad.

GENTLEMAN: Because *Billy* has one and you're gunfighters together and you saw him break Mr. Foster's window and swore you'd never tell.

Ethan is speechless now.

ETHAN: You're . . . Santa . . . ?

Michael is listening to this all, dumbfounded.

GENTLEMAN: And I know what else you want for Christmas, even though you haven't told a soul.

ETHAN: You do?

GENTLEMAN: You want your parents to stop fighting all the time and go back to the way they used to be.

Ethan takes a moment to digest this. Then, forlornly:

ETHAN: I don't think even Santa Claus can do that.

GENTLEMAN: You'd be surprised what kind of presents good little boys can get for Christmas . . . Heavens, look at the time. Run along and get your parents . . . You have to go.

Ethan runs out, and the old gentleman turns to where Michael is hiding.

GENTLEMAN: And you, young man—what is it *you* want for Christmas?

The Mike Van Dyke Show fades with this lingering question, as we leave its black-and-white world for

MICHAEL'S CAR—TRAVELING

Ethan, dejected, looks out the window as Michael drives him home. Michael looks over at him, not quite sure how to start a conversation.

MICHAEL: So, Eth . . . Whatcha gonna get for Christmas?

ETHAN: I don't know.

MICHAEL: You ever play gunfighters, you know, like who can draw fastest?

ETHAN: Gunfighters? Does that come with Xapticon and Trypticon?

MICHAEL: . . . Never mind.

They drive in silence for a moment.

ETHAN: Are you Jewish?

MICHAEL *(laughs unaccountably)*: Yeah, how'd you know?

ETHAN: Jews have Hanukkah. They get presents eight nights in a row.

MICHAEL: Yeah, but not big ones. You only get big ones the first night, after that it's like stuff from your aunt, you know, like pants, and wallets.

ETHAN: Jews can't put lights on their house.

MICHAEL: Yeah, well . . .

ETHAN: I'm glad I'm Christian.

MICHAEL: That's good. People should be glad they're what they are.

ETHAN: On Hanukkah, does everybody get presents together?

MICHAEL: What do you mean, Eth?

ETHAN: Does everybody get presents together, the moms and the dads?

MICHAEL: They try to. Yeah.

Ethan looks out the window again. Michael pulls the car up to Elliot and Nancy's house. Ethan stares at it for a moment.

ETHAN: Your dad's dead.

MICHAEL: Yeah.

ETHAN: Mine's separated.

Michael doesn't know what to say. Ethan opens the door.

ETHAN: 'Bye.

Michael can only watch as the boy goes.

EXT. THE SYNAGOGUE—LATER

Michael, as he drives by, impulsively stops the car to watch people going in and out, just as he did with Melissa. . . .

But this time is different, for this time Michael goes inside. A few people, going in for the service, smile as they pass. He sees them putting on *talisim,* talking and laughing quietly, greeting friends.

A rabbi walks to the pulpit and begins singing. As the others join in, an older man, preparing to close the door, looks questioningly at Michael. Michael smiles and backs off. The door closes, cutting off the singing.

Now, Michael looks around the old hallway: the donor plaques, the tiny gift shop, the prayer books in heaps on stacked chairs.

He turns a corner as he sees someone coming out of an office, who says, "Goodnight, Rabbi Markowitz."

Curious, Michael edges over, trying to get a glimpse at this guy Melissa was raving about.

IN THE OFFICE

the man is bending over, and we can't really see him. Michael turns away. Then:

MARKOWITZ: Who's that skulking outside my office?

MICHAEL *(caught):* Nobody.

MARKOWITZ: So, Mr. Nobody, you want to come *in* and skulk?

MICHAEL *(edging in):* Really, I was just walking b—

He stops as the rabbi straightens up and faces him. Good God—it's

Kris Kringle, the old gentleman from *The Mike Van Dyke Show!*
What's happening here?

GENTLEMAN: Hello?

MICHAEL: Hi, um . . .

GENTLEMAN: I'm terrible with faces . . .

MICHAEL: Oh, uh, my name's Michael Steadman, I'm not even
a member here.

GENTLEMAN: So get out. We don't allow intruders here.
Melissa Steadman is related to you?

MICHAEL: My cousin.

GENTLEMAN: Such a talent, such a lovely girl, can't you get her
to do something about that hair?

Michael laughs.

GENTLEMAN: So, Michael Steadman Melissa's cousin, what can
I do for you?

MICHAEL: Nothing, I was just . . . skulking by.

GENTLEMAN: Nonsense. Everybody wants something. Advice
on their love life, I should say a prayer over a sick poodle,
what's the point spread on the Eagles game . . . 'Course
nobody likes what I tell 'em anyway. So go ahead, what
can I tell you *you* won't like . . . ?

Michael looks at him, feeling an almost irresistible desire to un-
burden himself.

MICHAEL: No, really, I was just . . . in the neighborhood. *(on
the rabbi's look)* It's . . . been a lot of years—*(another look)* —
and I just wanted to . . . you know . . . see how the place
was doing.

GENTLEMAN: Ah.

MICHAEL *(likes this guy):* What do you mean—"Ah . . ."?

GENTLEMAN: So how're we doing?

MICHAEL: I don't know, I'm just walking through, how do I
know how you're doing?

The rabbi gives Michael what can only be called a bodhisattva look and turns his attention back to his desk. After a moment he looks up and sees Michael is still there.

GENTLEMAN: **We're doing fine.**

The "Hallelujah" Chorus is heard now, and it takes us to

INT. STEADMAN HOUSE—THAT NIGHT

as Michael enters to hear the offending music blaring from the stereo. The Christmas tree, presents stacked beneath it, is trimmed and lit. Michael regards this scene, then, realizing that no one's come to greet him:

MICHAEL: **Hello . . . ? Hope . . . ?**

Michael turns to the odd sight of Janey, standing alone in the doorway to the breakfast room.

MICHAEL: **Hi, sweetie . . . Janey?**

She's just standing there, looking at him.

MICHAEL: **Honey, what is it?**

She turns and goes into the kitchen. Michael follows. He finds Hope, on the floor by the sink; her eyes are closed, and she has a wet towel against her mouth. He runs over and kneels next to her. She opens her eyes, looks at him, and then, in a small voice—

HOPE: **I'm scared, Michael . . .**

He holds her—the music swells in the background.

ACT FOUR

INT. HOSPITAL ROOM—MORNING

Michael, almost dozing, sits across from Hope's bed. As she turns in her sleep he awakens to look at her. The magazine in his lap falls to the floor—and now she wakes up.

MICHAEL *(looks at his watch):* So much for seven-thirty.

HOPE: No more blood. No more needles.

MICHAEL: One more test.

HOPE: Essay or multiple choice?

MICHAEL *(looks at her):* I love you.

HOPE: Where's Janey?

MICHAEL: Ellyn's taking care of her.

HOPE: Oh, God.

Dr. Richards enters and picks up her chart.

DR. RICHARDS: What is *this?*

MICHAEL: You're supposed to tell *us.*

DR. RICHARDS: This is a fine way to start the morning. What are you doing back here?

HOPE: We just couldn't stay away . . .

DR. RICHARDS (*perusing the charts*): Hmmmm . . . No badness so far. Any more vomiting?

HOPE: No—

DR. RICHARDS: What can I tell you. According to this you're still fine, and we'll do more useless and painful tests just to be sure.

HOPE: I don't understand what this could be.

DR. RICHARDS: Some part of your body is clearly still reacting to the trauma. It isn't inner ear, it isn't concussion—

MICHAEL: In other words, you have no idea.

DR. RICHARDS (*after a moment*): Correct.

HOPE: Can I go home?

DR. RICHARDS: I don't really see much point in keeping you around . . . Let's just get through this last group of indignities, okay?

They look at each other.

INT. HOPE AND MICHAEL'S BEDROOM—DAY

Michael, Hope, and Janey lie in a tangle on the bed. Janey plays; Michael holds Hope's hand. It's a still moment, but not without intensity.

HOPE: Go.

MICHAEL: In a minute.

He doesn't move.

EXT. WESTON HOUSE—NIGHT

As Michael walks to the door, laden with gifts, he can hear the Chiffons' up-tempo version of "Sleigh Ride." He goes quietly to the window to look in. Ethan sits alone. Beyond the Christmas tree, Elliot and Nancy can be seen in the kitchen.

INT. WESTON HOUSE—MOMENTS LATER

Michael stands amid the debris of opened presents.

MICHAEL *(to Ethan):* **Wow, look at this haul! What'd you get?** *(bends down to look)* **Dino-Rider, check it out!**

Ethan sits down next to him to show him how it works.

MICHAEL: **So'd you have a good Christmas Eve?**

Ethan doesn't answer.

MICHAEL: **See . . . and when you press the button, this thing shoots. Oh, man, I'm gonna get this guy. Powww!**

Elliot and Nancy enter from the kitchen.

NANCY: **Don't worry, Michael, we got you one, too. How's she doing?**

MICHAEL: **Resting. Waiting for test results. Going crazy. Fine.**

ELLIOT: **What are you doing here, get out of here, are any of those for me?**

MICHAEL *(handing out gifts):* **Let's see now . . . Ethan . . . and Brittany . . . and this is for Nancy . . . uh . . . Gee. Elliot . . .**

Michael hands him an envelope he's kept hidden behind his back.

MICHAEL: **It's the bill from that recording session you double-booked and we couldn't get out of.**

ELLIOT *(opening it):* **It is *not*.**

Right. It's—

ELLIOT: **Courtside! All right!**

NANCY *(hugging him):* **I love it! Even though you don't know what it is and Hope picked it out, thank you.**

ELLIOT *(handing over gifts):* **Here. Don't open it in the car.**

Michael takes the gifts. They stand there for an awkward moment.

MICHAEL: **Well . . .**

ELLIOT: Yeah . . . I guess I'm kind of out of here, too.

ETHAN: *No!*

ELLIOT: Come on, guy, we talked about it. You're a big guy.
You understand . . .

Ethan runs out. Elliot looks helplessly to Michael and Nancy, then
starts after Ethan. Michael and Nancy watch as Elliot catches up to
Ethan, bends down, and hugs him. Michael takes this as his cue to
leave. He touches Nancy on the arm.

MICHAEL: I should have been home an hour ago. Hope's probably worried.

He leaves her there, the look on her face too painful to watch.

INT. STEADMAN HOUSE—LATER

Michael walks in with all the presents and calls out

MICHAEL: Hope? Ho-ope . . .

No answer. He goes to the kitchen. No dinner preparations are in
evidence—and also no Hope.

MICHAEL: Hope?

He runs up the stairs to check the bedroom . . .

Not there either. As he stands in the doorway his heart starts to
pound . . .

BACK IN THE KITCHEN

Michael tries to put dinner together, but he can't concentrate. He
starts at an imagined sound, waits . . . nothing. He picks up the
phone, dials.

MICHAEL: Hi . . . No . . . Right, Merry Christmas . . . Hope
wasn't with you, was she? . . . No, I was just . . . No, it's
okay, I thought she was gonna be here . . . It's okay.
(*reluctant laugh*) It's okay! 'Bye, Melissa. (*shakes his head*)
Good *yomtov* . . .

He hangs up. Fusses with dinner. Checks the clock . . . Then he
turns on the TV and—GUESS WHAT?

It's THE MIKE VAN DYKE SHOW

Ethan enters with the old Gentleman, who now looks resplendent in Mike's Santa suit. As Michael sees him:

MICHAEL: Oh, my Lord . . .

GENTLEMAN: No, just part of the family.

ETHAN: We gotta hurry, Mr. Kringle, or we'll be late.

ELLIOT *(entering)*: Ethan, come on, we'll miss the pag—*(he sees the old Gentleman)* What, are we playing musical costumes here? Mike, come on, we're gonna be late.

MICHAEL: Elliot, I want to tell you something and I think maybe you better sit down.

ELLIOT: We don't have time to sit, we'll sit at the pageant—

MICHAEL: Elliot—

ELLIOT: I promised the pageant committee that I'd supply the—

MICHAEL: ELLIOT!

ELLIOT: *What?*

MICHAEL *(points)*: This *is* Santa Claus. *(On Elliot's blank look) The* Santa Claus. St. Nick. Mr. Kringle.

ELLIOT: Hello, how do you do? Mike—*(pulls Mike aside)* Could you possibly have your nervous breakdown tomorrow? We're kind of busy tonight.

MICHAEL: Elliot—*I mean it.*

Elliot looks at Michael, at Ethan, and finally at the old Gentleman, who smiles calmly.

ELLIOT: St. Nick, eh? Okay. Tell me, Saint, what did I get for Christmas when I was thirteen, huh?

GENTLEMAN *(squinting)*: Oh, my, that's very difficult, it's been so many years . . .

ELLIOT: Mike, come on, would you change, please?

MICHAEL: Elliot, I'm telling you—

Nancy enters, her face all aglow.

NANCY: Elliot, oh, *Elliot,* and all this time I thought you were being so pigheaded—

ELLIOT *(while she kisses him):* Huh?

NANCY: It's guaranteed spotless and has a china cycle and it even matches our Formica!

MICHAEL: You bought her a dishwasher!? Oh, Elliot!

ELLIOT: Well . . .

He looks at Mike in panicked confusion. But Mike can only shrug. Which leaves the old Gentleman, who once again smiles calmly at Elliot.

ELLIOT: Well, I, you know, honey, I have your best interests at heart.

NANCY: I guess you do, my sweetie pie, lover boy.

She kisses him again, but as they clinch—

ELLIOT: Ow! *(looks down)* What's that?

Confused, Nancy holds up a set of keys that were attached to her pocketbook. Before she can respond:

ELLIOT: Oh, my Lord . . . You didn't . . .

He grabs the keys and runs to the window.

ELLIOT: Honey, you didn't . . . You *did!* Look at the fins! Look at the chrome wheels! Is that the most beautiful Thunderbird you've ever seen?! Oh, honey!

He runs over and kisses a totally bewildered Nancy.

ELLIOT: I guess we really have to believe in each other more, don't we?

NANCY: I . . . guess we do.

They kiss, and Ethan puts his arms around both of them.

GENTLEMAN *(as they leave):* Oh, by the way, don't hold me to this, but wasn't it the Captain Marvel Secret Decoder Set?

Elliot stares in amazement.

GENTLEMAN: **Merry Christmas.**

Mike turns to Santa.

MICHAEL: **But what about Hope? She's out there in the snow somewhere . . . If you're Santa, can you tell me where she is, can you tell me when she's coming back?**

The old Gentleman fixes Michael with a look and speaks to him in a straightforward, unaffected tone.

GENTLEMAN: **I'm sorry, my friend. Hope is never coming back.**

Mike looks at him in horror, backing away from the man's kindly smile. He looks to Elliot and Nancy helplessly and shakes his head as they stare balefully.

And then Mike's face slowly turns to color. He walks out of the room, past the others, who still remain in black and white. And now we follow Mike into the world of color, going back to

THE STEADMAN KITCHEN

where Michael is nodding off by the TV. There is the sound of the front door opening, and then Hope's offscreen voice as she calls out

HOPE *(gaily):* **Hi-eee . . .**

Michael goes into the living room, where he finds Hope and Janey.

MICHAEL: **Where were you?**

HOPE: **I know, I know, but I was feeling completely fine and I realized we hadn't gotten any cranberries, and I—**

MICHAEL *(seething):* **You were . . . *not* . . . supposed to go out.**

HOPE: **Michael . . .**

MICHAEL: **If there's something wrong with you and you're waiting for tests then you're not supposed to go out because—**

HOPE: **Michael, listen—**

MICHAEL *(looks up at her):* **No, because . . . I see you out there, you're dead on the highway, only this time it's true because you're bleeding inside and you're fainting and**

Janey's in the car and I see her lying . . . in a *ditch*—*(tears welling)*—and I can't . . . I've been . . . seeing that all week and I can't . . . *see* that anymore.

HOPE *(holds his head):* Oh, Michael . . . Michael . . . Michael—

After a moment, she can't help but start laughing. Finally:

MICHAEL: What? Why are you laughing?

HOPE *(looks into his eyes):* I'm not dying—I'm pregnant.

He stares at her in disbelief, trying to process the information. Then he's hugging her, fighting back tears, laughing with her. The door opens:

MELISSA: Knock, knock, knock. It's Hannahclaus. Merry Pagan Ritual, everybody. *(she looks at them)* What?

THE KITCHEN—LATER

Melissa comes and sits down next to Michael.

MELISSA: Mikey, you're pregnant, that's so great!

MICHAEL *(catatonic):* I know.

MELISSA: Aren't you happy?

MICHAEL: Are you kidding? Don't I look happy?

She peers sweetly into his eyes.

MICHAEL: I'm incredibly happy, I just—oh, never mind . . . Hope has this accident. And it makes me realize how much, I mean how *incredibly* much I love her, I mean like it's scary? And then she's not dying, she's pregnant. Oh. So we can have this wonderful life together and I can give her everything she wants, like Christmas, and make her happy.

MELISSA *(quietly):* So what's the problem?

MICHAEL: The problem is . . . I believe in God. I didn't think I did, but I think I do. And there's no way, I mean, I can't seem to find a way to live with that. My father believed in God, he didn't have a problem, but he didn't marry a non-Jew—

MELISSA: And he got divorced. Michael, you're trying to tell me, because you didn't marry into your own religion, you can't believe in God?

MICHAEL: No! But which God, who God, where God? I didn't have my *own* religion to marry into, and now, and now—I don't know what. And almost losing her is what—can't you see how weird this is? It's almost losing Hope that makes me want to . . .

MELISSA: Want to what?

As Michael looks to her:

EXT. SYNAGOGUE—NIGHT

Michael stands in the brisk night air. Somewhere, not far from here, Christmas carolers are singing.

INT. SYNAGOGUE HALLWAY—NIGHT

Michael approaches Rabbi Markowitz's office. The door is slightly ajar, and there's a light on inside. Michael knocks. No answer. He steps inside—

    —And there's no one there.

MICHAEL: Hello?

VOICE: Hello, I'll be right out—

The voice comes from an adjoining washroom.

VOICE: Who is it?

MICHAEL: It's Michael Steadman.

VOICE: Who? Wait a minute, I can't hear with the water running—

MICHAEL: It's okay, I can come back la—

Now the washroom door opens, and Rabbi Markowitz emerges. Only it's not the old Gentleman; this is a young man, balding, thin.
He sees the utter confusion on Michael's face.

MAN: How you doing? What's up?

MICHAEL: Nothing . . . I was, I was looking for . . . Rabbi Markowitz.

MAN: You found him.

A moment, as this registers.

MICHAEL: No, I guess I mean . . . the other . . . Rabbi Markowitz.

MAN: There's a frightening thought. Two of me. Really, what can I do for you?

MICHAEL (*completely at a loss*): No, I . . . Oh, man. Sorry, I . . .

Michael backs out and closes his eyes. He opens them again, turns, and peers back into the room. The same young man is staring back at him.

MICHAEL: Sorry, I guess . . . I was looking for somebody else . . .

Michael walks away from the office and the bewildered rabbi. He heads down the hall and turns a corner, approaching the chapel, where a service is in session. He goes to a door, opens it, and looks inside.

IN THE CHAPEL

A small group of mostly older men is praying. Michael enters, puts on a yarmulke, and finds a seat. He fumbles through the prayer book, trying to find the page, mumbling through the prayers until:

SERVICE LEADER: Mourners, please rise for the Kaddish.

Michael stands with a few others, and begins to recite the words.

MICHAEL WRITES A STORY

BY

JOSEPH DOUGHERTY

"Michael Writes a Story" isn't really about writing. It's about the fear of failure, not wanting to disappoint the people who love you, and the danger of using art to insulate yourself from the world. At least that's what I wanted it to be about. The basic idea got roughed up along the way, but enough of the message remained for me to select it as my contribution to this book.

My play *Digby* was produced off-Broadway in 1985. By the summer of 1987 I'd written two more plays, several screenplays, and a television pilot, all unproduced. I was beginning to feel like a literary footnote when I arrived in California and met Ed Zwick and Richard Kramer. Marshall was off being a father.

Ed and Richard explained to me that, through a clerical error, ABC had picked up the pilot for *thirtysomething* and had placed the series on the fall schedule. Ed was convinced the show wouldn't last more than thirteen episodes, so, if I wanted to write one, I'd better speak up.

I took the first four scripts back to my hotel and read them that evening. They were passionate, complex, and touched with a radical message: life is messy, full of terror and loss, but we're alive and capable of great love, so let's get on with it. Clearly *thirtysomething* would go down in flames, but it would give off a lovely light. I wrote two episodes during the first year, and, when the series wasn't canceled, I decided to write for it full-time. "Michael Writes a Story" came toward the end of the second season.

The way Ed and Marshall get you to do something is by presenting an irresistible challenge and then getting—more or less—out of your way. This is also how Oppenheimer ran the Manhattan Project. My challenge in this script was to create the definitive writing teacher—someone who would be a mixture of the teachers you had, the ones you dreamed of, and the one you hoped you'd be.

We outlined the episode and I went off to write it. None of us suspected we'd end up having hairsplitting arguments of religious intensity. All writers worship the same God, but we do so with the uniformity found in snowflake design.

With the collapse of The Michael and Elliot Company, our heroes were out of work and Michael decided to devote time to his neglected passion, writing. So he joined a workshop led by a writer named Ivy Dunbar, whom I based on the late novelist John Gardner. (There are books that promise they'll teach you to write, but if you want to find out if you *are* a writer, you should read Gardner's *The Art of Fiction.*)

What Michael didn't know—but I, unfortunately, do—is that being unemployed is the worst time to throw yourself into writing. Writing is a fragile process that doesn't respond to the pressure and desperation of job hunting. It also sucks time away from job hunting, which explains those chilled looks from family and friends. In this atmosphere the writing can become warped, because you expect too much of it. Each story, each script *must* be the golden key. "I won't have to take another depressing job. Not this time. I'm close; I can feel it." Actually, you're moving in the opposite direction; away from real life, and real art. That's the dilemma I wanted Michael to face, the story I wanted to tell.

But Ed and Marshall had an agenda of their own, and, with each subsequent draft, I felt my story becoming less important than the story Michael was writing in the workshop. The episode was suddenly about *dramatizing the writing process,* and script conferences took on a slightly confrontational tone. You might as well know it: we fight all the time at *thirtysomething.* We argue, rewrite, then argue some more, trying to navigate around each other's tastes and temperaments. And it's not like we fight about anything important; it's just writing.

To understand the differences I had with Marshall and Ed, compare Gene Kelly dancing with Cyd Charisse in *Singin' in the Rain* to Fred Astaire dancing with her in *The Band Wagon.* Ed and Marshall are Gene, I'm Fred, you can be Cyd.

Toward the end of *Singin' in the Rain* there's a fantasy number. Gene's in this MGM-meets-Dali set, working hard, dancing up a storm with Cyd in her dreamy little goddess outfit. The air is thick with choreography. In *The Band Wagon,* Fred and Cyd walk through Central Park on a summer evening. They're not fantasy figures, just two people wondering if they like each other. They stroll along until they casually, almost accidentally, start "Dancing in the Dark."

In one movie Gene seems to say, "You better just sit there and watch; this stuff is very difficult and it could get dangerous. But don't worry, I'm a skilled professional." In the other you hear Fred saying, "See, it just happens. It could happen to you. Why don't you go out, find a girl, and give it a try?"

I approach writing the way Astaire approached dancing. You're supposed to hide all the work, all the hardware. It's meant to look unforced and inevitable, and that's the sort of writing I wanted Michael to aspire to.

What follows is essentially the shooting script of "Michael Writes a Story." On a soundstage you often realize that what was written will play better if you turn it to one side; I've changed the script to reflect those improvements. However, under the pressure of production you're often forced to make other, less satisfying adjustments. Where those occurred, I've returned the script to the way I wrote it.

When I read the script now, I remember lobbying to keep the thing in balance. As Michael's "bad" story became more elaborate, Ivy Dunbar became more vehement in her stand on the relative unimportance of writing. Much of her eloquence is due to Marshall giving me a hard time. Thanks, Marshall.

I also want to thank Marshall for suggesting the addition of a character missing from the first draft. Miles Drentell was not there from the start. His arrival crystallized the show and led to one of my favorite scenes in which Miles and Michael discuss the parable of the samurai. Michael attributes the story to Nashiru's *The Art of Management.* There's no such book.

I took my inspiration for the story Michael writes from low-budget filmmaker Edward D. Wood, Jr., a man whose affection for storytelling far outstripped his abilities and budgets. His movies are incompetent, but they were made with unchallengeable love.

Most of the other writers work directly on their computers, but I can't compose at the keyboard so my episodes start on 8½-by-11-inch yellow pads, written with the fountain pen my wife gave me, the instrument of all serious work. It takes me about three weeks to write a first draft. When you're writing that fast you run certain risks. It's a struggle to keep scenes from bumping and to hold on to original intentions. The pace is grueling and it's easy to burn out, but your work gets performed and seen.

And there are prizes greater than an audience. You learn to write by writing, and in television you write day and night, inspired and blocked, on rainy winter days and on crisp October afternoons when you know you'd have Disneyland to yourself. The more you write, the less you censor, and the more comfortable you become trusting your instincts. You learn to get out of your own way, and start to experience that sense of spirit-writing, where scenes create themselves and characters find their own voices.

Will Michael ever become that kind of writer? I hope so. If he does, he'll find it was worth the depression and humiliation. He'll discover something else, too. I believe the most satisfying work a writer does is that for which she or he feels the least conscious responsibility. It simply flows from somewhere. You don't write it down so much as the paper is there to catch it. Ego is lost and you become transparent, something through which the story is seen and focused.

For a writer, this is a state of grace.

JOSEPH DOUGHERTY

ACT ONE

INT. STEADMAN HOUSE (LIVING ROOM)—DAY

Back in the corner, at the base of a damn-good-looking shaft of sunlight, sits Michael. He's on the floor next to a large cardboard box, reading a typewritten manuscript. The pages are at least a decade old. The front door opens. Gary and Elliot enter, dressed for basketball.

ELLIOT *(on the fly):* **It's great.**

GARY: **You're sick.**

ELLIOT: **No, really. Geraldo is the best thing about being out of work. Today he's doing "Nude Transvestites."** *(to Michael and his papers)* **Hey, Scooter, whatcha got?**

MICHAEL: **Just some stuff.**

ELLIOT: **What kind of stuff?**

Elliot moves in on the box. Michael tries to block him, but Elliot's got the moves and reaches past him to scoop up some of the manuscript.

ELLIOT: Oh, boy. Love letters. Typed love letters. You're such a perfectionist.

Gary dips into the box and comes up with the title page.

GARY: "The Girl with the Kool-Aid Soul."

ELLIOT: Wasn't Seka in that?

GARY: It's your novel.

MICHAEL: Okay, okay. Let's play ball. The unemployed against the untenured.

ELLIOT: You wrote a novel?

MICHAEL: Yeah, come on. Let's go.

ELLIOT: First we raid the larder for cookies with lots of pre-servatives.

He heads into the kitchen. Michael takes the title page from Gary.

GARY: I remember when you were writing this back at Penn; drinking too much coffee and smoking Gitanes. You were so dark and moody you didn't even reflect light.

MICHAEL: God, that was fun.

GARY: What happened to you taking that workshop with Ivy Dunbar?

MICHAEL: You know, I'm looking for work now.

GARY: A writing workshop would be good for you.

MICHAEL: You think so?

GARY: Yeah.

MICHAEL: Good, 'cause I'm doing it.

GARY: The workshop with Dunbar?

MICHAEL: Uh-huh. I start Wednesday night.

GARY: That's great. (*upon reflection*) You weren't going to tell anyone, were you?

MICHAEL: It's no big deal.

Michael turns to the manuscript, breaking eye contact with Gary. Elliot returns with a cracker smeared with white stuff.

ELLIOT: Hey, what's the half-life on this Marshmallow Fluff?

INT. WESTON HOUSE (LIVING ROOM)—DAY

Nancy and Matt Enwright are on the sofa, a big bowl of popcorn between them, watching television. On the screen, Yuri Zhivago sits down in the ice-encrusted summer house and struggles to write the first Lara poem.

MATT: Do that thing.

NANCY: What thing?

MATT: That thing you do with your tongue.

NANCY (*blushing*): Matthew.

MATT: Come on, do it. Do the popcorn lizard for me.

Nancy lifts the popcorn bowl close to her face. She sticks out her tongue, claims a big kernel with the moist end, then rolls it in like a nature film of a frog catching a fly.

MATT: I love that.

NANCY: What did you do for entertainment before I came along?

MATT: Oh, sharpened pencils, straightened paper clips, that sort of thing. (*off her look*) Something wrong?

NANCY: No, nothing wrong. Just . . . I got another rejection on the book.

MATT: Those publishers don't know what they're missing.

NANCY: They seem to know exactly what they're missing; I keep getting the same comments.

MATT: How can they not like your pictures?

NANCY: They like the pictures. But they keep telling me the story isn't right.

MATT: What are you going to do? Look for a writer to fix the story?

NANCY: If I do that it wouldn't be mine anymore.

MATT: So, you're going to work on it 'til you get it right. I can understand that. I just hope you don't think anything will change.

NANCY: What do you mean?

MATT: Ethan's not going to love you less if the book doesn't get published. No one's going to love you less.

They look at each other for a moment, then lean in for a kiss. One kiss turns into kissing. On the television in front of them, Lara reads the finished poem. "This isn't me," she tells Yuri. "It's you."

INT. STEADMAN HOUSE (KITCHEN)—DAY

Michael and Elliot enter from the lovely laundry pavilion. Elliot ends up against the cabinets across from what is still called in my mother's house the "icebox."

ELLIOT: Great, you'll write a big Stephen King novel with all the italics and I end up bucking cases of soda down at the Pick and Save. This is fair, this is equitable.

MICHAEL: I'm not doing it for the money.

ELLIOT: That's what they all say.

Elliot opens the refrigerator.

MICHAEL (*"Hey, you with your head in my fridge."*): Have a beer.

ELLIOT: Got some juice or something?

Elliot grabs a can of soda, and leans back against the counter, facing the closed icebox door.

ELLIOT: You'll be a famous writer. You'll have two refrigerators, one just for the champagne.

MICHAEL: I just want to sharpen the skills. Ivy Dunbar's good. I remember reading her stories at Penn . . . what's your problem?

Elliot's face has gone kind of cryptic, his eyes locked on a piece of paper held to the refrigerator door by a kitchen magnet. Elliot lifts his arm and points at the piece of paper.

ELLIOT: Mike.

Michael comes to his side and looks at the note.

ELLIOT *(reading):* "Miles Drentell called. Wants you to call back. Went out for cheese. Did you get real sweaty? Love, Hope."

Elliot reaches past Michael and tugs the message off the door. They look at each other.

MICHAEL: He probably just wants to torture us.

ELLIOT: So, call him and brighten his day.

MICHAEL: I don't want to call him. You call him.

ELLIOT: He called you. Come on.

Elliot drags Michael to the phone, dials the number from the message, and shoves the phone into Michael's hand.

ELLIOT: Be nice to him.

MICHAEL: *(someone picks up)* Miles Drentell, please. Michael Steadman returning his call. Thank you. *(to Elliot)* She's putting me through.

ELLIOT: That's a good sign, being put through.

MICHAEL *(the call goes through):* Hello, Miles?

INTERCUT WITH:
DRENTELL'S OFFICE—DAY

Miles is the calm eye of furious advertising activity.

MILES: Steadman. How are you? Sorry we kept missing each other. I was in Japan.

MICHAEL: How was the sushi?

ELLIOT: Where?

MICHAEL: Japan.

ELLIOT: Jeeze.

MILES: I miss you fellows. Why don't you and your faithful Indian companion come in, say, Thursday, for a nice chat?

MICHAEL: You're kidding.

MILES: Would you like me to be "kidding"?

MICHAEL: You want us to come in?

Elliot hears this and gives a silent cheer.

MILES: No, I dialed your number by mistake and now I'm covering.

MICHAEL: We could come in Thursday.

MILES: Say, seven-thirty?

MICHAEL: Seven-thirty in the morning?

MILES: Or are you accustomed to banker's hours?

MICHAEL: Seven-thirty's fine.

MILES: See you then. Have a care.

He hangs up.
    Back in the kitchen. Michael hangs up and turns to Elliot.

ELLIOT: We've got it.

MICHAEL: Got what?

ELLIOT: He's going to hire us.

MICHAEL: He doesn't like us.

ELLIOT: Like doesn't matter. Need is what counts.

Michael considers this and dismisses the idea.

MICHAEL: It's got to be something else.

He moves away from Elliot.

ELLIOT: That's what I like about you: your positive outlook.

INT. STEADMAN HOUSE (SUNROOM)—NIGHT

Hope is at the typewriter. Michael is scanning the stacks of books.

HOPE: Why would he call if it wasn't about a job?

MICHAEL: Probably just to taunt us. You don't know this man.

HOPE: But if he called, that indicates interest, and that could mean a job.

MICHAEL: Speculation is pointless with Miles Drentell. He's like a bear; you can never tell what he's thinking.

HOPE: A job. We could stop playing leapfrog with the Visa cash advances and I could stop worrying about them keeping the baby to pay for the delivery room.

He finds the paperback he's been looking for, *Ivy Dunbar: Early Stories.*

MICHAEL: Here it is. I should read them again.

HOPE: Would the workshop conflict with the job at DAA?

MICHAEL: Read my lips: There is no job at DAA.

He opens the book and heads for the sofa.

INT. CLASSROOM—NIGHT

Beginning with Michael's notebook and two number two pencils on a desk. Michael's there, so are six other adults of various shapes and sizes scattered in the first two or three rows of the room. Michael looks toward the open hallway door. Ivy Dunbar appears at the threshold, talking to someone just out of our sight. Dunbar is dark-haired, in her late forties (and doesn't care who knows it), given to sweaters and long skirts, wears little or no makeup, and presently carries a seventeen-year-old soft leather briefcase. Michael straightens himself in his chair as Dunbar motions for the person she's been talking with to precede her into the classroom. Her companion does so. It's Nancy, with a notebook and pencils of her own. Michael sees her before she sees him. Dunbar moves to the teacher's desk and drops her briefcase on the blotter. It sounds like it weighs a ton.

DUNBAR *("Let's get down to business.")*: I'm Ivy Dunbar. Let's fill in the first rows and pretend we're all in the same room with each other.

Ivy grabs an unoccupied desk and pulls it around for herself. Nancy, connecting with Michael for the first time, goes to him.

NANCY: I didn't know you were taking this workshop.

MICHAEL: I didn't know *you* were.

NANCY: I guess there's no reason why we should have known. Is there?

MICHAEL: I guess not.

But it still feels kinda weird, doesn't it, kids? They sit next to each other.

DUNBAR: I'm not going to teach you to be writers. You already are. If you weren't, believe me, you wouldn't be here. But you all need to get past where you are. Past the need to stand between the reader and the work so they'll know how clever you are. Because good writing is writing that appears not to have been constructed, but to have ripened. Like a banana. The key to that is honesty. There are no rules in fiction, except honesty. If you learn that, you will have spent your money well. *(she scans their faces)* The first thing I'll ask you to write . . . don't spend more than an hour on this, we want to check the basic wiring . . . will be about a parting.

She reaches for her briefcase. Michael and Nancy look at each other. The class continues.

INT. COFFEE SHOP—NIGHT

Someplace old and collegiate, near the university. Michael and Nancy enter from the street and are pointed toward a booth.

NANCY: I wanted the words to be as good as the pictures. I studied drawing, why shouldn't I study to make the writing better?

MICHAEL: I can understand that. Me, I wanted to get back in shape.

NANCY: Isn't Ivy wonderful?

MICHAEL: She's not what I was expecting.

NANCY: What were you expecting?

MICHAEL: She doesn't seem to take it very seriously. Writing.

They reach the table and sit. Michael listens to Nancy. She's excited, her color is high, her thoughts intensely focused. Michael's never seen her like this.

NANCY: I like her. She's just like her stories. We're going to learn so much. I mean, she opens this window and clears out all the cobwebs and theories. It's like riding a motor-cycle. You're so scared you can hardly breathe, but it's so exciting. God, I feel good about this.

MICHAEL: Me too.

Nancy looks past Michael's shoulder.

MICHAEL: We expecting somebody?

Nancy smiles.

NANCY: Maybe.

MICHAEL: I'm finally going to meet the guy who owns the hardware store.

NANCY: He owns several stores. It's a chain, actually.

MICHAEL: Sounds like a solid guy.

NANCY: He is. It makes for a welcome change.

MICHAEL: You seeing him regular?

NANCY: I don't know if I should tell you.

MICHAEL: Why not?

NANCY: Because I don't like the idea of Elliot knowing every-thing I do and who I'm seeing.

MICHAEL: That's not why I asked.

NANCY: You see Elliot, you talk to him. And don't you feel we all know too much about each other as it is? I want to keep Matt to myself for a while.

There's something playfully wicked in Nancy's eyes, something Michael's never seen before. It's gone so fast he's not even sure he saw it. Nancy looks past Michael's shoulder.

NANCY: Matt.

Michael turns to see Matt Enwright approaching the table. He comes to Nancy's side of the booth and leans down to kiss her hello.

It's a standard, public kiss, but Michael looks away until it's over.

NANCY: **Matt, this is Michael Steadman. Michael, Matt Enwright.**

MICHAEL: **Hi.**

They shake hands, Matt sits close to Nancy. He puts his arm around her.

MATT: **Hello. Steadman?**

NANCY: **He was my husband's partner.**

Matt and Michael have eye contact. Matt almost removes his arm from Nancy's shoulder, but doesn't.

NANCY: **We ended up in the workshop together.**

MATT: **And you didn't know 'til you got there?**

NANCY: **No.**

MATT: **That's funny, isn't it?**

MICHAEL: **I guess so.**

The waitress arrives to take their order.

STEADMAN HOUSE (BEDROOM)—NIGHT

Late. Hope is asleep when Michael makes his quiet way down the hall and enters the bedroom. He slips out of his shoes and tiptoes into the bathroom. The phone rings. Michael lunges out of the bathroom to grab the bedside phone before the second ring. Hope stirs.

MICHAEL: **Hello?**

ELLIOT *(V.O.):* **Michael. Am I calling too late?**

MICHAEL: **What if I say yes?**

ELLIOT *(V.O.):* **I'll hang up. What are you wearing to Drentell's tomorrow?**

MICHAEL: **Are you serious?**

ELLIOT *(V.O.):* **Come on.**

MICHAEL: **Something conservative. Maybe Hope's cranberry Leslie Fay suit.**

ELLIOT *(V.O.):* Cranberry. That's like a deep red, isn't it?

MICHAEL: I'm hanging up now.

Michael hangs up. He turns toward the bed. Hope is sort of awake.

HOPE: Hi.

MICHAEL: Hi.

HOPE: Who was that?

MICHAEL: Nobody.

HOPE *(nodding her head):* Elliot. How was the class?

MICHAEL: Nancy was there. She's taking the workshop too.

HOPE: Good for her.

MICHAEL: I met her boyfriend.

HOPE: The one who owns the hardware store?

MICHAEL: Several hardware stores.

HOPE: What's he like?

MICHAEL: Okay.

HOPE: Serious?

MICHAEL: Could be.

HOPE: Go Nance. Come to bed. You've got to get up early for Drentell.

MICHAEL *(pretty flat):* Yeah.

HOPE: You could have a job tomorrow.

MICHAEL: Probably not.

HOPE: Don't worry. You'll get it if you want it.

She turns over and pulls up the covers. Michael looks at the Hope shape under the sheets.

ACT TWO

INT. DRENTELL'S OFFICE—DAY

Clean, simple, balanced. There's a floor plan partially unrolled on the placid surface of Drentell's desk. Miles faces Michael and Elliot.

MILES: So. Boys. How are we doing?

MICHAEL: Swell, Miles. How's by you?

MILES: Fine. Glad you could make it.

ELLIOT: We were kind of wondering why you called.

MILES: Does a man need an excuse to call up friends?

ELLIOT: No, but what's that got to do with us?

Miles assembles a smile on his face.

MILES: Two days ago I was in Osaka, at a foundry where they make these huge temple bells. Fascinating. The Buddhist monks come and throw prayers etched on pieces of metal into the molten steel before they pour the bell. When it cools and comes out of the mold, the master of the foundry strikes it once and only once before it's delivered to the temple. I was there when they struck one of those bells. It's the deepest sound you've ever heard. You feel it here, in the sternum, more than you hear it. And do you know what I heard in the reverberations of that ancient sound?

ELLIOT: Haven't a clue.

MILES: I heard a voice, and the voice said: "Hello, my name is Mr. Squeeze." Across the international date line, getting my zen adjusted, and I'm haunted by a radio commercial you guys did. Profound or trivial?

MICHAEL: Depends on what you plan to do about it.

MILES: We're making some changes. *(he slides the floor plan toward them)* What do you think?

Michael and Elliot examine the floor plan.

ELLIOT: Looks cozy.

MILES: I'm trying to find the right ergonomic flow . . . and get the maximum square footage. The way this is coming along, I'm going to have the space to bring in a new creative team.

ELLIOT: Do tell.

MILES: Yes. They'd go right about here.

He indicates a simple white box on the floor plan. He does so by pressing his thumb into the center of the box. The choice of gesture is not lost on Michael. The office door opens and Drentell's secretary looks in.

MILES: Excuse me, boys.

Miles exits. Michael and Elliot look at each other, then turn their attention to the empty square on the floor plan.

ELLIOT: I love this building. This is a great building.

MICHAEL: He's jerking us.

ELLIOT: He's dancing with us.

MICHAEL: There probably isn't even a job.

ELLIOT: There's a job all right.

MICHAEL: He's got such an attitude.

ELLIOT: He can afford one. That's DAA out there, Michael. An agency so cool they don't even have to be in New York. We've got to figure out what he wants us to do.

MICHAEL: Grovel.

ELLIOT: I can do that.

MICHAEL: So we can sit in his ergonomically designed work space listening to him pontificate on how he reinvented advertising?

ELLIOT: Hey. What's the matter with you? You like being in purgatory?

MICHAEL: He wants us to beg.

ELLIOT: Yeah, well, so?

MICHAEL: I got this trick knee. Before I get down on it to beg, I gotta know what I'm begging for.

Drentell's secretary returns, curtailing the conversation.

EXT. STEADMAN HOUSE—DAY

Michael pulls the Volvo into the driveway and heads for the porch. Hope comes out to collect some of Janey's toys. Michael reaches the porch.

MICHAEL: Hi.

HOPE: How'd it go?

MICHAEL: It went.

HOPE: How was Miles?

MICHAEL: Pompous.

HOPE: Is there a job?

MICHAEL: Maybe.

HOPE: Maybe there's a job, or maybe you'll get it?

MICHAEL: I don't know. We'll have to see.

He enters the house. Hope wants more information, but she doesn't want to lean on him . . . not yet, at least.

INT. STEADMAN HOUSE (LIVING ROOM)—DAY

Michael with pad and pens sits in the chair by the fireplace and makes himself comfortable. He adjusts himself, squares his shoulders, and places pen to paper. Nothing happens. He readjusts himself. Yeah, that's it. No it isn't. Michael moves to the sofa. Much better. Pen to paper. A car with a shot muffler rumbles outside the window. Michael reacts to the sound, shrugs it off, and tries again. A carload of kids, yelling and blasting the radio, drives by. This is followed by a garbage truck, two police helicopters, and a dramatic five-hundred-foot flyby from the Blue Angels. Finally things quiet down and Michael writes his first words.

MICHAEL *(V.O.):* "The clock over the counter stood at two forty-three."

INT. COFFEE SHOP (MICHAEL'S STORY)—NIGHT

It's the coffee shop Michael and Nancy went to after the workshop. The color is pale, bled to a faint pastel. The whole place is kind of fuzzy and flat. Michael is at the counter, looking up at the clock.

MICHAEL *(V.O.):* "Harrison watched the progress of the minutes."

Everything is slow, way too deliberate, and full of meaning.

MICHAEL *(V.O.):* "He lifted the tarnished spoon, dipped it into the cup, and stirred deliberately. Once again, his eyes were drawn to the clock. The second hand moved with the thoughtlessness of an underwater plant caught in a lethargic current."

Dunbar's voice interrupts.

DUNBAR: Well, this isn't very interesting, is it?

Michael looks to his side. A couple of stools away he sees Melissa, behind the counter, dressed as a waitress and chewing gum as she pours coffee into Ivy Dunbar's cup. They're both looking in Michael's direction.

MELISSA: I don't understand. Michael used to be very imaginative.

DUNBAR: I'm very disappointed. It lacks focus, intent, detail.

The man on the other side of Michael lowers the newspaper he's been reading. It's Gary.

GARY: I'll say. Look at this. He's got me reading a blank newspaper.

Gary opens the paper to show that the pages inside are completely blank.

INT. STEADMAN HOUSE (LIVING ROOM)—DAY

Michael starts to cross out what he's been writing. The sound of his scratching carries over into:

INT. COFFEE SHOP (MICHAEL'S STORY)—NIGHT

There's a ragged erasure of a dissolve going from the clock in the coffee shop the way we know it to another version with hot neon piping all around. From the clock to Michael, now in seriously cool club-hopping clothes. The coffee shop has changed. It's now ruthlessly chic. Really beautiful extras (male, female, and those not bound by such arbitrary labels) move in wholly artificial traffic patterns.

MICHAEL *(V.O.):* "People drifted through his field of vision like lost, soulless leaves. They lived to aimlessly move . . ."

DUNBAR: I know I told you there weren't any rules . . .

Michael turns back. On the other side of the counter is Dunbar. Now she's dressed as a waitress and pouring coffee.

DUNBAR: . . . but could you tell me exactly why you felt you had to split an infinitive?

INT. STEADMAN HOUSE (LIVING ROOM)—DAY

Michael balls up the page he's been working on and chucks it toward the fireplace. He starts again.

MICHAEL *(V.O.):* "People drifted through his field of vision like lost, soulless leaves . . ."

INT. COFFEE SHOP (MICHAEL'S STORY)—NIGHT

Back to the neon and primary-color version. Michael looks across the room.

MICHAEL *(V.O.):* "He singled her out amid the motion." No.

There's the sound of furious scratching out. The people freeze and disappear from the shot three or four at a time until the only one left is Nancy sitting across the room in the booth she shared with Michael after class. She's dressed in a drop-dead outfit and looks worldly, bored, and beautiful.

MICHAEL *(V.O.):* "The coffee shop was empty except for her. She wore her ennui the way lesser women wore diamonds."

Michael pushes off from the counter and starts across the shop. We make a subjective move toward Nancy.

MICHAEL *(V.O.):* "Her dress was the color of summer wine." No it wasn't.

The sound of more scratching out. The forward movement stops. We retreat a few steps as Nancy's dress changes color. We start moving again.

MICHAEL *(V.O.):* "Her dress reminded him of fresh-squeezed orange juice." Right, like a day without sunshine.

Scratch, scratch, scratch. We stop, retreat, then move forward as the dress changes color again.

MICHAEL *(V.O.):* "Her frock was the color of polished emeralds." As opposed to what? Unpolished emeralds?

Scratch, scratch. The dress turns black.

MICHAEL *(V.O.):* "He approached the woman in the black dress."

Closer to Nancy now, looking down at her. She is illuminated by the light coming in through the window next to her.

MICHAEL *(V.O.):* "The rain on the window streaked a pattern along her face . . ." No.

Scratch, scratch. The rain disappears and sunlight pours in.

MICHAEL *(V.O.)*: "The sun through the window bleached . . ." No.

Scratch. Deep-red neon replaces the sunlight.

MICHAEL *(V.O.)*: "Neon blinked beyond the window at her side."

Michael sits across from Nancy.

MICHAEL: Nice dress.

MICHAEL *(V.O.)*: "He said."

NANCY: I'm in mourning.

MICHAEL *(V.O.)*: "She replied."

MICHAEL: For what?

NANCY: My life.

MICHAEL *(V.O.)*: "Sorrow hung about her like wet chemise."

INT. STEADMAN HOUSE (LIVING ROOM)—NIGHT

Michael writing and looking awfully pleased with himself.

INT. WESTON HOUSE (DINING ROOM/LIVING ROOM)—NIGHT

Looking through the French doors to the living room, where Matt and Nancy are slowly dancing. Soft music fills the air. We look down at the dining room table. There, next to the computer printer, are the neatly formatted pages of Nancy's writing assignment.

NANCY *(V.O.)*: "She was never able to figure out why he had chosen that particular moment to leave. Did he make up his mind during the drive home? Or did he decide to leave in the split-second before he told her?"

INT. CLASSROOM—NIGHT

Nancy finishes reading her story to the workshop. We clock Michael's reaction. He's clearly impressed.

NANCY: "He packed a few things in a small bag and left. Was she supposed to stop him? Was she supposed to want to stop him? He left and later she couldn't remember if they'd said good-bye or kissed or shook hands. The only thing she could remember was how dark the house seemed after he'd left. She remembered going from room to room, turning on all the lights."

She looks up from the page to the face of a pleased Ivy Dunbar. Nancy smiles that particular Nancy half-smile and straightens her papers.

We distill the class, dissolving through several other assignments.

FIRST WRITER: "If he hadn't failed the driver's test, he would not be faced with the humiliating and tactical nightmare of kissing her good night while his mother sat parked at the curb in the station wagon . . ."

SECOND WRITER: " 'Go. Just go,' she thought to herself. 'Get on the stupid plane and stop pretending any of this means anything to you.' "

THIRD WRITER: "But it would be sunny outside the theater and he wasn't ready to give up the dream, give up this cool cave where things worked out, life had resolutions, and people could actually tell each other how they felt . . ."

Michael's turn.

MICHAEL: "Sorrow hung about her like wet chemise."

INT. COFFEE SHOP (MICHAEL'S STORY)—NIGHT

Back to Michael's mental coffee shop right where we left it during the writing process.

NANCY: What's the point?

MICHAEL *(V.O.):* "She asked the air."

NANCY: We move through life, trapped by time and events. Our empty days piling up like discarded socks in God's hamper.

MICHAEL: "She was depressed."

NANCY: We struggle and what does it get us?

MICHAEL: Perhaps nothing. Perhaps love.

MICHAEL *(V.O.):* "She looked at him and smiled."

NANCY: You're a funny sort of guy, aren't you?

MICHAEL *(V.O.)*: "It was a sad smile just the same."

NANCY: But I'm afraid you're a lifetime too late.

MICHAEL *(V.O.)*: "The door of the coffee shop opened with the sound of a sad bell. He took his eyes off the woman and watched a man walk in."

Enter Elliot, looking dapper, smug, and with his arm around a girl for whom the bustier was invented. Nancy stands, dipping her hand into her purse. She comes up with a nickel-plated revolver.

NANCY: Clive!

MICHAEL *(V.O.)*: "She said."

Elliot sees her and the gun. The girl splits.

ELLIOT: Rebecca! I can explain.

NANCY: I know. That's the problem, isn't it?

Nancy drills Elliot. Six slugs right in the pump. Elliot dies all over the coffee shop. Michael grabs Nancy's gun. She collapses into his arms and looks into his eyes.

NANCY: We met . . .

MICHAEL *(V.O.)*: "She whispered."

NANCY: At a carnival.

Up we swoop, looking down at Michael and Nancy . . . and Elliot who is struggling to his feet in order to die some more.

INT. CLASSROOM—NIGHT

Michael looks up from his pages. After a hell of a pause:

DUNBAR *(real slow)*: Socks? In God's hamper?

MICHAEL: It's a metaphor.

DUNBAR: That'd be one way to describe it, yes.

Someone in the class laughs once and shakes his head. Nancy covers her mouth. Michael looks around. This isn't going the way he thought it would.

DUNBAR: How long did you spend on it?

MICHAEL: Not too long.

DUNBAR: How long is "not too long"?

MICHAEL: A couple of hours.

DUNBAR: Then a couple of hours *was* too long. You really worked on this assignment.

MICHAEL: Yes, I did.

DUNBAR: But I didn't want you to work, I wanted you to write. You polished this, revised it. Weren't you here last week when I talked about the danger of being clever, being cute?

MICHAEL: I was here.

DUNBAR: Couldn't you hear the difference between yours and, say, Nancy's? *(she lifts her attention from Michael, turning to the class)* This gives us a chance to look at some common pitfalls. Let's start with Michael's dialogue. What kind of impression did it make on you?

Michael can't bring himself to turn his head and have eye contact with the other workshop members as they start to take his story apart.

FIRST WRITER: Well, they didn't sound like people. At least not people in this century.

It's downhill from there.

INT. COFFEE SHOP—NIGHT

Michael facing Nancy.

NANCY: It wasn't *that* bad.

MICHAEL: Not for you. They liked yours.

NANCY: It isn't about being liked. It's about learning to be a better writer.

MICHAEL: What did you think of it?

NANCY: It did seem rather . . . well . . . studied.

MICHAEL: Studied?

NANCY (*knowing bloody well who they are*): **The woman and the man she shot . . . who were they supposed to be?**

MICHAEL: **What do you mean?**

NANCY: **Who were they? Who did you model them on?**

MICHAEL: **They weren't supposed to be anybody. They were just characters. I made them up.**

Her expression indicates she isn't convinced.

MICHAEL: **Honest.**

NANCY: **What I wrote . . . to the others in the class, it must have seemed like I made that up too. You're the only one who would have known differently.**

MICHAEL: **I guess so.**

NANCY: **I talk to Hope, you talk to Elliot, Hope talks to you. We probably know more about each other than we think. We probably know things we shouldn't know.**

MICHAEL: **I don't think so. I mean, do we have secret lives or something?**

NANCY: **Private lives.**

MICHAEL: **But if we don't write about the things we know . . . you did it yourself.**

NANCY: **That was different.**

MICHAEL: **How was it different?**

Nancy is about to answer when Matt arrives at the table.

MATT: **Hi. Sorry I'm late. You ready to go?**

Nancy starts to collect her things. She reaches for her purse.

NANCY: **Let me give Michael some money for the check.**

MICHAEL: **I've got it. Don't worry.**

She gets up and, with Matt, starts to exit. A round of good nights. Michael watches Matt and Nancy reach the door. In the doorway Matt says something and they kiss. It's a less public kiss than the other night. Nancy looks back and catches Michael watching.

Michael quickly looks down to figure the check. Nancy turns her attention to Matt and they exit.

ACT THREE

EXT. STEADMAN HOUSE (DRIVEWAY)—DAY

Michael and Elliot are washing the Volvo.

ELLIOT: So, what are we going to do about Drentell? We've got to move on this before he cools down. What can we do to really sell ourselves?

MICHAEL: Oh, Elliot, he wants us to crawl and beg for the job. Then he'll let us linger for a week and then, maybe, he'll hire us.

ELLIOT: Go team.

MICHAEL: And that would be the pattern for the whole time we're there. That would be our life.

ELLIOT: We can deal with that. We're homo sapiens. We survive, evolve, make tools.

Michael sponges with a vengeance. Elliot decides to try another approach.

ELLIOT: How's the workshop?

MICHAEL: Okay.

ELLIOT: Knocking 'em dead?

MICHAEL: Not exactly.

ELLIOT: How's Nancy doing?

MICHAEL: Better than me.

ELLIOT *(kind of proud)*: No kidding? She still seeing that guy?

MICHAEL *(knowing full well)*: Which guy?

ELLIOT: The one with the hardware store.

MICHAEL: He owns more than one.

ELLIOT: Uh-oh, a hardware magnate. What's the story?

MICHAEL: How should I know what the story is?

ELLIOT: You see her at the class, you see her with this man. You know what I'm asking.

MICHAEL: No, I don't.

ELLIOT: Yes, you do.

Michael does know.

MICHAEL: Yeah, they kinda look like a couple.

Elliot looks away, then heads for the front porch. Michael follows.

ELLIOT: She's getting prettier. Nancy. You notice that?

MICHAEL *(he has)*: Not really.

ELLIOT: The way she looked at the party when Miles and I had our slap-fight, jeeze, she was beautiful. Mike, do me a favor? Keep an eye on Nancy and if she does something would you tell me?

MICHAEL: Does what?

ELLIOT: Let me know if she starts wearing a man's wristwatch.

Michael doesn't know where this is coming from. Elliot explains.

ELLIOT: In college, the first time I went someplace for a couple of days, she kept my watch. Wore it 'til I came back so she'd always have something of mine touching her. When I got back, we made love at three thirty-six in the afternoon. I know because she left the watch on. She was naked except for my big clunky Timex and a black leather band. Things got . . . to a certain point, and she slammed it against the nightstand and cracked the crystal. "It takes a licking, but keeps on ticking." So, could you let me know if she starts wearing his watch?

MICHAEL: Okay.

Elliot snaps the moment. He moves back to the car. Michael watches him go.

INT. MELISSA'S LOFT (DARKROOM)—DAY

Melissa and Michael in safety light as Melissa makes enlargements.

MELISSA: If I give you one of Ivy Dunbar's books will you ask her to autograph it for me, or would that jeopardize too much of your "cool"?

MICHAEL: We're really not on those kinds of terms.

MELISSA: It's so great that you're writing again.

MICHAEL: Yeah, well . . .

MELISSA: You know what I was thinking about the other day? "The Adventures of Milt and Penny."

MICHAEL: Oh, God, no.

MELISSA: I took the pictures with the Instamatic, you wrote the cartoon balloons; our own comic strip. We should do it again. I take much better pictures now.

MICHAEL: My writing may be stuck back with "Milt and Penny."

MELISSA: Michael?

MICHAEL: So far my work has been called artificial, overly clever, and dishonest.

MELISSA: Is it?

MICHAEL: Thank you very much.

MELISSA: I'm just asking.

MICHAEL: I'm a little rusty, that's all. I thought it was going to be a more technically advanced workshop. I didn't know it would have novices and we'd be burning time on minor details.

MELISSA: Minor details. Like honesty.

MICHAEL: Want me to turn the lights on in here so you can see what you're doing?

MELISSA: Pardon me.

INT. STEADMAN HOUSE (LIVING ROOM)—DAY

Michael enters through the front door, fresh from Melissa's. Hope gets up from her desk in the sunroom and meets him.

HOPE: Elliot called. Drentell invited you to a shoot.

MICHAEL: Drentell invited us?

HOPE: That's what Elliot said.

MICHAEL: Did he say Drentell called him, or the other way around?

HOPE: I think he said he called Miles.

MICHAEL: Damn it. What's he trying to pull?

HOPE: Is this about the job?

MICHAEL: Hope, there isn't a job. It's just an opportunity for humiliation. He shouldn't have called.

Michael walks away from her, into the kitchen. Hope follows.

INT. STEADMAN HOUSE (KITCHEN)—DAY

Hope enters. Michael is at the refrigerator. Hope watches him for a moment. This isn't easy for her.

HOPE: Michael.

He looks at her.

HOPE: Would you mind explaining to me just what's going on? There is a job, isn't there?

MICHAEL: Maybe.

HOPE: Excuse me, but why don't you want it?

MICHAEL: It's not that simple.

HOPE: Wouldn't it be a better job than Pressman's? You're always talking about the great work they do at DAA, what a "sexy shop" it is.

MICHAEL: It wouldn't have cost me anything to work at Pressman's. It would have been just like Bernstein-Fox only I'd get a discount on garden tools. But you don't know Miles Drentell. Every day I'd have to smile and bathe in his arrogance, and I don't know if I could do it. Can you understand that?

HOPE: Yes, I understand, but Michael, what good does that do us? We're still racking up debt, digging a deeper hole with every check, and I don't see you trying to get a job, if not this one something else. This isn't the way it was supposed to happen. Not for us. And that frightens me. Can *you* understand *that?*

They stand there.

INT. STEADMAN HOUSE (LIVING ROOM/ SUNROOM)—NIGHT

Michael back on the sofa with his legal pad. He's stretched out facing the back of the house. When he looks up from his writing he can see Hope at her desk, diligently working on something that actually brings money into the house. Michael writes.

MICHAEL *(V.O.):* "Harrison looked down at the check and reached for his wallet."

INT. COFFEE SHOP (MICHAEL'S STORY)—NIGHT

Back to the coffee shop, but in a realistic mode. Michael sits opposite Hope, looking down at the check for their dinner and inspecting the thin contents of his billfold. Hope eyes him critically.

MICHAEL *(V.O.):* "Harrison heard the woman laugh."

Michael looks past Hope to a couple necking in a nearby booth. We can see the woman is Nancy, but we don't get a good look at the man. Hope indicates Nancy and her escort.

HOPE: First date.

MICHAEL *(V.O.):* "She said with an edge in her voice. Their fight fresh in his mind, Harrison tried to concentrate. But his eyes were drawn to the couple in the other booth."

We focus, with Michael, on Nancy and her date.

MICHAEL *(V.O.):* "Who were they? What gave them the right to be so happy? Harrison resented the happiness of these strangers and it bothered him that their passion should make him feel so uncomfortable. Why?"

The last "why" is answered by a revelation of just who Nancy's kissing. It's Michael.

INT. STEADMAN HOUSE (LIVING ROOM)—NIGHT

Michael's pen jerks up from the page. Michael looks up, startled by what he's just written. He looks at the paragraph. Where the hell did that come from? He looks toward Hope, who continues to work. He's pricked by a guilt he doesn't understand, then starts crossing out the last description.

INT. COFFEE SHOP (MICHAEL'S STORY)—NIGHT

The sound of scratching. Michael is crudely erased from Nancy's arms and replaced by Matt. In the story, Michael looks from the couple to Hope, who still sits across from him but has gone all coy and melodramatic. Michael writes.

HOPE: I suppose you wonder why I'm telling all this to you
. . . a perfect stranger.

MICHAEL *(V.O.):* "The girl said."

HOPE: But really strangers, I've found, are the only ones you
can trust. Or do you think me wrong?

MICHAEL *(V.O.):* "He told her . . ."

MICHAEL: No.

MICHAEL *(V.O.):* "And she went on with her story. But Harrison's mind wandered, his eyes constantly drawn back to
the couple."

Michael watches Nancy and Matt.

MICHAEL *(V.O.):* "He watched them kiss and felt it ripple
through him, startling him. He tried to think of something else, something to distract him. The woman's pale
arm rested on the table. At her wrist was a man's watch.
Was it her lover's or did she buy it for herself?"

Tight on the black-faced Timex around Nancy's wrist. There's a
crack in the crystal.

MICHAEL *(V.O.):* "What tight burst caused the silver crack in
the crystal?"

INT. BEDROOM (MICHAEL'S STORY)—NIGHT

The watch again, still on her arm, as it bangs the edge of a night
table, then moves against sheets and a man's back.

MICHAEL *(V.O.):* "Did she take it off when they made love or
leave it on, time strapped to her wrist? Harrison heard the
ticking in his head."

INT. CLASSROOM—NIGHT

Nancy's simple gold wristwatch, her arm resting on the desk top.
She covers the watch with her other hand. We move to her face. She
can't believe what she's hearing. Michael finishes reading aloud.

MICHAEL: "He thought the sound would give him away, like
the man in 'The Tell-Tale Heart.' So he concentrated on

the menu, counting the periods that separated the entrees from their prices."

Michael looks up, straight into Dunbar's eyes. She's leaning on the edge of the desk. She squints at him unreadably. Then:

DUNBAR: I like the watch.

Michael smiles. He turns toward Nancy who avoids his eyes.

INT. CLASSROOM—NIGHT

Later. The workshop is breaking up. Nancy and the others move toward the door, while Michael, smiling, approaches Dunbar at the desk. She's stuffing papers into her faithful briefcase.

DUNBAR *(looking up):* Hi there.

MICHAEL: Hi.

DUNBAR: You did better.

MICHAEL *(fishing):* I'm glad you liked it.

DUNBAR: I didn't say I liked the whole thing. I said I liked the watch. That was real. If you can do that, there's really no excuse for all that other crap you wrapped around it. You have some terrible bad habits, Michael, and you need to learn the difference between eloquence and masturbation, but you did manage to get one small thing right. That'd be a miracle for anybody and you should be happy about it. Just don't try to ride it too far.

She turns back to her briefcase. Reeling, Michael heads for the door.

INT. CLASSROOM ENTRANCE/HALLWAY—NIGHT

Michael comes out of the classroom. Nancy is waiting. She practically pins him to the wall, furious but controlled.

NANCY: All right. I'm going to say this to you once and I'm never going to mention it again. I don't know if you wanted to hurt me or not, but you did.

MICHAEL: Nancy . . .

NANCY: You had no right. Elliot shouldn't have told you about the watch, but you had no right to use it. You want to be clever, use your own damn life and leave mine alone.

Before he can respond Nancy turns and walks away, leaving him against the wall.

INT. COMMERCIAL SET—DAY

The idea is to fake the act break and come up on: swirling mist and pounding music. Black high heels come into the shot and we're looking at several intimidatingly beautiful women, all in black and holding high-tech laser guns with which they guard something of great value: a gleaming office copier on a pedestal.

DIRECTOR'S VOICE: Cut.

We drop back to include the crew filming the commercial as the playback barks off and the women lean on their space rifles. Miles steps in to block our view.

MILES: So, you decided to grace us with your presence.

Michael and Elliot are there at the edge of light and activity.

ELLIOT: Did you really think we wouldn't come?

MILES *(simple):* No. Come into the circle, boys.

He leads them onto the set, ducking industrious crew members. The Amazons walk past them.

ELLIOT: This the new p.s.a. for the Girl Scouts?

MILES: Sakamoto Office Technologies. Thirteen million in network prime time. Sort of a mid-level account for us.

ELLIOT *(pointing off):* Who's the geek in the shirt?

Mr. Weston has indicated a short, pugnacious man in the loudest Day-Glo Hawaiian shirt you've ever seen.

MILES *(no big deal):* Trevor Bundt.

MICHAEL: The director?

ELLIOT: He makes actual movies.

MILES: I also let him direct my commercials.

MICHAEL: Why does he bother with this kind of thing when he could be making real movies?

MILES: He's getting paid fifty grand for three days' work. It doesn't get any more real than that.

ELLIOT: Maybe he thinks of them as epics for people with short-term memory problems.

MILES: Don't tell me Michael thinks there's a distinction between work and art.

Elliot and Miles laugh.

MICHAEL: Yes, I do.

ELLIOT: Is he a card, or what? So do we get to meet the babes?

MILES: I like you. You're predictable. *(he points him at the Amazons)* Be my guest.

Elliot heads for the models, who have moved over to the caterer's table. Miles and Michael stay put.

MILES: Steadman, you've got this puritanical hitch in your shoulders, like an Amish in Atlantic City. Relax.

MICHAEL: I'm having a fine time, Miles.

MILES: Good.

Miles looks off to where Elliot is chatting with one of the towering women.

MILES: Ever wonder what a mind like his would come up with given these resources?

MICHAEL: So, Miles.

MILES: Michael.

MICHAEL: Have you found anybody for that empty office yet?

MILES: What empty office? Oh, right. Not yet. Any suggestions?

Miles looks at Michael. Michael looks at the devil's smile. "Come on," it whispers to him. "Ask me for it." But Michael can't bring himself to do it. Instead:

MICHAEL: You know, Miles, I don't like you.

Miles just stands there and smiles.

MICHAEL: I'm not kidding. I mean it. I really don't like you.

MILES: I'm a little hazy on what it is you expect me to do with this information.

MICHAEL: I'm just being honest.

MILES: Am I supposed to be hurt or something?

MICHAEL: I'm just telling you the truth.

The others are watching now; Elliot, the women, and the crew.

MILES: No, you said you were being honest, not truthful. You told me your opinion, you didn't give me any facts. And your opinion, as such, has no weight. No significance. No relevance. But I do find the "fact" that you think I should care what your opinion is of me rather pathetic. Sorry if that insults you. I'm just being honest.

Miles turns his back on Michael and goes to Elliot and the Amazons. Michael stands there a moment, then turns and leaves the circle of light. Elliot watches him go.

ACT FOUR

INT. COMMERCIAL STUDIO (STAGE ENTRANCE)—DAY

Elliot trails Mike. They reach the padded doorway leading from the stage. In the distance behind Elliot is the circle of light surrounding the commercial shoot.

ELLIOT: Give me a clue, okay? At least a hint about what you were trying to accomplish in there.

MICHAEL: Forget it.

ELLIOT: Forget it? After the heat you gave me over Pressman you pull something like this?

MICHAEL: Pressman was different.

ELLIOT: Damn right it was different. That was over a job, this is just personalities. You were set to eat anything Pressman dished, but here, here where we could really do ourselves some good . . . I don't get it.

MICHAEL: Look, I'm not like you. Maybe I wish I were, but I can't fake it with him. It burns too much.

ELLIOT: He knows that and he loves it. That's part of the deal. There's a price, no matter what you do there's always going to be a price. So you decide what's important and you make boxes. In one box is what you do to work for somebody like Miles. In the other is who you take home to Hope and Janey and that's how you get through.

MICHAEL: That's the road to happiness? Self-induced schizophrenia?

ELLIOT: Hey, you want a soul like a perfect ball of light? Go to Osaka with Drentell's Buddhists. You want to have a life right here, today? Then pick your battles and learn how to compromise. Now, where do you want to have lunch?

Without waiting for an answer, Elliot brushes past Michael, opens the door, and exits. Michael looks back at the pool of light, like a cold star at the center of the stage.

INT. WESTON HOUSE (LIVING ROOM)—DAY

Beginning with Matt looking down at one of Nancy's illustrations on the drafting board. Nancy enters from the bedroom, putting on a jacket.

NANCY: All set.

MATT: I've been meaning to ask you something.

NANCY: What?

MATT: Does Ethan realize he's the prince?

It was the last question she was expecting.

INT. CLASSROOM—DAY

Michael enters. It's a different space in the sunlight. Dunbar is there, on the wrong side of the desk with her feet up. She's reading a manuscript. The remains of a brown-bag lunch are on the blotter.

DUNBAR: Hello.

MICHAEL: Hi. You busy?

DUNBAR: Not inordinately. Want an apple?

MICHAEL: No, thanks. I wanted to tell you I think I'm going to have to drop out of the workshop.

DUNBAR: I see. What kind of problem have we got here?

MICHAEL: No problem, it's just not working out.

DUNBAR: This isn't because I roughed you up the other night, is it?

MICHAEL: No, it's just, well, can we just say there are conflicts. How's that?

DUNBAR: Sounds plausible.

She reaches down for her war-weary briefcase, rifles around inside, and comes up with his two assignments and his writing sample. She puts them on the desk.

DUNBAR: There you go.

Michael looks from the papers to Dunbar.

DUNBAR (*light, nonthreatening*): Oh, I'm sorry, did you want me to talk you out of quitting? That's a little too clichéd for me. Besides, writing isn't that important.

MICHAEL: How can you say that?

DUNBAR: Because I'm a writer.

MICHAEL: I can't figure out if you're kidding or not. I mean, a writer . . . a writer is the greatest thing in the world you can be.

DUNBAR: What would you give to be a "great" writer?

MICHAEL *(automatic):* Anything.

DUNBAR: Anything?

Michael realizes what anything might include.

DUNBAR: You see? If a writer disappears, it doesn't even leave a hole. But if a wife disappears, or a father, or a friend. When you learn the proper scale of things, that's when your writing will change.

Michael picks up the papers. He can't leave like this.

DUNBAR: You could be good. But a guilty conscience makes a lousy editor, so if there are demands on you in the real world, you're right, you should attend to them. Writing is not a replacement for living. If you don't believe me, ask my ex-husband.

MICHAEL: Then why do you do it?

DUNBAR: I don't have a choice in the matter. Do you?

Michael looks at her.

INT. WESTON HOUSE (LIVING ROOM)—DAY

There's a knock at the door which pulls Nancy from her work at the drafting table. She answers the door. There's Michael.

MICHAEL: Hi.

NANCY: Hello.

MICHAEL: Could I talk to you for a couple of minutes?

NANCY: I'm going out in a little while.

MICHAEL: Just a minute. I have to try to clear something up.

She thinks about it, then stands away from the door. Michael enters. They stand there in the living room.

MICHAEL: The thing in the story. The watch. I didn't use that to hurt you. And I don't think you'd be mad at Elliot if you knew why he told me.

NANCY: It was a shock; your reading that out loud in front of the others, in front of Ivy.

MICHAEL: But Nancy, we were the only two people in the room who knew.

NANCY: I'm not angry because you used it. Who cares about that? That's just writing. I'm angry because you knew. Now, whenever I think about that afternoon with Elliot, there's always going to be another person in the room, watching us. It was a lovely memory, and you've changed that.

MICHAEL: That wasn't my intention.

NANCY: Which means you did it carelessly, which makes it even worse.

How come nothing's ever easy?

MICHAEL: The thing is, I changed the story to *keep* from hurting you. I faked it, went back to something safe and full of noise, but I couldn't hide everything.

NANCY: What were you trying to hide?

He looks at her a moment before answering.

MICHAEL: You're right. We do know too much about each other.

INT. STEADMAN HOUSE (KITCHEN)—NIGHT

Janey in her high chair watches her father make dinner. The front door opens, then closes, and Hope enters from the living room.

MICHAEL: Hi.

HOPE: Hi. What's cooking?

MICHAEL: "Chicken-Oh-My-Gosh." It used to be Chicken Paprikash, but Janey likes the new name better.

Hope looks through to the dining room. The table is set for dinner.

HOPE: Pretty damn sneaky, being nice to me when I'm angry at you.

MICHAEL: Is it working?

HOPE: Not yet.

She goes into the sun room. Michael turns down the stove and follows her.

INT. STEADMAN HOUSE (SUN ROOM)—NIGHT

MICHAEL: I don't want this to come as a shock to you, but sometimes I can be really thoughtless.

HOPE: I wish it was a shock.

MICHAEL: I didn't want you to see me crawl for somebody like Drentell, see me turn into somebody other than the man you married.

HOPE: It wouldn't have made any difference to me.

MICHAEL: I know. And that's part of what was bothering me. You see, I don't think I'd want you to love me then. I made promises to you. I don't want you to let me off the hook or settle for ten cents on the dollar.

HOPE: My husband, the Blue-Light Special.

MICHAEL: I'm going in to talk with Miles tomorrow.

HOPE: Is that something you want to do?

MICHAEL: Yes, I want to do it. Because it's time I do it.

HOPE: What about the writing?

MICHAEL: The writing. I could take workshops from now till doomsday, I could wear down enough pencils to make a forest, but I could never come up with a sentence that'd be worth as much to me as you are.

They stand there. Michael touches Hope's face. They kiss.

INT. DRENTELL'S OFFICE—DAY

Miles stands alone, facing a monitor running the footage from the commercial shoot. After a moment, Drentell realizes he's not alone and turns toward the door. Michael's there.

MILES: Steadman.

MICHAEL: Miles.

MILES: Come, take a look.

Michael moves to Drentell's side and watches the monitor.

MILES: What do you think?

MICHAEL: It's very hot.

MILES: But?

MICHAEL: But I don't think it'll sell many copiers.

MILES: A couple of thousand dollars worth of trade magazine ads will sell the copiers.

MICHAEL: So what's the point of the commercial?

MILES: You tell me.

MICHAEL: You win more awards, get more clients. You make more money.

MILES: That's the point.

He turns off the tape, hits the eject button, and retrieves the cassette. He turns the black rectangle in his hand.

MILES: Stupid way to make a living, isn't it?

MICHAEL: It has its rewards.

MILES: Yes, it does. That's true. What can I do for you, Michael? What do you want from me?

MICHAEL: Something you're not going to give me.

MILES: And what's that?

MICHAEL: An invitation. I want you to ask us if we'd like to come to work for you.

MILES: Instead of what?

MICHAEL: Instead of our begging for it.

MILES: You ask me, I ask you, either way you end up here. What difference does it make?

Michael smiles.

MICHAEL: I took your advice; read Nashiru on the art of management. He tells the story of two samurai warriors standing in the rain, swords out, each ready to strike. But neither of them moves. They just stand there in the storm, poised.

MILES: Why?

MICHAEL: You tell me.

MILES: Because whoever moves first loses the advantage.

MICHAEL: So they stand there getting soaked, accomplishing nothing. Stupid way to make a living, isn't it?

They stand there. Then:

MILES: Why don't the two of you come in and we'll have a more substantive discussion?

MICHAEL: Sounds like a good idea.

MILES: It is.

The secretary appears at the open doorway. Miles sees her.

MILES: Excuse me.

MICHAEL: Sure.

Miles heads for the door. Just before he exits, he turns to Michael.

MILES: Remember: you came to me.

Miles turns and walks away. Michael watches him go. During the voice-over, we move off Michael, panning across the office.

MICHAEL *(V.O.):* "Watching his straight back as he walked away, I realized how busy the office had been around us. I hadn't noticed it. I'd been aware of a sound, but not a human one . . ."

We have panned out of the office and into. . .

INT. CLASSROOM—NIGHT

. . . the workshop. Michael is reading the end of his story. Nancy is there, listening intently, as is everyone else in the class.

MICHAEL: "I had turned the sounds of the office into the sounds of a storm. Rain. Thunder. If I'd closed my eyes I might have seen the lighting reflected on our swords."

Michael looks up at Dunbar who sits on the edge of the teacher's desk. A beat.

DUNBAR: It's about time.

MR. RIGHT

BY
JILL GORDON

"**M**r. Right" was about being single and over thirty. It's a very important subject—one I knew absolutely nothing about—so why was I hired to write it? Because I'm a unique and sought-after talent, maybe, and maybe because it was the last show of the season, no one else wanted to do it, and my husband, Scott, is the supervising producer. Okay?

Writing a script for *thirtysomething* is different from any show that I've ever worked on. They respect writers. They give you the freedom to create something that is honest and in your own voice. And, therefore, they rob you of the satisfaction of being able to say, when it's on the screen—"Hey, I didn't write that crap. The producer screwed it up."

Melanie Mayron and Polly Draper came up with the idea for this script. They wanted to do a comedy about what might happen if their characters, Melissa and Ellyn, went to a video dating service. Melanie also thought it might be interesting if Melissa got involved with a younger man. She told me about a friend who fell in love with a man who was ten years younger. She was ready for marriage and children; he was still bouncing checks. But they were truly in love, and it was out of that love that she gave him an ultimatum: If he stayed, it was for the whole nine yards. If not—go now, because it would be too painful if he left in a few years. What intrigued me is that he did leave her—but he left out of love.

Which, many episodes after "Mr. Right," is what ultimately happened with Lee and Melissa. In the end, she loved him enough to know she had to let him go. No one ever said Melissa wasn't wise.

Corey Parker, who played Lee, got a leading role on a pilot for another series. Was I trying to say that the tragic inability of people to ever really connect could be blamed on a network's fall schedule? I don't know. All I know is that if Lee and Melissa get back together, it means true love prevailed, Corey's pilot didn't sell, and the studio was able to make a deal.

But back to "Mr. Right." I had the actresses' ideas, a meeting with Marshall and Richard, and full creative freedom, which is my personal vision of hell. I didn't have a clue as to what the story was about, so I decided to divorce my husband and start dating.

I didn't date; I stayed married. I was fortunate because the art director of *thirtysomething,* Brandy Alexander (I swear that's her real name), had just joined a video dating service. Her testimony was crucial to the script, as was that of the other single women I interviewed, who so generously shared with me the raw truth about their electronic quest for love so I could exploit it on television. Their stories, pain, and sense of humor wrote "Mr. Right" for me.

Story meeting number two . . . Marshall, Richard, and I talked about the kind of men Melissa and Ellyn would want to find at video dating, and how what they found might affect the other characters on the show. My meeting was brief, and so was my deadline; the first draft was due in eight days. (Now, I could have handed the script in late, but then I'd be screwing over the director. Who was my husband, Scott Winant.)

The story wasn't happening. Nothing seemed to work. But don't think that I took my frustrations out on my husband. We had a very good working relationship. I'd walk into the kitchen and say, "What about a scene in an auditorium?" He'd say "No. It's impossible to light." I'd say, "You're sleeping in the living room."

First, I had to figure out what the scenes were. That too, in the end, had a lot to do with Scott. I remember that I was really stuck trying to find the core of the story. Scott kissed me, and I thought of the magic of a kiss, and Cinderella, and what that meant to all of us as little girls. I thought of Ethan and what his first kiss might be like. And I saw that the moment of Ethan's first kiss would be the moment Melissa lets go of her own long dream of Cinderella-hood.

There was a time when we were taught to believe in knights on white horses, that some day a prince would come and rescue us. A lot of people, I think, never let go of that fairy tale. That's why, in the script, when Melissa turns down Mr. Right, there just happens to be a prince waiting for her, dressed, for the moment, in painter's clothes.

By the way—in the time it took to write and shoot "Mr. Right," Brandy Alexander did find someone. Last Saturday, Scott and I went to her wedding.

JILL GORDON

ACT ONE

INT. NANCY AND ELLIOT'S LIVING ROOM—DAY

Nancy backs in the front door, holding a shopping bag stuffed with clothes. Hope follows, carrying two more bags.

HOPE: This is it. Thanks.

NANCY: They said they'd be here at noon.

The phone rings. Nancy answers it as Melissa enters, dragging two large trash bags of clothes.

MELISSA: Hi, am I late? Did they pick it up already? I'm not putting these back on hangers . . . Actually, I included the hangers.

NANCY (*on the phone*)*:* I'll get him . . . Ethan—it's for you!

MELISSA (*re the bigger bag*)*:* This is the guilt bag—clothes I

199

couldn't afford and never wore. *(re other bag)* **This** is the stuff I can't believe I went out in public in.

HOPE: Don't you wonder if what you're wearing today you'll be horrified you wore two years from now . . . ?

As Ethan reluctantly enters, Nancy hands him the phone.

NANCY: It's Susie Burrows. Be nice. *(to Hope and Melissa)* Ethan's drama class is putting on *Cinderella*. He's playing the prince. Susie's Cinderella.

The three women, variously entranced by this notion, watch Ethan as he talks to Susie.

ETHAN: Yeah . . . No . . . I don't know . . . How am *I* supposed to know? . . . 'Bye.

Ethan hangs up. Nancy calls after him as he walks out angrily.

NANCY: I'll be there in a minute!

MELISSA: I loved *Cinderella* . . .

NANCY: We were actually kind of excited about getting the lead until we found out that the prince has to *kiss* Cinderella.

Nancy follows Ethan into his bedroom.

MELISSA: Every time the prince was going to leave before Cinderella had a chance to put on the shoe, my heart would seriously stop. Then he'd see her and they'd live happily ever after, and you'd be depressed because you could never be Cinderella, because you were fat and she was skinny. Which is how it is in all fairy tales.

HOPE: Oh come on, Melissa. Anyone can be a princess.

MELISSA: Yeah? Name one fairy tale with a redhead in it.

Nancy returns.

NANCY: Name one fairy tale that came true. How long did you wait for a prince to come rescue you?

MELISSA: What? You mean he's not coming? Did he call?

HOPE: How's Ethan?

NANCY: He threw up a testosterone force shield. I'll get Elliot to talk to him . . .

MELISSA *(re the clothing bags):* Maybe we should tie them up . . .

INT. ELLYN'S LIVING ROOM—THAT DAY

Melissa follows Ellyn as she goes to the couch, stoops down, and looks underneath.

ELLYN: Sophie? You want to meet Melissa? *(to Melissa)* She's still a little scared.

Melissa looks under the couch to see.

MELISSA: Oh, it's an adult cat. She's beautiful . . . Is that hissing?

The phone rings.

ELLYN: Let the machine pick it up . . . They have great animals at the pound . . . There was this really cute kitten . . . and then there was Sophie. We connected . . .

A hiss—and Ellyn quickly pulls her hand out from under the couch.

ELLYN: Maybe she's hungry . . .

BEEP! A man's voice is heard on the phone machine.

MAN'S VOICE: My name's Devon Marks, your Aunt Lorraine gave me your number . . . She thought maybe we should get together. My number's 555-6217.

The machine clicks off. Ellyn turns to Melissa.

ELLYN: Aunt Lorraine is dead meat.

MELISSA: Everyone in *my* family knows better. Everyone in my *life* knows better.

ELLYN: I love it when someone says they've got a guy they want me to meet. Blind dates are so much fun and stress-free.

Ellyn goes to the kitchen to prepare food for Sophie.

MELISSA: But I got all the rules down. Always meet them at the restaurant—it's much faster to say good night in a parking lot with your motor running.

ELLYN: Never order an appetizer. It extends the evening.

MELISSA: And just say you're not drinking coffee these days.

ELLYN: And it's bad enough your friends do it to you, but I
even got this stuff in the mail for, you know, video dating.
It's like a conspiracy. I must be on a mailing list marked
"Pitiful" . . .

MELISSA: I get them too!

Ellyn sneaks the most tentative of glances at Melissa.

ELLYN: It's not like I think it's a *totally* weird thing to do . . .

MELISSA: Well, no. It's just the whole idea of it . . . I'll take
one perfect man who's not hung up on his mother or ex-
girlfriend. To go, please.

Ellyn slides the cat's food under the couch.

ELLYN: I know someone who met her husband through video
dating. She's like us. Really! And he's actually almost
cute. He's a lawyer, they have a kid, a house, a shower
made of glass blocks . . . They're really happy. *(on Melissa's
hairy eyeball)* All right. The kid is hyperactive, but still—

MELISSA: Yeah, well, that's okay for some people, but I still
have faith that I'll *meet* someone . . .

ELLYN: You know, if we're thinking about this—even though
we're not and never would—maybe there are guys like us
thinking about it, too. Cute guys.

MELISSA: With nice arms?

ELLYN: That, too.

MELISSA: We're not having this conversation.

ELLYN: Right. I would never—unless you—

MELISSA: What happened to fate? *It had to be you . . . Strangers
in the night . . .* Hearing bells when he kisses you? It
happens, you know.

They look at each other.

MELISSA: We tell no one.

INT. STEADMAN HOUSE—BEDROOM—DAY

Hope hands Ellyn a black bolero jacket from her closet.

ELLYN: Thanks. *(playful)* Hope, what was Michael's roommate's name? The one he was living with when you first met him?

Hope quickly closes the bedroom door and turns to Ellyn.

HOPE *(low voice):* You know what his name was. I can't *believe*—Michael is right downstairs and we weren't even really dating officially when that happened . . . Once! And you are sworn to secrecy.

ELLYN: I just wanted to point out how important it is to keep a secret . . .

INT. STEADMAN HOUSE—LIVING ROOM—DAY

Melissa reads the instructions as Michael struggles to assemble a dollhouse for Janey.

MELISSA: It says that these come pre-made, too.

MICHAEL: Real men build their own dollhouses.

MELISSA *(hedging):* Hey, you wanna hear a kick? Ellyn knows someone who met her husband through video dating. Interesting, huh? Do you think it's interesting? What do you think of it? Video dating, that is.

MICHAEL *(preoccupied):* Video dating. Does that really exist? I always thought it was a myth of the eighties—you know, like concern for your fellow man and "just say no."

MELISSA: So what are you saying? You think it's stupid . . . ?

INT. STEADMAN HOUSE—BEDROOM—DAY

HOPE: No, I think it's great—

ELLYN: At least I know the men I'll be meeting aren't afraid of getting involved. They spent too much on the application fee.

HOPE: It's kind of exciting. It kills the whole concept of the blind date . . .

ELLYN: Yeah. This is more like a seeing-eye date, I guess *(tries on the jacket)* Maybe Melissa will back out, and—can I still borrow the jacket?

INT. STEADMAN HOUSE—LIVING ROOM—DAY

Michael stares at Melissa. He just can't take it seriously.

MICHAEL: Nooooo . . . No . . . No . . .

MELISSA: As long as you have an open mind about it. You know, Michael, the only men I meet who are willing to make a commitment are married.

MICHAEL: I want to support you on this. I really do. *(unable to handle it)* Give me time.

MELISSA: Thanks . . . All right, it's not exactly romantic. But neither is praying they'll show *Breakfast at Tiffany's* on cable Saturday night. We don't all get lucky and meet our perfect mate. You're out there now and it's "Hi, I'm Melissa Steadman, I've been tested." That's what it's like in the real world, Michael. I could wait forever . . . *(defiant)* Or I could try this. Please, please, please don't tell anyone, even though I know you will . . .

INT. STEADMAN HOUSE—FRONT DOOR—DAY

Good-byes are exchanged as Ellyn and Melissa leave together. Hope closes the door and turns to Michael. Her look says "I've got a secret and I'm not telling." Michael calls after her as she heads upstairs.

MICHAEL: I know what you're thinking. I can't keep a secret . . . *(quickly backtracks)* If I even had a secret.

INT. MELISSA'S LOFT—DAY

Melissa talks to Ellyn on the phone as she labors over her video-dating member's profile.

MELISSA: What did you put down for number three—"What I'm looking for in a relationship . . ." Oh, that's good . . . Don't use it, let me . . .

A little antique clock chimes noon, and there's a knock at the door.

MELISSA: Yeah, thanks.

Melissa hangs up, erasing what she's written as she goes to open the door. Standing there is Lee Owens, who's twenty-five, attractive in a nontraditional way, and carrying a book of paint samples.

LEE: Melissa? I'm Lee.

MELISSA: You showed up on time. You're supposed to call to apologize for not showing up, then miss two more appointments before showing up an hour and a half late for your last chance to get this job.

He smiles, unflustered by her barrage of words, and looks around the loft.

LEE: Actually, your watch is fast. I'm five minutes early.

MELISSA: You're hired.

LEE: Good. You need me.

Melissa tucks away her member's profile. Lee chips some paint from the wall.

LEE: This is new paint.

MELISSA: Yeah, I just—

LEE: Did you pay the dip who did this?

MELISSA: I did it.

LEE: Don't spread it around.

His examination continues.

MELISSA: Is there hope?

LEE: I'm gonna have to remove most of this crap. You want this same color?

MELISSA: Yeah.

LEE *(too bad):* Oh.

MELISSA: What do *you* think?

Lee hands her his book.

LEE: See if there's a color in there you like.

As she opens the book a piece of sheet music falls out.

MELISSA: You're a musician.

LEE: No, I'm a painter.

MELISSA: Oh, you're an artist!

LEE: No. *(re sheet music)* I needed something to write on.

Melissa is a little tongue-tied. Lee crosses to her work space.

MELISSA: Oh, I—I want to keep that wall white. But maybe you can suggest something for this wall?

LEE: Well, I don't like to impose my vision on people until I'm absolutely sure they have no vision of their own.

He takes a final look, adding up all the possibilities.

LEE: The problem is—you work where you live. So I want to find a color that can sort of let you get away from that . . . You must get great light here in the morning.

MELISSA: I do. You know, I'd also like you to repaint the bathroom. I keep putting it off.

Melissa leads him to the bathroom while we remain in the loft.

LEE'S VOICE: This should be easy . . .

MELISSA'S VOICE: It's cracking above the shower . . .

LEE'S VOICE: I use that shampoo!

MELISSA'S VOICE: I've been using it for years.

And they return.

MELISSA: So what's the damage?

LEE *(taking it literally):* Oh, well, there's no real damage. You just used bad paint.

MELISSA: No, I meant—what do you think this will cost?

LEE: Oh! *(comes back, playful)* A lot . . . Let me just go out to my truck and write up an estimate.

"THE RIGHT ONE" VIDEO DATING CLUB—DAY

We are greeted by Kelly, a perky android with very large teeth.

KELLY: . . . So we take your photos and profile and put them in a book that's alphabetized by first name only. You look through the men's book and decide whose video you'd like to view . . .

We now see that Kelly's target is Ellyn. She struggles to take all this in.

KELLY'S VOICE: Then if you'd like to meet that person, we tell them. He looks at your video and if the interest is mutual, we exchange your phone numbers and last names. And whenever you come in, we'll give you a computer readout of who'd like to meet *you* and who's responded to your requests. 'Kay, is that clear?

We now discover the other half of Kelly's pitch—Melissa, who is sitting next to Ellyn and wearing dark glasses.

"THE RIGHT ONE"—VIDEO ROOM—ELLYN

A small room, with a chair in front of a simple gray backdrop. Ellyn's sartorial statement reads "Sophisticated Business-Gal." A male interviewer's voice floats in—warm, friendly, almost flirtatious.

INTERVIEWER #1: Hi.

ELLYN *(nervous):* Hi. *(to the video camera)* Is that on yet?

INTERVIEWER #1: We'll talk a little bit and then I'll turn the camera on. Okay?

Ellyn nods, unconsciously biting her lower lip. Then, worried she might have gotten lipstick on her teeth, she "subtly" rubs her finger along her teeth to remove it, just in case.

INTERVIEWER #1: Now you can remake your video as much as you like.

ELLYN *(takes off coat):* On or off? *(puts on coat)* On . . . No. Off is better . . . *(takes off coat)* But on is more professional. *(puts on coat)* On?

INTERVIEWER #1: Either way.

ELLYN: Right. I'll just throw it over my shoulder.

INTERVIEWER #1: So just relax. I'm going to ask you a few questions. And, ah, have fun with it . . .

ELLYN: Great. I feel relaxed. I do . . . Would you excuse me for just a minute . . . ?

Ellyn gets up.

"THE RIGHT ONE"—VIDEO ROOM—MELISSA

Melissa has chosen more casual clothes for her ordeal. A second male interviewer's voice speaks to her.

INTERVIEWER #2: Why don't we start with who you are.

MELISSA (*a bit nervous*): Okay, I'm ah, Melissa Steadman and . . .

INTERVIEWER #2: You don't have to tell me your last name. (*realizes*) Melissa Steadman? Were you in Mrs. Byler's ninth-grade math class? You used to be fat? Wow! How ya doing?

Melissa, her worst nightmare realized, forces a casual smile.

"THE RIGHT ONE"—VIDEO ROOM—ELLYN

Ellyn sits back down, smiling at the interviewer. One piece of hair stands straight up.

INTERVIEWER #1: Ah, Ellyn . . .

"THE RIGHT ONE"—VIDEO ROOM—MELISSA

Melissa, struggling to be serious, recites her bio as if by rote.

MELISSA: I'm Melissa Steadman and I'm looking for someone who's fun, but mature . . .

She starts to giggle.

MELISSA: Sorry. Let me try that again.

She takes a deep breath to compose herself.

MELISSA: I'm Melissa Steadman and I'm looking for—

Melissa cracks up again.

MELISSA: I'm sorry, it's just that is so—

Okay. One more deep breath, and one more stab at seriousness.

MELISSA: I mean, it's not silly . . . Of course not . . . Okay. I'm ready. I'm Melissa Steadman—

And she loses it completely.

"THE RIGHT ONE"—VIDEO ROOM—ELLYN

INTERVIEWER #1: What do you want to say to the special guy waiting out there just for you?

ELLYN: Call me at seven . . . can you take that out? I don't want to be funny, then you're expected to be funny. The camera's not on yet, is it?

"THE RIGHT ONE"—VIDEO ROOM—MELISSA

Melissa laughs uncontrollably, almost falling out of her chair.

"THE RIGHT ONE"—VIDEO ROOM—ELLYN

Ellyn is now more composed.

ELLYN: "What do I want . . . in a relationship?" . . . Oh, I think a relationship should bring out the best in you . . . I want to have fun . . .

She continues with a totally straight face.

ELLYN: "I want to shine like the sun. I want to be the one that you want to see. I want to knit you a sweater, write you a love letter, I want to make you feel better. I want to make you feel free. I am on a lonely road and I am traveling—"

INTERVIEWER #1: Joni Mitchell.

ELLYN: I couldn't think of what to say.

"THE RIGHT ONE"—VIDEO ROOM—MELISSA

Melissa drinks some water in an attempt to calm herself down.

MELISSA: Thank you. *(a pause, then:)* Okay . . . Ask away.

INTERVIEWER #2: Okay. What are you looking for in a relation—

We now hear the interviewer totally crack up, which causes immediate hysteria in Melissa.

MELISSA: Look, we all know this is ridiculous . . .

Silence.

MELISSA: Isn't it? I mean—I'm looking for something I can't

find. It's like the lottery. You know you won't win—but
you keep buying tickets . . .

We stay with her, for just a moment past comfortable, and
then . . .

ACT TWO

INT. "THE RIGHT ONE"—LIBRARY—DAY

Long tables, little cubicles, rock music piped into the room. Ellyn
flips through a black book while Melissa looks around the library.

MELISSA: Right now people could be looking at our pictures,
rejecting us.

ELLYN: Then we'll reject them.

MELISSA: Then we won't get our money's worth.

ELLYN: But we'll have ego satisfaction.

MELISSA: I can't do this—

ELLYN: Melissa—

MELISSA: Okay, I'll just glance under the "D's." I'll find someone named David—my mother would like that.

Melissa and Ellyn look through their books.

ELLYN (*hopeful*): Oh, he's kind of—(*looks harder*) Ugly.

MELISSA: This is too weird.

ELLYN: It's reality—

MELISSA: I know it's reality. But I think reality is overrated.

And now, she freezes: she's turned to the "E's" and there's a picture of
Elliot! Closing the book, she looks up to make sure Ellyn didn't see.

MELISSA: I've got to get out of here. I feel a stress zit waiting to
erupt . . .

A photo in Ellyn's book catches her eye. It's "William"—thirty-five,
kind eyes, infectious smile. Ellyn quickly senses Melissa's interest.

ELLYN: Your hormones are showing.

MELISSA: I don't want to be premature, but I promise I won't
make the bridesmaids wear Empire.

They start reading William's profile.

ELLYN: He's a journalist.

MELISSA: That's too perfect. This hurts . . . He's politically
active . . . But is he politically correct?

ELLYN: "Homeless relief" and "anti-Apartheid Committee."

MELISSA: There's a God. I never doubted it. There's *got* to be
something wrong with him. He isn't real. What a smile
. . . Do you see that smile? Don't look. He's mine.

ELLYN: Well, go for it, girl! Tell them you want to meet him.

MELISSA: No, I can't . . . I want him to find *me* first . . . You
know?

Of course she knows, and for a moment she and Melissa silently
contemplate the workings of the ideal romantic universe. Melissa
checks out William's photo one more time.

MELISSA: I don't believe it. He's perfect. I mean he *seems* perfect . . . Is that shallow? You know, to judge somebody basically from their picture?

Ellyn just looks at her.

MELISSA: Okay. I'm shallow. I want him.

INT. STEADMAN HOUSE—LIVING ROOM—DAY

Michael and Elliot watch an Eagles game on TV, screaming for the play, jumping up and down and hugging each other. Hope comes down the stairs holding one of Janey's sweaters.

HOPE: Jocks.

ELLIOT: Oh, it's okay to act like jocks on weekends as long as you've been in touch with your feminine side during the week. Right, Michael?

MICHAEL *(grabs Hope):* Or someone else's . . .

Hope holds up Janey's paint-spattered sweater.

HOPE: She definitely has artistic talent. I've just got to teach her how to paint on the paper.

As Hope goes to the kitchen Melissa comes in the front door.

MELISSA: Hi, everybody . . .

Melissa fishes in her bag and pulls out a single man's loafer.

MELISSA: Michael, is this yours?

MICHAEL: Not mine.

MELISSA: I found it in my closet when I was getting stuff to bring to Nancy's. It's so stupid, I can't imagine whose it is. Someone left it.

Michael and Elliot look at her.

MELISSA: Trust me. I'd remember. The last time a man dressed at my place he needed both shoes for a running start.

Elliot checks out the shoe on his way to the bathroom.

ELLIOT: My feet are much bigger.

Michael approaches Melissa as soon as Elliot is gone.

MICHAEL: Did you meet Mr. Right yet?

MELISSA: Yes. Maybe. I think. *Now* he has to meet me.

And she heads off for the kitchen.

INT. STEADMAN HOUSE—KITCHEN—DAY

Hope washes the paint out of Janey's sweater. Nancy rehearses with Ethan at the table. As Melissa enters:

MELISSA: Hi . . .

HOPE: Shh . . . We're in rehearsal.

NANCY *(reads):* "Sire, you must get back to the dance."

A very reluctant Ethan picks up his cue.

ETHAN: "I must find her" . . . I'm not kissing her. "She left her slipper" . . . I'm not kissing her.

NANCY: All right, Ethan. Do you want to practice the dance?

ETHAN: You're kidding me, right?

NANCY: How will you be any good if you don't practice?

ETHAN: I'll fake it.

Ethan storms out.

NANCY: He refuses to learn how to waltz.

EXT. STEADMAN HOUSE—FRONT YARD—DAY

Ethan kneels on the ground staring at a bug. Melissa joins him.

MELISSA: What kind of bug is that?

ETHAN: Dead.

MELISSA: Oh . . . So! You're going to be the prince.

No response.

MELISSA: Well, I think it's really neat.

ETHAN: It's a stupid play.

MELISSA: Oh no, Ethan, it's a wonderful play. Do you know how important the prince is? Everyone wishes they could be Cinderella so they could marry the prince. I was in love with the prince for so long—until I saw Mark Lindsay with Paul Revere and the Raiders.

ETHAN: Who?

MELISSA: Never mind. Can I come see your play?

ETHAN: Why does he have to dance with her?

MELISSA: That's the best part. I mean, when he picks her out of everyone else, your heart stops and it's like he picked *you* . . .

Ethan throws a rock. Melissa throws a rock.

MELISSA: I remember—he took her hands . . .

Melissa takes Ethan's hands.

MELISSA: Now, I'm not very good at this. I hope you won't mind.

Slowly, carefully, Melissa shows Ethan how to waltz. They both look down at their feet.

MELISSA: See . . . You step right, then left, right . . . Left, then right again.

She starts to hum the waltz from Tchaikovsky's *Sleeping Beauty*—the same waltz most of us are stunned to learn was not composed by Walt Disney.

MELISSA: You're good!

And now they are really dancing as—

INT. "THE RIGHT ONE"—RECEPTION DESK—DAY

Kelly, even more cheery than usual, hands Melissa and Ellyn two computer printouts.

KELLY: These are the gentlemen who've requested you view their videos. Good luck, ladies.

As Melissa scans her list for William's name, she and Ellyn both subtly hold up their lists to compare whose is longer.

"THE RIGHT ONE"—VIEWING BOOTH—MELISSA

Melissa sits in front of a small screen, armed with a stack of videos labeled "William." A "William" flashes on—but it's not *the* William.

WRONG WILLIAM: Hi. I'm a stockbroker. I was born and raised here. I work a lot of hours, so it's hard to meet new people . . .

"THE RIGHT ONE"—VIEWING BOOTH—ELLYN

Ellyn watches the end of a video.

MAN ON VIDEO: I like horseback riding and tennis. I'm a real tennis fanatic—

As she pulls out the cassette Melissa scoots over from her viewing booth.

MELISSA: I'm feeling the need to eat something very bad for me.

ELLYN: Not one of them was my type. Not even close. I mean they seemed nice . . . I don't know what they saw in my tape. This is the type of guy I attract?

Ellyn puts in another tape, and this time Melissa's William—Mr. Right, that is—comes on the screen. A moment, then quietly, carefully:

MELISSA: He chose you.

And now we all meet William.

INTERVIEWER'S VOICE: William, what are the few key words that describe what you're looking for in a woman?

MELISSA: Not me . . .

WILLIAM: You know, I'm a little uncomfortable with all this. I really just want to say I'm looking to meet someone who's not afraid to be involved . . . I guess we've all been crushed at some point, and none of us wants to go through that again . . . There are a lot of men who always think the grass is greener . . . I'm, ah, not that way. I think loyalty and commitment are essential to a good working relationship . . . I guess I'm really looking for a best friend.

Melissa lets her forehead fall on the monitor.

INT. ELLYN'S APARTMENT—DAY

Ellyn slides cat food under the couch. Melissa, depressed, sits on the floor eating ice cream.

ELLYN: Melissa, I'm an "E," he probably hasn't even gotten to the "M's" yet—

MELISSA: I'm very happy for the both of you. Have a wonderful life. Your kids will call me Aunt Melissa. I'll come for Thanksgiving.

ELLYN: No, you won't! Because you're going back to tell them you want him to see your video!

MELISSA: What if he *rejects* my video? Worse—what if I have to go out with him?

ELLYN: Oh, God, those first five minutes . . . you just want to Xerox your bio and hand it over.

MELISSA: Love means never having to go on another date—

ELLYN: —*After* William . . . *(preoccupied)* You know what? I'm going to redo my video, I think I came off too serious . . . Hope has this little red jacket . . . I'm going to call her . . .

Melissa considers Ellyn's advice as she goes to call Hope.

MELISSA: So you really think I should go for it?

ELLYN: Absolutely . . . Come on, Hope. Answer . . . *(to Melissa)* She doesn't know how good she has it . . .

MELISSA: Right. The picture-perfect couple . . .

INT. STEADMAN HOUSE—KITCHEN—NIGHT

And here they are, gathered around the dinner table. Janey screams, her face covered with food. Michael wears a T-shirt, his hair's a mess, and he has a five-o'clock shadow. Hope sits across from him in a robe, looking exhausted, her hair in a ponytail on top of her head. Michael stares into space. Hope burps. The phone rings. And rings. And rings.

HOPE: You wanna get that?

MICHAEL: Let it ring.

INT. MELISSA'S LOFT—DAY

Melissa looks over some proof sheets as Lee paints a test strip on the wall. As Lee stands back to consider his work:

LEE: Have you ever been to the Grand Canyon?

MELISSA: No. Nature hates me . . .

LEE: You gotta go. When the sun sets, the mountains turn this incredible color. It's so beautiful. *(re the wall)* It's this color. It's a subtle change, but it'll work great with the light . . . You haven't been? I'm surprised, you're a photographer, I would think—

Lee shakes himself out of his own intensity. Hey—this is just a job.

LEE: Well—you gotta go.

MELISSA: You want some more coffee?

He smiles. Their eyes meet, but just for a moment. Lee checks his watch.

LEE: No thanks. Listen—if it's not a problem, I'm gonna take off for about two hours.

MELISSA: Ah-ha! It starts. You'll never be back.

LEE: Believe me, I'd rather not go. It's this thing—my brother's having my nephew christened. I think all that stuff is pretty out there, but he's heavy into religion, so I really gotta show.

MELISSA: No problem.

LEE: It's not like I'm putting it down. I mean, I know religion's important to you—

MELISSA: It is? I mean not that it isn't, but how did you know?

LEE: Well—the menorah. Some of your books. It's a habit, you get to know people in my work. You see what's behind the bookshelf. *(playful)* I also know you're into some pretty steep lingerie.

Lee refers to an open drawer with Melissa's underwear in it.

MELISSA: "Steep?" A colloquialism of your generation?

LEE: Hey—it'll never be as embarrassing as "groovy."

MELISSA: I'm not a hundred and four, you know. I was still a kid when "groovy" hit the big time.

LEE *(laughs):* I'll be back in about two.

He goes. The minute he's out, Melissa runs to close her lingerie drawer.

INT. "THE RIGHT ONE"—VIDEO ROOM—DAY

Ellyn, for today's interrogation, has replaced "businesslike" with "trendy"—and she looks great.

INTERVIEWER'S VOICE: So we'll just try the whole thing over again . . .

ELLYN: Great . . .

INTERVIEWER'S VOICE: I see here from your profile that you work a lot. But what do you do with your free time?

ELLYN: Well, I do work a lot, but I've cut down. I like to go to movies and read . . . And I love running.

INTERVIEWER'S VOICE: Ellyn, what would you say are the few key words that describe who you are?

She considers this for a moment, then:

ELLYN: Oh . . . I like to have a good time. I like to escape, you know, and get out of the city. And I love to dance all night long and go to breakfast before I go to sleep . . .

We start to approach her now, and, as we do, we sense a just-perceptible darkening of her mood.

ELLYN: "Who am I?" . . . I mean—I'm somebody who wants to share my life with someone. I wouldn't *be* here if I wasn't . . . Wouldn't it be nice if it could just *happen?* It's like everyone you meet is potentially "the one." Because you gotta be a couple. It's become a crime to be single. So you gotta get out there and sell yourself . . .

Our approach now becomes a retreat—slowly, slowly—until we bend time to find Ellyn in her

PSYCHIATRIST'S OFFICE

as her monologue continues to him.

ELLYN: . . . It's this—this *pressure.* You know—hurry up, all the good men are getting taken . . .

And now it all pours out—all the anger and frustration behind her reasonable analysis of contemporary romantic life.

ELLYN: You're the one who said I should try this video thing . . . All right, you didn't say "go do it." But you did say maybe it would be good for me . . . Maybe it is. At least, I'm out there trying. You know the worst thing about being single isn't being alone. It's the way everyone perceives you. You feel weird because you're not in a relationship . . . I got a cat, did I tell you that?

A pause.

ELLYN *(quietly):* She likes the couch.

INT. DAA—MICHAEL'S OFFICE—DAY

Michael is outside his office with his back to the wall. He's holding a basketball and concentrating intensely as Melissa appears.

MELISSA: Hi, I was nearby and—what are you doing?

MICHAEL: Shhh . . . This is very important.

He flips the ball over the wall, turning to see it land in the basket.

MICHAEL: All right!

MELISSA: I can see you're really busy. I'll go—

MICHAEL: No, come in, I'm on a creative break.

They go into his office together. Melissa starts to sit down but Michael stops her.

MICHAEL: Block me.

Huh? She just looks at him.

MICHAEL: Here . . .

He puts her hands up in blocking position and dribbles around her. She stands there passively, not interested in playing along.

MELISSA: I just stopped by to say hi . . .

She nonchalantly puts out her hand, blocking his shot.

MICHAEL: Melissa, you're only supposed to *pretend* to block . . .

Now they sit down together, to gather the yarn of the extended conversation they've been having since they were old enough to talk.

MELISSA: This guy I told you about—

MICHAEL: From the video? Did you meet him?

MELISSA: No. But I could. If he *ever* sees my picture . . . Or— if I tell *them* I'd like to meet *him*.

MICHAEL: So? Tell them.

MELISSA: So? It's not so easy.

MICHAEL: Melissa, that's why you went to this thing. It's what you're supposed to do.

MELISSA: Yeah. Right . . . Michael—did you ever think that maybe you and Hope would have met, you know, no matter what?

MICHAEL: Yeah, I guess I did. Because I can't see my life without her . . . Yeah.

MELISSA: Well, then maybe there's someone out there *I'm* supposed to meet.

MICHAEL: Maybe it's this guy.

MELISSA: I'll have to tell my grandchildren I paid to meet their grandfather. It's not exactly *Wuthering Heights*.

MICHAEL: Tell them you were *meant* to pay to meet him . . .

He's not teasing her. She knows that, and it allows her to laugh with him. Then she grows pensive, maybe even a little sad.

MELISSA: Right . . . thanks.

INT. "THE RIGHT ONE"—RECEPTION DESK—DAY

Melissa, about to go to the desk, reconsiders and starts to leave—but too late! There's Kelly, her optimistic talons bared and ready.

MELISSA: Hi! I, um—there's someone . . .

KELLY *(a little too loud):* You want someone to view your video? Great! What's his video number?

MELISSA: His name's William. He's in that book.

KELLY: We'll just find his number—

MELISSA: Six-one-seven-seven.

ACT THREE

INT. WESTON HOUSE—LIVING ROOM—NIGHT

Two model dinosaurs maul each other to gruesome sound effects by Ethan. Elliot's feet appear.

ELLIOT'S VOICE: There's a rumor that you tried to push Susie Burrows.

The dinosaurs fight on as Elliot kneels down. Ethan pushes one of the dinosaurs over to Elliot, who picks it up and joins in the battle.

ETHAN: She tried to kiss me.

ELLIOT: It's in the play, Eth . . .

Well—so much for the logical approach.

ELLIOT: This is going to sound totally gross, but you're going to want to kiss girls someday.

ETHAN: Na-ah.

ELLIOT: Ah-ha.

ETHAN *(whines):* Dad . . .

ELLIOT *(whines):* Son . . .

Now, as the triceratops comes from behind:

ELLIOT: Don't tell your mother this, but I used to not know how to kiss girls . . . Yeah! But I found out it's real easy. I used to practice by kissing the back of my hand.

Ethan doesn't seem to hear Elliot's warm, Folksy-Guy wisdom, so Elliot takes another tack.

ELLIOT: Even dinosaurs had to kiss, Eth. Or else there wouldn't have been any new dinosaurs.

ETHAN: There *aren't* any new dinosaurs.

ELLIOT: That's not the point. Ethan, you have a responsibility to do the play, and that means you're going to have to kiss Susie Burrows.

ETHAN: I don't have to.

ELLIOT: You *do.* The prince has to kiss Cinderella, otherwise they can't live happily ever after.

Ethan looks at his father, not buying it.

ELLIOT: And because his father will prevent him from watching music videos for a month if he doesn't.

Ethan pounds all life from Elliot's dinosaur. Elliot gets up to leave.

ELLIOT: Someday you'll thank me . . . *(cringes)* I didn't say that
. . . But someday you will.

Elliot goes. Ethan raises his hand, puts it up to his mouth—and
then goes back to his dinosaur.

INT. MELISSA'S LOFT—DAY

Melissa is about to make coffee. Lee carries a can of paint toward the
bathroom.

MELISSA: You want me to make some coffee?

LEE: You make terrible coffee. You take real nice photos, but
your coffee's bogus . . . *I'll* make it. I brought real coffee
beans.

Lee gets to work, and as he does Melissa watches him.

MELISSA: So . . . do you like photography? Have you seen
anything of Alfred Stieglitz, or Edward Weston—

LEE: No. But I like what *you* do.

He considers her work.

LEE: You get people—even though you seem like you keep to
yourself a lot . . . That's kind of funny, but I like the way
you look at people . . .

He turns to her now, and they both somehow sense he may have
gone one step too far. So he reclaims that step.

LEE: I want to set up in the bathroom. Then I'll make drink-
able coffee.

He heads for the bathroom, then—

LEE: Where do I find the stuff you keep in there that you'd be
embarrassed for me to see?

Melissa smiles, and just as Lee vanishes Gary appears at the door,
holding some proof sheets. They're very polite—in that nails-on-a-
blackboard way that can't quite hide what's beneath the smooth,
agreeable surface.

GARY: Hi.

MELISSA: Oh, hi . . . I guess you guys decided what shots you want.

GARY: I really appreciate your doing this. Maybe it'll help get us the funding we need. Why not? I saw *Mr. Smith Goes to Washington.* I believe in fairy tales.

Now, seeing Gary, Melissa remembers the unclaimed loafer.

MELISSA: This isn't yours, is it?

Gary looks at the shoe and shakes his head. Lee enters from the bathroom.

LEE: Okay, coffee . . . *(seeing Gary)* Hi . . .

MELISSA: Ah, this is Lee Owens, he's painting my place. This is Gary . . . Shepherd.

GARY: Nice color.

LEE: Thanks. I talked her into a pale shade so when she decides she hates it, the next guy won't have trouble painting over it.

Lee, playful and casual, knocks shoulders with Melissa—a move that does not go unnoticed by Gary.

LEE: This one's an easy read. I'm cashing the check the minute I get it.

MELISSA: If the paint job's not shabby, the color will stay.

And now Melissa playfully punches Lee, not aware of her former lover's X-ray emotional eyes.

LEE: You gotta start punching the other arm. *(to Gary)* You want some coffee? It's not hers, so you don't have to worry.

GARY: Thanks. I've got to go.

MELISSA: I'll get the pictures done right away.

GARY: I'd appreciate it. *(to Lee)* Nice meeting you.

LEE: You too.

GARY *(whispers to Melissa):* Righteous.

Melissa gives him a sharp look. Gary leaves. Lee waits for a moment, then:

LEE: How long you been pissed at him?

MELISSA: Pissed at him? I'm not pissed at him.

Lee finishes the coffee, crosses to the bathroom, and looks at Melissa as if to say "I know better."

MELISSA *(irritated):* I'm not.

INT. "THE RIGHT ONE"—RECEPTION DESK—DAY

A nervous Melissa twirls her hair until Ellyn finally stops her. Kelly hands them two long computer readouts.

KELLY: These are the gentlemen who've requested to meet you. And Melissa, you requested to meet William . . . Well, he'd like to meet you, too. So, here's his number and we gave him yours.

Melissa wants to scream like a fifteen-year-old, but she remains composed.

MELISSA: Really? How nice.

INT. DEPARTMENT STORE—THE NEXT DAY

Ellyn, Hope, and Melissa stare at a mannequin wearing a black leather dress.

MELISSA: So what do you think?

ELLYN: You have to get it.

HOPE: He will die when he sees you in that dress.

MELISSA: He *has* to die when he sees me in this dress . . .

ELLYN: He won't be able to get up from the table. Do *not* wear a bra . . .

HOPE: So tell me what else he said on the phone.

MELISSA: Well, it was brief, but he has this really sexy voice. And he was very straightforward; he just said he wanted to meet me and we set a time . . .

ELLYN *(admiring a blouse):* This is pretty.

HOPE: You know the only problem with that dress is it might be too hot for it tomorrow night. They said on the news we can expect a heat wave. I hate when it's humid . . .

MELISSA *(touches her hair):* Great. Frizz City. I'll look like Bob Dylan in a dress. Very pretty.

Ellyn, meanwhile, is off on her own tangent.

ELLYN: You know, I think I'm going to change my video again. The guys who are responding just aren't . . . I'm doing something wrong.

HOPE: What about that one guy? Dave. You said he was cute.

MELISSA: He was. You showed me his video.

HOPE: You have to go out with one of these guys. I'm reliving being single through you.

ELLYN: Fine. I'll call him. Okay? *(to Melissa)* So are you getting the dress?

MELISSA: I'm getting the dress. *(to Hope)* When did you hear there'd be a heat wave?

EXT. GARDEN RESTAURANT—NIGHT

A television, set to the news, is on above the bar.

NEWSCASTER: So, how about that humidity, Sandy . . .

Melissa, her hair frizzed out, waits at the bar in the black leather dress. The hostess leads her to a table.

HOSTESS: Your table is ready.

MELISSA: Excuse me, do you think we could sit inside?

HOSTESS: The reservation requested outside.

WILLIAM'S VOICE: Melissa?

Melissa looks up to see William, who is, of course, dressed appropriately for the weather. A tiny bead of sweat makes its way down Melissa's chin.

MELISSA: Right . . . hi . . . It's nice to meet you.

WILLIAM (*as he sits*): I hope you don't mind sitting outside. I can't stand air-conditioning.

MELISSA: No! I don't mind at all.

The bead of sweat continues down her cleavage; she casually tries to stop it.

WILLIAM: I liked your video.

MELISSA: Thanks. I—ah—I liked your video, too. It sounds like we both have albums out . . .

William gazes at her, all sincerity. Albums? Melissa wishes she were either dead or in another city.

MELISSA: You know. Because we both have videos . . .

WILLIAM: Haven't you found that so many of the people you've gone out with are totally different from their videos?

MELISSA: How many? I mean—not really. I just joined.

WILLIAM: Now you're—right, the photographer. I have a book of Ansel Adams photographs. You look at them and they just take you away . . .

Buzzword. Bingo. Melissa could melt from this.

WILLIAM: Last year I gave a copy to everyone I knew for Christmas. What kind of photographs do you take?

MELISSA: Well, all sorts of stuff. Ad work and album covers and I'm going to—

WILLIAM: Album covers? For who?

MELISSA: Well, last year I did Carly Simon . . .

WILLIAM: I once met Mickey Dolenz when I was covering a rally in D.C. for the homeless. I *think* it was Mickey Dolenz. Maybe it was Peter . . .

MELISSA: I think what you do is so fascinating. I mean you have this opportunity to expose things to so many people. It must be great.

WILLIAM: Yeah, well, I free-lance mostly, human interest stories, battered wives, whatever's the sociological disease of the week. It keeps you in business. Does Carly Simon really look like that in person?

As William blathers on, his Rolex taps the table. The sound is magnified, for we have now entered the heart of Melissa's perception of this date. The only sounds we hear are those that divert Melissa's attention. Ice clinks in a glass. A match is struck. A woman laughs. Melissa struggles to focus on William.

WILLIAM: So what do you think? Can I order for you? I love the food here.

INT. ANOTHER RESTAURANT—NIGHT

Ellyn enters. She approaches the host.

ELLYN: I'm supposed to meet Dave . . . I can't remember his last name. Is there anyone waiting for someone?

HOST: No.

ELLYN: I'll, ah, I'll wait. Thanks.

She stares out at the restaurant, where it seems as if she's the only one not part of a couple. Her mind wanders, and then Geraldo Rivera walks in, holding a microphone. The whole place breaks into applause as his theme music plays.

GERALDO: "Single Women over Thirty" . . . Who are they? Where do they come from? What do their friends and family think? Let's explore how this phenomenon has penetrated our society.

Geraldo walks over to Ellyn, who's now seated in the Geraldo studio stage.

GERALDO: This is Ellyn, a victim of this condition. Ellyn— what can you tell us about it?

ELLYN (*defensive*): Well, I just started video dating.

GERALDO: Ah. So you felt desperate.

ELLYN: No!

GERALDO: How does your family feel about all this?

ELLYN: Well, my parents are divorced and—

GERALDO: Ah! Maybe *that's* why you're still single!

ELLYN: No! I'm single because I haven't met anybody I want to be not-single with. I'm sorry!

Geraldo turns to the audience.

GERALDO: We have a couple who know Ellyn, but prefer to remain anonymous.

We now see, behind a blue screen, the shadowed outlines of Hope and Michael.

GERALDO: Did you ever think this would happen?

HOPE: We love Ellyn. We're proud of her—no matter what.

GERALDO: Then if you're not embarrassed—why won't you expose your identities?

MICHAEL: Well, it's not like we're embarrassed or anything. It's just—you know—we have a kid, I have this job . . . And like other people—I mean, who knows what they might think? I gotta protect my family.

GERALDO: Ellyn—let me ask you something. When you were a little girl, didn't you always believe you'd get married?

ELLYN: Yes. Of course I did—

She'd like to go on, but Geraldo interrupts.

GERALDO: —We're going to break for a commercial . . .

ELLYN: Wait! I want to say something to the other survivors out there. You don't have to give up hope!

Applause—and the fantasy is over. The host approaches Ellyn.

HOST: Dave called and said he'd be five minutes late. His last name, by the way, is—

ELLYN: Could you please tell him I had an emergency? Make up something. Anything. I just have to get out of here . . .

And she's gone.

EXT. PARKING LOT—NIGHT

Melissa sits in her car, the motor running. William stands over her.
They struggle for things to say.

MELISSA: So. Thanks—

WILLIAM: That fish? That fish was great—

MELISSA: *Really* great. Oh, and the sauce—

WILLIAM: Just the right level of spicy—

MELISSA: Not too spicy—

WILLIAM: Just right.

An awkward pause. Then William launches into what he does
best—a moist, halting, protestation of sincerity. Anyone would buy
it.

WILLIAM: Melissa, I'm, ah . . . Look, I'm not one of those guys
    with all the smooth moves and great lines. I just know
    how to be honest. I think it's essential in a relationship.
    And the truth is I'd like to see you again. You're very—
    real. That's hard to find. Can I call you?

MELISSA: Yes.

He leans in to kiss her . . . What's missing? Her eyes open. A car
drives by. A dog barks . . .

ACT FOUR

EXT. MALL—DAY

Ellyn and Hope come out of an ice cream store, eating giant cones complete with jimmies and colored sprinkles.

HOPE: How'd you get me to do this? You're bad . . . You know, you've got to call this guy to apologize.

ELLYN: I know, I will, I will . . .

HOPE: You think maybe you'll go out with him?

ELLYN: Why is it so important to everybody that I'm seeing someone?

HOPE: I think it's because people care and want you to be happy.

ELLYN: Oh, and I can't be happy if I'm not with someone?

HOPE: Ellyn, what is it?

ELLYN: I don't want you to feel sorry for me, Hope. I'm alone, but it's okay. That's really okay right now.

HOPE: Ellyn, nobody's judging you.

ELLYN: Right. You don't know what it's like—you bump into people, the first thing they say is, "Are you seeing anyone?" "Are you in love?" No one asks me about my job, or my cat.

HOPE: So, how's your cat?

ELLYN: She hates me. Another failed relationship. But it's not my fault.

HOPE: No one said it was.

ELLYN: Oh, come on, Hope. I know you and Michael must think I'm not seeing anyone because of something I'm *doing*.

HOPE: That's not true—

ELLYN: Right. Like you never thought I brought it on myself—

HOPE: I hate when you assume what I think. I have an idea of how hard it is out there. If I hadn't met Michael I doubt I'd be seeing anyone right now—

ELLYN: It's like no one gets it. God forbid I should be alone. I lie sometimes when people ask if I have plans for the night. Because if you say you just want to hang out by yourself, there's always this silence, and then—"Well, why don't you join *us?*" *(pissed)* I want to be alone. Okay?

HOPE *(supportive):* Bitch 'em out, girl!

They look at each other and laugh, each pleased and surprised by the other's reaction. Ellyn sees something and drags Hope toward it.

HOPE: No way!

ELLYN: Come on! Let's just be thirteen again . . . You'll have no boobs, and I'll buy Kotex, pretending I'm not the last one to get my period . . .

So they pile into a Fast Foto booth—

HOPE: I'm not making funny faces . . .

—and pull the curtain shut. Flash . . . Flash . . . Flash . . . And the sound of their laughter . . . And four double portraits appear, Hope and Ellyn crazier in each one.

INT. MELISSA'S LOFT—DAY

Lee stands on the ladder, touching up spots in the living room. Melissa enters from an interview, carrying a portfolio.

MELISSA: Honey? I'm home!

LEE: What a day—but don't ask.

MELISSA: I won't ask.

LEE: That's the thanks I get . . . Did you get the job?

MELISSA: I got the job.

LEE: You should celebrate. *I* should celebrate, I'll take any excuse to have a good time . . . So—I have these tickets to Lyle Lovett tonight—

MELISSA *(a little too quick):* You like Lyle Lovett?

LEE: Yes. And so do you. I saw your CDs . . . Are you surprised I actually appreciate music that doesn't have a name like "Scream Blast" or "Drug Sluts"? Or are you surprised I asked you out? Whatever you say, I'm still going to overcharge you for my work.

MELISSA: I'm very flattered . . .

LEE: Oh, God, you're going to patronize me. Is it the age thing? Because we can just tell people you're my mommy.

MELISSA: Lee, look . . .

Lee turns back to his painting.

LEE: It's okay, I can take a no . . . *(shrugs)* But there goes your discount—

MELISSA: It's just there's this guy.

LEE: William Aaron?

Melissa looks at him, shocked.

LEE: He left three messages on your machine. *(stiff, uptight voice)* "This is William Aaron, I must be honest, I had a good time . . ." *(deadpan)* Party guy.

MELISSA *(irked):* You know, I really don't appreciate that. He happens to be—important. To me—

LEE: Right—

MELISSA: Where do you get off? You don't know anything about him . . . Or me!

LEE: I know he isn't "important"—

MELISSA: You're wrong!

LEE: I don't think so . . .

MELISSA: How could you possibly know what I would like?

LEE: You're not that complicated. And that's not an insult.

MELISSA: I don't believe you! This is none of your business . . .

LEE: Oh, come on, Melissa! If you were hot for this guy, the minute you walked in the door you'd have run to the phone machine. You still haven't checked the message.

MELISSA *(flustered):* I was going to check them—

LEE: Forgive me—but I can't believe you'd like a guy who leaves his last name on your machine. Three times.

MELISSA: Three times?

LEE: Check!

MELISSA: I will!

Melissa grabs her phone machine and takes it to the bathroom for privacy—only the cord won't reach. She turns haughtily to Lee.

MELISSA: When will you be done? Completely?

LEE: Tomorrow.

She puts the phone machine down and makes an impressive show of checking her watch.

MELISSA: I have someplace I have to be.

And she goes.

INT. "THE RIGHT ONE"—VIEWING BOOTH—DAY

Melissa watches William's video.

WILLIAM: . . . There are a lot of men who always think the grass is greener . . . I'm, ah, not that way. I think loyalty and commitment are essential to a good working relationship . . .

MELISSA *(quietly):* Me too.

WILLIAM: I guess I'm really looking for a best friend.

The screen goes blank, now reflecting Melissa's face.

INT. ELLYN'S APARTMENT—DAY

Ellyn—two little bandages on her fingers—slides cat food under the couch. Melissa is with her.

ELLYN: Sophie's really starting to interact with people . . . So? Come on! What was he like?

MELISSA: He's very smart. He's read all seven volumes of Proust. His pants crease correctly. Oh—and he's into honesty.

ELLYN: Great! Now what's *really* important—how does he kiss?

MELISSA: Well-rehearsed.

ELLYN: Well, don't overreact . . .

MELISSA: Did I forget to mention that *he* didn't forget to mention how he wants kids and is looking to make a commitment?

ELLYN: *Never* see him again. Melissa—what's the problem?

MELISSA: I don't know. I mean—I really want all the nauseating stuff I wrote in my profile. I want a guy I can have a life with. And I'm sorry if that includes a home and kids. I want to take family vacations and fight in the car the whole time . . .

She has just sketched a picture of Paradise; she and Ellyn regard it together. Then:

ELLYN: I don't know . . .

Melissa looks at her; what's not to know?

ELLYN: I just don't think you can go through life with a checklist. You try to make everything fit into the plan, and you know what you get?

MELISSA: William?

ELLYN: Maybe . . . But if you force things to work the way you think they should, you never know what else there is . . .

Both women think about this. Then, almost sadly—

MELISSA: Is that true?

ELLYN (*gently*): I don't know. Is it?

MELISSA: Look—I gotta go. I'll see ya . . .

She's on her way to the door when she turns to face Ellyn.

MELISSA: You got plans Saturday night?

ELLYN: No . . .

MELISSA: Want to see what's on cable?

ELLYN: I'll make pasta.

Melissa goes. Ellyn puts on some music and stretches out on the couch. She starts to read; as the book interests her, she doesn't see the cat come out from under the couch and walk quietly into the kitchen.

INT. ETHAN'S SCHOOL—AUDITORIUM

Onstage—the dreaded *Cinderella*. The Wicked Stepmother pushes her daughters up to the Prince (Ethan), who holds out the shoe.

ETHAN: Well, I did say every maiden in the land.

The audience laughs. On stage, hiding behind a bush, is Cinderella—Susie Burrows, the picture of innocence with her soft blond hair and big eyes. Nancy, Elliot, and Melissa are in the audience; Melissa is particularly intent on what's going on.

ETHAN (*to Cinderella*): Come, young maiden. Do *you* want to try on the slipper?

WICKED STEPMOTHER: Don't bother with her!

Ethan pushes the Wicked Stepmother aside and holds out the slipper for Susie. She slips it on. Nancy and Elliot watch, anxious to see what Ethan will do. And so, as the Prince looks down on Cinderella's perfect face—

ETHAN: Will you marry me?

SUSIE: Yes.

As Susie looks hopefully up at Ethan, he looks out to his father in the audience. Elliot nods his encouragement. Ethan looks back at Susie. And suddenly

IN THE AUDIENCE

everyone is gone but Melissa, for this moment is entirely for her. She watches as Ethan summons his nerve and kisses Susie sweetly on the cheek. He looks at her; something he'll never forget has just happened. Bells chime, and he kisses her again, and as the Prince's Assistant sounds a triangle we go
BACK TO REALITY
The audience applauds. Ethan takes Susie's hand, Nancy and Elliot beam with pride, and Melissa, as much as anyone here today, knows it's the beginning of something wonderful . . .

INT. MELISSA'S LOFT—DAY

Lee, his job done, is packing up his things as Melissa enters.

MELISSA: Hi.

LEE: I'm done. I was just going to pack up.

MELISSA: I'll write you a check. (*remembering*) Oh, yeah, wait a minute . . .

Melissa goes to the closet and takes out the loafer.

MELISSA: Is this yours? You're the only one who could have left it.

Lee slips it on. It fits perfectly.

LEE: No. I hate loafers, they're like old-man shoes. But if you find the other one I'll take 'em. They'd be good to work in. I won't have to ruin my tennis shoes.

Their eyes meet. Then, hesitant, Melissa turns away and looks around her place.

MELISSA: It really looks great . . . So how was Lyle Lovett?

LEE: You missed a great concert.

MELISSA: Yeah . . . I'm sorry I did.

LEE: So, what happened to William Aaron? What, is he a lawyer?

MELISSA: Journalist.

LEE: Impressive.

He moves closer.

MELISSA: Not really.

LEE: Oh? No kidding . . .

MELISSA *(re the wall):* You missed a spot . . . No. I guess you didn't—

LEE: I'm driving to the Cape next weekend. I could use some company.

Melissa turns toward him.

MELISSA: Look—I'm not looking to be just—"company" . . .

LEE: It wasn't a casual invitation.

He touches her face.

MELISSA: This would be a big mistake.

LEE: Then it should be great . . . Sometimes things just happen . . .

She walks away. He follows.

LEE: You want me to say I'm not seeing anyone else?

MELISSA: No . . .

LEE: I'm not seeing anyone.

MELISSA: That's none of my business—

LEE: It could be . . . Are you scared?

MELISSA: Yeah.

Lee comes up from behind and brings her into him.

LEE: I am too . . . *(practically whispers)* So don't worry.

He kisses her neck. She turns to face him. As, up on the shelf, the clock chimes twelve . . .

LOVE AND SEX

BY

LIBERTY GODSHALL

"But that's too embarrassing to write about," I wail to Marshall and Edward when they ask me to write about Hope and Michael's sex life. Not just their sex life, but something going wrong with their sex life and possibly something wrong with their marriage. "This is a show about embarrassment," they chorus from their respective telephones.

It's 1989. I am in Savannah, Georgia. Edward is on location here directing the film *Glory*, and I'm holed up in a hotel room with our three-year-old son, several weeks' worth of moldy room-service trays, and a serious case of writer's block. And now Marshall and Ed want me to write this. I can't write this. I am happy *not* writing this because in order to write it, I have to examine my own marriage. I have always clung to the theory that the unexamined marriage is the only kind worth having.

Okay, marriage. Ellyn said to Hope in a script I wrote last year—"So Nancy's mad at him for marrying her. First, they get us to fall in love with them, then they systematically destroy us with dry cleaning and dinner and returning rented videotapes." I could have added: then there is the moment of truth when your husband stands in the kitchen sweetly blinking at you and asking, "Where does this bowl go?" Luckily for him, all the knives are in drawers with kid—safety latches. If you throw in a child who is the center of the universe, and half a dozen frantic midnight calls to 911, of course it throws your timing off for about twelve years. This is all normal stuff, I thought; the domestication of passion.

"No," says Marshall, long distance, "it's not normal. It's something worse. There's something really wrong in their marriage." But what could it be? Hope and Michael are television's dream of a couple, they discuss everything. Endlessly. She laughs at his anxieties and sighs "Oh, Michael," with that lovingly reproachful grin. They talk before bed. (I love them in bed. Often when Ken and Mel are doing a scene in bed I want to crawl in with them, to take refuge in their safe, cozy cave.) They're like baseball. The *Times* on Sunday. They endure—and reassure me, somehow, that life will go on; that there is, if you will, hope.

And now Marshall and Ed want to blow all that to shit? I can't do it.

"But something has happened to their marriage when none of us was looking," Ed says. He's lying facedown on the hotel bed, caked in Georgia clay, having just reenacted the battle of Antietam. "What?" I bark. "They have a great sex life." Ed, meanwhile, has fallen asleep with his clothes on. "Okay, maybe their sex life isn't so great. Maybe trying to time sex to have a baby sets it off. I would buy that." All this time I'm praying— please God, don't let that happen to us.

"But it's more than that," says Marshall at the end of the longest long-distance phone call in Bedford Falls history. "Women change after they become mothers—" "No, no, no!" I cry. "Don't start with that women/men stuff." Marshall knows I still believe the sexes are fundamentally alike—a sixties notion he treats as seriously as the belief that smoking banana peels will get you high. He, meanwhile, maintains that men and women are fundamentally unsuited to each other, and that the longer they stay together, the more this becomes apparent.

Okay. Fine. We agree to disagree. I'll just start to write, see what comes out, because how do I know what I'm thinking until I see it on the page? And so it comes out badly. I hate it. I tell Ed I'm going to quit. He ignores me. I call Marshall in California to quit. He won't take my call.

For a while I consider titling the episode "Love Stinks," after the song on the tape Lauren returns when she meets Bernard. But the more I write, the more I come to realize it's not love that stinks, it's how marriage gets in the way of love.

I write all night long. My son sleeps beside me, each tiny breath puncturing me, the polluted Savannah River sighing outside my hotel window. Edward is off somewhere blowing something up. Marriage . . . What I do love about marriage is its deep thicket of intimacy. Later, peeing alone in the igloo cool of the bathroom, I stumble upon Edward's silent shadow weaving by the door, still asleep but standing sentinel, waiting for me to emerge so he can pee because I woke him up by peeing. There are no words. Our rhythms are like sea creatures that scientists trap in boxes, still waking and sleeping to the pull of dawn and stars they can no longer see. I love listening to my husband swear as he tries to fix something, locking up the house at night, fighting, making up, changing our son's puke-filled sheets as our eyes crash in concern. I still love *us*. We are different now, yes, but what more could I possibly want?

By the time I finished writing "Love and Sex," I felt older. Like I had washed up on a distant shore where natives stared at me with knowing eyes. Suppose Hope finds someone else she can feel "like a pressure and a sound inside of me, in a place so deep I didn't think anyone could ever reach"? Or, as Susan wrote so wonderfully in her script "Courting Nancy": "It just hasn't happened to you yet," meaning when some nameless dreadful thing enters a marriage. And indeed, in the scripts to come, we all eventually decide there are more places in Hope's heart that she will dare to explore.

So I turn in the script. And Susan polishes it. And Marshall and I fight some more. Marshall directs it and gets nominated for the Directors' Guild Award. I even kind of like the show when it's done, although I have no idea who wrote it. In retrospect, I guess Marshall and I were actually a good marriage for this story. (Sorry, Ed.) I tend to think that people having problems should jump around and throw things and scream at one another. Marshall knows the drama inherent in a look, a pause, a question that goes unanswered.

In rereading it now, I ask myself, what was I trying to say? Perhaps only that love is that point of catching up to yourself. Of most profoundly embracing a single moment. That there is no imitating this. This is what Hope realizes when she sees Lauren race out the door in the fading light to meet her destiny on a motorcycle. Michael realizes it when he sees two kids locked in a shameless embrace in the street in front of his home. We can all point to moments like this in our lives—"Oh, those people must be in love," we realize with a stab—then tally up the check and leave the restaurant.

But when Hope stumbles upon Lauren and Bernard locked together making love in her living room, it is akin to fate. Indeed, had she not seen it, I think she would have dreamed of their lovemaking. For what roused her from slumber if not her deepest sense that something was calling to her, a feeling she would miss if it never happened to her again? That sensation of love and urgency that is almost like death but is, in truth, the postponement of death.

But this is Hope and Michael we're talking about. Or is it . . .

I suppose there is a way that we who write this show often find ourselves playing a kind of "Whisper Down the Lane"; sometimes the ideas are transformed from their original states to what we hoped they would be. Sometimes we discover that life has a funny way of slopping over the edges of fiction. I know that Marshall and Susan and Edward and I have used these stories to talk about our marriages, what we fight about, and what we secretly cry over. Sometimes I even suspect we've found ways to articulate in public things that we have never quite been able to put so well when looking into each other's eyes. Often we reveal ourselves in the guises of others, and sometimes we sketch others disguised as ourselves. We caucus and lobby and rewrite and reinvent. And so it goes, the whispering back and forth, until we end up not with a portrait of one marriage, not even of two, but finally, an occasionally amusing, occasionally truthful version of a thing that ultimately defies description.

LIBERTY GODSHALL

ACT ONE

INT. STEADMAN HOUSE—LIVING ROOM—LATE DAY

CLOSE on two funny handmade sock-puppets talking.

PUPPET #1: So, the prince and princess live together in this magical land. And you can fly there on your moon tiger whenever you want.

PUPPET #2: Remember, you can never tell anyone, or you will never find this place again.

MICHAEL: But if Mommy and Daddy eat all their lima beans, you'll take them with you, okay?

PULL BACK

to reveal Janey, delighted (maybe), and a very embarrassed Lauren, the fifteen-year-old baby-sitter, coming up from under the coffee table with the puppets on her hands. Lauren is trembling on the brink of hormones, a colt about to run, her face not yet touched by Clearasil.

LAUREN: Hi.

Michael, just home from work, drops his briefcase and scoops Janey up in his arms.

MICHAEL: Hi, Thumper . . . Hi, Lauren . . . You guys having fun?

LAUREN: Well, *I* am.

Hope is in the sunroom, on the phone interviewing someone. She hangs up and comes into the living room.

HOPE: Hi.

MICHAEL: Hi.

This is weird but we don't know why.

LAUREN: You're home early.

Ah, that's it. Lauren picks up Janey, who plays with Lauren's necklace. It is clear how fond they are of each other.

MICHAEL: Yeah, well. Hope and I sort of—

HOPE: We have to—we have some things that we have to discuss—

MICHAEL: It's not serious—

HOPE *(trace of a smile):* But it is kind of pressing, I think.

MICHAEL: Shall we—

He makes a gesture with his thumb—"upstairs?"—out of Lauren's sight. They go up separately.

HOPE *(turns to Lauren):* We'll be right back.

LAUREN: Take your time.

INT. STEADMAN HOUSE—BEDROOM

Hope and Michael burst through the door like thieves.

MICHAEL: She knows—she *must* know—

HOPE: I'm sure this happens a lot in her line of work.

He pulls her toward him.

MICHAEL: Loved your message—

HOPE: It was cute—

MICHAEL: "Urgently needed at home to deal with addition to house."

HOPE: Right, I should have said, "The mucus is kind of stretchy and will soon be sticky and by then it'll be too late."

MICHAEL: Drew would have thought we were wallpapering the bathroom together—

Hope laughs as she undresses.

HOPE: Lauren's got to leave in fifteen minutes.

MICHAEL: Fifteen minutes? I'm not sixteen anymore—

HOPE (over him): Thank God.

MICHAEL: —lucky for you.

Hope, finished with undressing, unceremoniously hops in bed.

MICHAEL: As I'm leaving, Drentell stops a meeting with a client so he can yell at the guy who details his car . . .

HOPE: He's such a prince—

Now Michael gets into bed.

MICHAEL: Mmmmm.

HOPE: See? We should do this more often.

MICHAEL: It's four o'clock in the afternoon. I can actually see you . . . Who *are* you?

HOPE: I'm your wife. Kiss me.

Michael kisses her, pulls back, looks at her.

HOPE: What?

MICHAEL: Nothing. I'm not allowed to look at you?

She can tell from the look on his face that this isn't working terribly well . . .

HOPE: The earth doesn't have to move *every* time, does it?

MICHAEL: Sure it does.

HOPE: Michael . . .

She kisses him. They do some experimental rolling around. There is an arid quality to the proceedings. We hear strains of Lauren and Janey laughing. They stop and listen for a moment.

HOPE: Listen, it's our house. We're allowed to do this.

MICHAEL: I know that . . . This is weird.

HOPE: We can't waste another whole month.

She pulls Michael on top of her. They do some nestling in. Michael is smiling; this is *really* not working now . . . And Hope gets the giggles.

MICHAEL *(not mad):* Oh, shut up. Women are lucky, they have no moving parts to wear out.

HOPE: We'll just lie here and not think about it—

They grin. They fondle one another, but there is desperation in the air. Finally, Michael rolls on top of her and they begin to make love. Michael moves a pillow away from them on the bed.

Later, the same pillow is being put under Hope's bottom. They pull apart, collapsing in what looks mainly like relief.

HOPE: I have to stay like this for half an hour?

LAUREN *(V.O.):* Hope? I have to go—

We hear her climbing the stairs.

MICHAEL *(rising panic):* Just a minute—*(to Hope)* Have fun.

INT. DAA—DAY

Michael and Elliot, unusually tense, fiddle at their respective desks.

ELLIOT: Why do I feel like I'd rather be having a root canal done right now?

MICHAEL: Because if Drentell hates this idea he'll hate it forever and a root canal only lasts an hour *and* you get drugs.

ELLIOT: I gotta get out of here. I'm gonna make a Milk Duds run—

At the door, Elliot comes face to face with Drentell.

DRENTELL: Elliot.

ELLIOT: Miles. Can I get you some Milk Duds?

Drentell stares at him.

DRENTELL: No, thank you, I'm not a Milk Duds kind of guy
. . . So, gentlemen. Kenwa phones. Tomorrow at ten?

MICHAEL: Couldn't you just tell us now?

DRENTELL: That would be presuming I had a chance to look at
your proposal . . .

Which of course he did, and he didn't like it. Michael ponders how
to get him to admit it when Gary, dressed to play squash, opens the
door of the office. Drentell eyes Gary with curiosity.

MICHAEL: Hey.

GARY: Hey.

MICHAEL: Miles, this is Gary Shepherd. Gary, this is Miles
Drentell.

DRENTELL *(shakes Gary's hand)*: Hey . . .

GARY *(so this is Drentell . . .)*: Nice to meet you.

DRENTELL: Good to meet *you*. *(to Michael and Elliot)* Ten o'clock.

He leaves.

ELLIOT: 'Bye, Miles—

GARY: What charm.

MICHAEL: Isn't it time you started wearing long pants?

GARY: What a tragically hip tie, Michael.

ELLIOT: So what do you think?

GARY *(looking around)*: This is quite a place . . . You didn't tell
me about the incredibly beautiful android receptionists
out front.

MICHAEL: Only the best for Miles.

ELLIOT: He's a guy's guy.

They all look at each other.

MICHAEL: So—Dad. Any day now.

GARY: Hah.

ELLIOT: You nervous?

MICHAEL: Just remember your Lamaze. It'll give you something to do while she's having the baby.

Michael pulls out his squash racket and hands it to Gary.

ELLIOT: Meanwhile, you gonna quit outraging the public morals by then or what?

GARY: Not if I can help it.

Michael and Elliot look at each other.

ELLIOT: Really.

GARY: Why ruin what we have with marriage?

MICHAEL: That's a good one . . .

GARY *(to Elliot):* Why is he such a big fan of the conventional nuclear family?

ELLIOT: Beats me. I believe in stretching the envelope myself.

GARY: In stable societies—

MICHAEL: Oh no—

GARY: Oh yes . . . In stable societies, marriage is an economic agreement. It has nothing to do with love, or sex. In fact, it's a tool for the suppression of dangerous sexual impulses, so that lust and passion don't threaten the rate of production.

ELLIOT: Amen.

GARY: If you want to stay alive, you don't get married.

MICHAEL: Oh come on, you don't believe that—

Gary smiles at him.

GARY: I don't?

INT. STEADMAN HOUSE—KITCHEN

Hope struggles in the door, lugging groceries and research material.

LAUREN *(reading to Janey):* "So the queen said, mirror, mirror on the wall, who's the smartest of them all . . ." Hi, Hope. Need help?

HOPE: No, it's okay—

Hope almost collapses with the weight of the groceries. Lauren helps her get the bags on the counter.

HOPE: Look, Janey. Mommy didn't forget—pretzel sticks.

Hope gives Janey a pretzel as she and Lauren put groceries away. Lauren points to the bottle of spaghetti sauce that Hope is holding.

LAUREN: There's pesticides in that.

HOPE: When you get your license, *you* can go to three different stores before you find organic spaghetti sauce.

LAUREN: It's too late for me. I grew up on pesticides and radiation. I practically glow in the dark.

HOPE: Very funny.

LAUREN: I read your article on ozone. I liked it.

Hope looks at her, surprised and interested.

HOPE: Thanks.

LAUREN: It's scary, you know? It seems like we're running out of everything good.

She turns away from Hope to tend to Janey. Hope watches her, briefly troubled.

LAUREN: Do you need me to stay longer?

HOPE: Well, actually, I was going to ask if you could baby-sit tonight . . . *(on Lauren's look)* What?

LAUREN: I can't tonight.

HOPE: Oh . . .

Hope knows Lauren is dying to tell her something.

LAUREN: It's Bernard . . . we're going out tonight . . .

HOPE: Oh, *Bernard.* This is serious. Three weeks now?

LAUREN: Almost four. He's picking me up here. I'm sorry about tonight—

HOPE: Don't be silly. You have a date with destiny. I was just talking about dinner.

Lauren stares dreamily at her reflection in the toaster oven.

LAUREN: He's so intense and we're totally completely telepathic. And he has these beautiful shadows on his face. And his eyes kind of . . . pierce through you . . . Do you think maybe you could French-braid my hair like you had yours when you went to that party?

HOPE (*a little touched and a little bored*): Sure.

They move to a mirror. Hope starts to brush Lauren's hair as Janey watches, interested.

HOPE: So it's going good, huh?

LAUREN: He gave me a book with this story in it—Tristan and Isolde—it was the most beautiful thing I've ever read . . . Maybe I should wear it down, I'm getting a zit.

Hope holds out the half-finished braid. Lauren examines her flawless face with the ruthlessness of a scientist. Hope steps back, watching her.

HOPE: How did you meet him, at school?

LAUREN: I saw him in a music store when he was returning this defective CD. *Love Stinks.*

HOPE: Excuse me?

LAUREN: J. Geils. It was an anthology album and so anyway I told him that I liked oldies too, and we just got talking about stuff. He's *so* sensitive.

The roar of the largest motorcycle ever built—a Harley chopper—screams up the driveway.

LAUREN: That's him!

She undoes the braid, shakes out her hair, and turns to Hope, who is picking up Janey. Lauren gives Janey a kiss.

LAUREN: 'Bye, bunny. (*to Hope*) How do I look?

Like she has been lit from within, yet completely unaware of the effect.

HOPE *(heartfelt):* You look beautiful.

Hope follows Lauren to the door, to watch her race into the fading light.

INT. STEADMAN HOUSE—JANEY'S ROOM—NIGHT

Hope and Janey are giggling and jumping up and down on her bed. Hope is sticking glow-in-the-dark stars to the ceiling.

HOPE: There . . . Where do you want the moon, Janey? Here? See, these are the Pleiades . . . I think that's such a pretty word, don't you?

Michael is watching Mom and daughter from the doorway.

MICHAEL: Hi.

HOPE: Hi. I kept her up to see you . . . All right, Janey, one more.

MICHAEL: Sorry. Drentell came gunning for us. We had to plan a new line of attack.

HOPE: There's some dinner, sort of.

MICHAEL: Hey, Janey, remember me?

He tries to cuddle with Janey, who doesn't seem to want too much to do with him.

HOPE: She's tired . . .

This is about Janey but it's not about Janey.

MICHAEL *(looks at the stars):* Great, Janey, you can wake up and think you've been kidnapped by a band of gypsies—

Hope picks her up, giving Michael a look—"Thanks a lot."

HOPE: Let's get some pj's, Janey . . .

INT. STEADMAN HOUSE—KITCHEN—NIGHT

The kitchen is a mess. Hope is trying to clean up the dinner dishes when Michael comes in.

HOPE: She asleep?

MICHAEL: Finally. Maybe she'd go to sleep better if she stopped taking her nap.

Michael is foraging for food in pots on the stove.

HOPE: In the oven.

MICHAEL: Was I supposed to take the car in today?

He finds a foil-covered plate containing his now rather unappetiz-ing-looking dinner. Still standing, he digs into it.

HOPE: Yes.

MICHAEL: I'm sorry. You should have reminded me. I'll do it next week, I promise.

HOPE: Hand me the pan—

He hands her a dirty pan.

MICHAEL: I'll do that—

HOPE: No, it's okay.

MICHAEL: What do you think? About her nap?

HOPE: I think we should all get a blanky and a Fig Newton every day at two o'clock. She still needs her nap.

She leaves the pan soaking, opens the cabinet above the sink, and roots around for the steel wool. As she leans up on tiptoe, her cropped T-shirt pulls away from her waist, revealing the smooth skin of her back. Michael sees her suddenly, how pretty and lithe she is. He steps up and retrieves the steel wool, puts it on the counter, and puts his arms around her.

MICHAEL: Want a back rub?

HOPE *(teasing):* A back rub? A *real* back rub? Or a Michael version of a—

MICHAEL: Well . . .

She lets him kiss her, but shrugs off his arms.

MICHAEL: You look so smooth . . .

They stand for a moment, not moving. He reads from her body language that it's not going to happen, and lets go of her.

HOPE: I can't just switch gears like this . . . There are some things—I have to finish . . .

Suddenly they are looking at one another as if they haven't met yet.
And would just as soon skip the introduction.

MICHAEL: Okay.

Michael stands very still for a moment. Hope walks past him out of
the kitchen.

INT. STEADMAN HOUSE—LIVING ROOM—NIGHT

Michael is working with a can of beer beside him. Hope walks past,
collecting books and papers.

MICHAEL: I'm dead.

HOPE: Come up.

MICHAEL: I will.

She looks at him.

HOPE: Come up soon.

MICHAEL: I'll be there.

But he won't.

MICHAEL: Good night.

HOPE: Good night.

She goes up the stairs.

ACT TWO

EXT. STEADMAN HOUSE—DAY

Bernard has Lauren practically bent over backward on top of his Harley, in one long endless kiss . . . As we
PULL BACK to reveal Michael looking intently at them from behind a shade at the living room window. Hope is at the front window, not bothering to hide. Janey is between them, playing one monotonous note after another on her flute.

HOPE: That girl's never comin' up for air.

Michael drops the curtain, trying to act like he wasn't really looking.

MICHAEL: Hope—they'll see you.

HOPE: Are you kidding?

MICHAEL: I wanted to run before I met Elliot.

HOPE: Just wait a minute—

MICHAEL: This is ridiculous. I'm trapped in my own house because I'm afraid to disturb some prepubescent baby-sitter who's having sex with a Hell's Angel in front of the whole neighborhood, including Miss D'Ascenzio who's probably having a coronary about now—

HOPE: They're not having sex, they're kissing. Do you know how lucky we are to have a baby-sitter who'll come on Saturdays?

MICHAEL: That motorcycle's bigger than my car—

HOPE *(delighted)*: You're jealous!

MICHAEL: I remember guys like that. I got to be vice president of the junior class and they got to have sex.

HOPE: Lauren says he's very sensitive. Go.

EXT. STEADMAN HOUSE—DAY

Michael walks out, trying to look cocky in his sweats and wrist-bands. He throws his gym bag and briefcase into the car.

LAUREN: Mr. Steadman?

Michael, wincing slightly at the "mister," feigns seeing them for the first time.

MICHAEL: Oh, hi, Lauren.

Bernard gets on his bike, looking like he's off to drink someone's blood.

LAUREN: This is Bernard. Bernard, this is Mr. Steadman.

BERNARD *(cool)*: Hi.

Bernard grabs Lauren for one more down-the-throat kiss.

MICHAEL *(while he watches this)*: Nice meeting you.

Michael gets in the car and backs out of the driveway. As he changes gears, attempting to peel out—he stalls the car.

INT. DAA

Michael and Elliot are at Drew's empty desk, looking through the drawers as they eat a late breakfast of donuts and juice.

ELLIOT: **Can Drew really be *this* boring? There aren't even any dirty magazines.**

Michael looks around the office; it's almost half full.

MICHAEL: **People are supposed to play ball on Saturday—not work.**

ELLIOT: **So we'll come up with three more exploitatively sexual uses for a cordless phone and then we'll go play ball.**

Drentell emerges from his aerie.

DRENTELL: **Gentlemen—I trust you're not missing your favorite cartoons this morning?**

ELLIOT: **Our wives are taping them for us.**

DRENTELL: **Isn't it more relaxed here on the weekends? I find I get a lot more work done.**

He's carrying a shotgun. Michael and Elliot stare as he polishes the barrel with a chamois.

DRENTELL: **Heading up to Bucks County later. Ever hunt?**

ELLIOT: **Several times a week.**

DRENTELL: **Should try it sometime.** (*sits down with them*) **So, how's the new, new Kenwa approach coming?**

ELLIOT: **Swimmingly.**

Drentell picks through some papers Elliot has brought.

DRENTELL: **Too bad about your *New Yorker* idea, it's really very droll.**

He holds up Elliot's mock-up, an ad in the form of a Steinbergesque cartoon. A man stands with a cordless phone on the Palisades cliffs of New Jersey, talking to a tiny dot of a man on the other side of the Hudson. A balloon from the man's mouth holds the words: "It's for you." Drentell laughs, then:

DRENTELL: **But we're not targeting *The New Yorker,* are we?**

ELLIOT (*looking at Michael*): **We're giving you lots of skin, don't worry.**

MICHAEL: **You don't think people are smarter than that, you** don't think people are beyond that, and they'd rather laugh at themselves?

DRENTELL: Nobody laughs at himself, Michael. First rule of advertising. *(gets up)* Have a good day, gentlemen. I must shoot some quail.

He leaves. They stare after him, and then stare at each other.

MICHAEL: Guy on a huge Harley, ripping the clothes off a teenage baby-sitter.

ELLIOT *(not again):* You've got motorcycle on the brain—

MICHAEL: She's sixteen years old, for God's sake! And the worst thing is, seeing them together, I realized that no one's ever going to look at *me* that way again.

ELLIOT: Man, I walked through Penn the other day, I discovered a new affliction of old age, worse than balding: Invisible to Teenage Girls.

Michael shudders.

ELLIOT: It's better this way. Now we're not susceptible to their plan.

MICHAEL: What plan?

ELLIOT: Bait and switch.

Michael shakes his head, but Elliot's off and running.

ELLIOT: Oh, yeah, Mike, they start out these unbelievably luscious and sexy creatures, like your Lauren—

MICHAEL: She's not *my* Lauren—

ELLIOT: Their bodies like these *offerings,* and the clothes, and all they want to do is entice you and drive you crazy so you'll do anything just to have them, just to touch them . . . *(sits back)* Then you get them and it's "Let's get married, let's have a baby, let's have a house, let's not, the kids'll hear us, I'm too tired, really, you want me to wear *that?!*"

MICHAEL: You're sick—

ELLIOT: It was all just advertising, Mike. Time-honored principles: the right package and the public'll buy.

MICHAEL: And that's why you want Nancy back, because she's
a frigid shrew.

ELLIOT (*stopped dead*): Okay, it's a little more complicated . . .

Michael picks up his trash and heads into the office. Elliot follows.

ELLIOT: So, what's it like, driving her home at night, after she
baby-sits for you?

INT. LINGERIE STORE—DAY

Hope, Ellyn, and Melissa are pulling things off a table filled with an
array of underwear, crotchless panties, G-strings, and bras with
holes cut out of them.

MELISSA: I should get something for my grandmother—

ELLYN: Here?

HOPE: White cotton bikini underpants. That's all I was looking
for, you know. White cotton.

Ellyn holds up something tasteless.

ELLYN: I have these—

HOPE: I remember when the raciest thing you ever wore was
panties with the days of the week on them.

ELLYN: *You* were the first girl in our class to have a black bra—

Melissa holds up a simple satin teddy.

MELISSA: This would look good with black stretch pants—

ELLYN: I want something sort of see-through lace, but discreet, for under my white suit.

Melissa pulls something off a rack.

MELISSA: Here—

HOPE: Guys, I don't want to be hopelessly out of it, but you
wear this stuff on the street?

MELISSA: Well, I don't parade down Broad Street in garter belt
and stockings . . . Do you, Ellyn?

ELLYN: Rarely—

MELISSA: But yes, I wear it out. Don't you?

HOPE: I'd feel so—on display.

MELISSA: Hope, you didn't wear *any* underwear freshmen year at college—

HOPE: I was twenty for God's sake—

ELLYN: Look, dating isn't what it used to be.

MELISSA: Yeah, you spend a whole evening trying to be witty and sexy and fascinating and then you whip out an ammo pack of condoms at the last minute.

ELLYN: And there aren't any single men left anyway—

MELISSA: But you can't just give up. You have to keep the possibility alive, the fantasy. Of something great happening—

ELLYN: So at least you try to feel privately sexy, even if the real world's gone sort of—gray . . . I'm going to try this on.

HOPE: Am I hopelessly out of real life now?

MELISSA: Yes. But we like you anyway.

Hope picks up a garter belt.

HOPE: In nineteen sixty-four we thought these were ugly things that only old ladies wore. What a difference twenty-five years makes . . .

Melissa takes it from Hope and throws it over the curtain into Ellyn's dressing room.

MELISSA: Try this on.

ELLYN: Ooohh.

EXT. STEADMAN HOUSE—STREET—DAY

Ellyn and Melissa are driving Hope home.

ELLYN: Who's that on your lawn?

HOPE: What?

MELISSA: Looks like she's got her hands full.

Lauren and Bernard are having a rather intense discussion on the front lawn. A large ghetto blaster is blaring.

HOPE: Let me out. Let me out here.

ELLYN: Okay—

Hope, furious, leaps out of the car and strides across the lawn to Lauren.

HOPE: Where's Janey?

LAUREN: She's asleep . . . I checked her, we're just—

HOPE: I want to talk to you. Now. Inside!

INT. STEADMAN LIVING ROOM

Hope, still upset, comes downstairs from checking on Janey to face Lauren.

HOPE: You never would have heard her if she had cried with that music on—

LAUREN (*looks like she's been crying*): I'm sorry . . . I checked on her twice. I didn't know he was coming over—

HOPE: Look, we have never discussed this and I guess—(*she takes a breath*)—we should have. I don't know who this guy is—

LAUREN: I'm so sorry. I wanted you to meet him . . . We just had to talk about something—

She bursts into tears and walks away. Now Hope is stuck.

HOPE: Janey *must* be your first, your *only* priority when you're here—

LAUREN: I love Janey, I'd never do anything to hurt her—

HOPE: I know that, I guess . . . Did something happen?

Lauren turns a tear-stained face to Hope.

LAUREN: His mother is— She got a job at a nursing home somewhere, I don't know, real far away from here—and they have to move. Bernard wants to quit school, he wants to be with me and—

Hope sighs, taking a long look at Lauren.

HOPE: **You love this guy.**

Lauren starts to say yes but it comes out as a sob. She stops, nods. Hope shakes her head—why is this happening to me?

HOPE *(the easy way out):* **I think you should talk to your mother about this.**

LAUREN: **She doesn't care what I do as long as I make dinner and don't bug her. My father left ages ago.**

HOPE: **Lauren, I know it's tough, but—**

Lauren jumps up, shaking with emotion.

LAUREN: **You don't understand! I want to be with him. I love him . . .**

Now Hope sees her intensity. She considers this for a moment.

LAUREN: **I have to go.**

HOPE: **Wait.**

Hope goes to her, trying to lighten the situation.

HOPE: **I mean, wait before you do anything. I don't think you're ready for your whole life to happen to you just yet.**

LAUREN: **He *is* my whole life.**

And she's gone. Hope watches her like she's never seen her before.

INT. STEADMAN HOUSE—DINING ROOM—NIGHT

Two places are set at the table. Michael is finishing his dinner and reading a magazine. At Hope's place is a crumpled napkin and a half-eaten plate of food. We hear Hope coming down the stairs.

HOPE: **I think she's having nightmares again.**

MICHAEL *(doesn't look up):* **Mm.**

Hope sits down to finish her dinner.

HOPE: **She was never completely awake.**

MICHAEL *(without much interest):* **So she wasn't even in the house?**

HOPE *(mouth full of linguine):* **She's in love, what can I do?**

MICHAEL: **Oh. Drentell tried to do a number on us again today.**

HOPE: Oh yeah?

Michael walks into the kitchen.

MICHAEL: God, I'm so tired.

He rotates his tense shoulders. Hope watches him. She has no choice.

HOPE: You want me to rub your back?

MICHAEL: Would you?

INT. STEADMAN HOUSE—HOPE AND MICHAEL'S BATHROOM—NIGHT

Hope is at the mirror brushing her teeth. Michael crosses behind her. We hear the sound of the toilet seat being raised, and Michael peeing. Finally:

MICHAEL: He knows I'm not going to play his games. He can criticize my work all he wants, but he can't convince me I'm not right.

Michael flushes the toilet and leaves the bathroom. Hope dries her face and follows him to the bedroom. Michael climbs into bed, going through various small rituals relating to watches, Kleenex, books, medications, whatever. Hope sits down on her side of the bed, removes her sweat socks, and methodically removes the lint from between her toes.

Michael looks at her—for the first time, really, since she came into the room. She's his wife, and he loves her, but

HOPE: What?

MICHAEL: Nothing.

She picks at a toenail, climbs under the covers, and opens her book. Michael does the same.

MICHAEL: So you told Lauren that guy's never to show his face around here again, right?

HOPE: Not in those words, no, but I told her. They're just so overwhelmed, by their bodies, and each other, and, and, I don't know, love, it's so—

MICHAEL: Can you imagine being fifteen again?

He shudders. But yes, she can.

HOPE: It wasn't all bad . . .

MICHAEL: It wasn't?

Hope considers this for a moment, then:

HOPE: I can't believe I have to pee again.

MICHAEL: Go for me too, will you?

She's still thinking.

HOPE: Michael—I wish you would . . .

He looks at her. What? Wish I would what? Is this going to be serious, because I'm kind of tired right now and it looks serious.

HOPE: Nothing. I just wish we had more time, to talk—no, not to talk. To—

Hope sits up for a moment. She's gearing up to really tell him what she misses. But she can't. She lies down again and opens her book.

MICHAEL *(watching her):* We'll go out tomorrow night, okay? *(no answer)* Okay?

HOPE: Okay.

And he opens his book, too. They read for a moment, then they both drift into the same
FLASHBACK
A bedroom. Not theirs. It feels like winter. There's a party in a distant room, scored to the clink of glasses and jazz and cocktail banter. Hope and Michael are taking off their coats and putting them on a bed piled with coats and parkas and scarves.

Hope, sleek in a cashmere sweater dress, casually pulls up her stocking in front of the full-length mirror. Michael goes to her, holds her breasts in his hands.

HOPE: Just don't do that when I introduce you to my friends—

But she is intoxicated by his breath, which is now so close to hers.

MICHAEL: I don't want to meet your friends.

He lifts her dress. They move to the bed and fall down, the snowy softness of coats all around them. Michael caresses her softly between her legs.

HOPE *(breathless):* **This is crazy—what if someone comes in—**

MICHAEL: **You won't even know . . .**

He unbuttons her dress. She's not wearing a bra. He kisses her breasts, she closes her eyes, and
THE FLASHBACK ENDS
and Hope opens her eyes in bed, still holding her book in front of her. Michael is turned away from her, staring past his book to the wall. She sighs, looks at his back for a moment, then starts to get out of bed.

ACT THREE

INT. *SYNERGY* **MAGAZINE—CAFETERIA—DAY**
Hope is waiting for Nancy. Val Shilladay, Hope's editor, is dumping her tray and sipping her coffee from a paper—not Styrofoam—cup

VAL: All I'm saying is it's going to be an awfully "down" piece.

HOPE: Is this my Val talking? Are you going for the *Readers' Digest* market or something?

VAL: Murder, Hope, I think I'm safe in calling that a downer—

HOPE: He was trying to save the rain forests, he was getting somewhere, it's a hopeful story. Look, it's the rain forest, we'll have nice pictures . . .

Nancy joins them.

NANCY: Hi—am I interrupting?

Ad-lib introductions.

NANCY: I really admire your work here.

VAL: Well, I'm glad somebody does. My staff doesn't appreciate me . . . Hope? Think about it.

She's gone. Nancy raises her eyebrows. Hope just waves her hand, it's nothing. They get in line at the counter.

HOPE: So how were the agents?

NANCY: I walked into the room and there were these two young guys—and I mean *young*. And they're here from New York, they think they're slumming, and all I could think was you're such babies, you should be in school, does your mother know you're out alone?

Hope laughs and touches Nancy's sleeve.

HOPE: This is great . . . Is it from that place near you?

NANCY: Yeah, you like it? Dating clothes.

HOPE *(to server):* Do you have any more chef's salads? *(to Nancy)* Are you dating Elliot? Is that what's going on?

NANCY: I guess that's what you'd call it. He's trying to get me into bed, and I'm holding out against the inevitable, because I know three weeks later it'll be like he never left . . .

HOPE: I want to date.

NANCY: Simone De Beauvoir and Jean-Paul Sartre, they had the right idea living next door to each other for fifty years.

HOPE: What was the weirdest place you ever made love?

NANCY *(laughs):* With my boyfriend before Elliot at RISD, we tried it standing up in his mother's swimming pool. Boy, did that *not* work.

HOPE: Michael and I made love on a train in Switzerland once, right near Montreaux. All those tunnels and flashing lights. It was incredible.

Hope notices the woman behind her is listening openly. Hope smiles at her and moves closer to Nancy.

HOPE: Why does the good stuff always go away?

NANCY: That's easy. You have no time. You have kids, and one of them is usually sick. You worry about money, you worry about work—

HOPE: *We* worry about work, *they* obsess about it—

NANCY: Yes, but *they* worry about the kids and *we* obsess about them.

HOPE: I know I do, but I remember when all I had to do was look at Michael, and everything else fell away, I just wanted him so much—

NANCY: But Michael's crazy about you.

HOPE *(sadly):* No. Not crazy. Not anymore.

Nancy looks at Hope. This is more serious than she thought.

NANCY: How long have you been married now?

Hope has to think a second.

HOPE: Five and a half years.

Hope looks at Nancy, who shrugs.

NANCY: Comes with the territory . . .

Hope's assistant interrupts them.

ASSISTANT: Hope, sorry, your baby-sitter called. Everything's okay, she just needs you to call her.

HOPE: Thanks, Michelle.

Hope and Nancy look at each other.

INT. STEADMAN HOUSE—LATE AFTERNOON

Lauren's been crying again. Nancy watches, amused and sympathetic, as Hope tries to cope.

HOPE: Isn't there anyone else you could have called?

LAUREN: No one. I wouldn't ask if it wasn't really important—

HOPE: How far is it?

LAUREN: Not too far, just past Lansdale—

HOPE: That's twenty miles from here—

Lauren's starting to cry again.

LAUREN: I'll never see him again.

Hope sighs. She's giving in.

NANCY: I'll take Janey. Go ahead. I'll call Michael and tell him where you are.

Hope looks at Nancy and shakes her head.

INT. DAA—MICHAEL AND ELLIOT'S OFFICE

Michael and Elliot pore over Drentell's comps. There's a cropped picture, where all we see is a woman's torso as she floats in a pool, holding a Kenwa phone.

MICHAEL: You know this is not even good. Just because it's vulgar and sexy doesn't make it good.

Elliot just looks at him, trying to control his irritation.

ELLIOT: I think women should stop wearing bathing suits like this, to protest this kind of exploitation.

Michael shakes his head.

ELLIOT: Tell Hope to stop wearing bathing suits like this . . .

MICHAEL: You two ever going to like each other again, or what?

ELLIOT: I like Hope.

MICHAEL: Yes—but do I?

ELLIOT: Whoa—what?

MICHAEL: Never mind. I love my wife. Anyway, you wouldn't understand—

ELLIOT: Oh, I wouldn't understand this stuff—

MICHAEL: We don't have problems like you guys, we're healthy.

ELLIOT: Except for—

MICHAEL: Shut up. I don't know. It's like, sometimes, it seems like I'm not as . . . attracted to her as I used to be, or it's not automatic anymore—

ELLIOT: Oh, yes . . .

MICHAEL: I used to only have to look at her, even like her neck or something, or smell her, and I'd be trying to tear her clothes off, but now . . . And she's . . .

He doesn't know how to finish the sentence.

ELLIOT: I thought sex was great for you guys—

MICHAEL: I'm in advertising, remember? No, it's just . . . calmer. Too calm. It scares me.

ELLIOT: No kidding.

MICHAEL: So what are we supposed to do?

ELLIOT: Walk out on her. She'll start looking great . . . *(on Michael's look)* Worked for me.

EXT. SERVICE ROAD—NIGHT

Hope pulls her car up near a bridge and kills the engine. Balmy night air spills in the windows. The sound of crickets. Time suddenly slows down.

HOPE: This is beautiful.

LAUREN: No one knows about it. Bernard and I found it together.

HOPE: Beats the mall, I guess. Twenty minutes.

LAUREN: I really, really appreciate this. It's been so—

A Mustang convertible rumbles up, stops. Lauren leans forward.

LAUREN: That's him. And his friend.

HOPE: I'll just take a little walk. You guys can stay here—for a very little while.

Hope gets out. The sky is heavy with stars. She walks to the retaining wall, looks out, inhales the night and shivers. A car door slams. A stone tumbles near her, she whirls around—
    —a boy, a rather beautiful one, is standing in the moonlight. They exchange brief hellos.

BOY: I'm Danny. Friend of Bernard's.

HOPE: Okay. *(to herself)* I guess.

Danny sits up on the railing, oblivious to the drop below him.

DANNY: Nice of you to do this. Means a lot to Bernard.

HOPE: Oh, well—it's no big deal.

DANNY: How long have you known Lauren?

HOPE: A few months. Not too long.

DANNY: She's a good kid. You want something to drink?

HOPE: No, no, I'm fine.

Danny jumps off the railing and moves closer to Hope. Danny looks at her, then turns to the view.

DANNY: You see shooting stars when it gets hot like this at night.

HOPE: Indian summer.

Danny studies her.

DANNY: I haven't seen you before—

HOPE: Look, I'm—I'm not—listen, it's pretty *dark* out here and—

DANNY: Hey, I like older women, I always have.

HOPE: I'm older than your—well, I'm older than you think I am. I'm gonna get Lauren. I have to get back. To my life.

DANNY: Sure.

INT. THE CAR—NIGHT

Hope furiously tries to start the car, but all she gets is a dead "click." Lauren is nervous.

HOPE: It's the starter—it—oh, damn. Maybe now Michael will take this thing back to the dealer.

She keeps trying. Danny appears at her window.

DANNY: Can I offer you ladies a ride?

Hope looks up at him, exasperated. Janey's car seat is visible behind her.

HOPE: I don't believe this.

Hope gets out of the car. Danny jumps lightly into the Mustang's backseat as Lauren slides in front. Bernard holds the seat forward for Hope, who climbs in back and sits down beside Danny.
DRIVING
It's windy with the top down. Lauren is snuggled close to Bernard. The radio plays the Righteous Brothers' "You've Lost That Lovin' Feeling." Hope keeps trying to find a way not to be near Danny's casually draped arm.

LAUREN (*turning around*): Bernard got accepted to art school. And a scholarship—

HOPE: That's great . . . Listen, I'm going to Bryn Mawr Avenue . . .

Lauren and Bernard do their famous soul-kiss while the light keeps changing.

HOPE: Guys . . . ?

The light goes back to green, Bernard roars off, and Hope is flung backward next to Danny. The music, the wind, the night, and yes, this boy, whose breath smells like clover—it's all melting her. They drive into the night, music blaring. Hope smiles, remembering. And then laughs out loud.

EXT. STEADMAN HOUSE—NIGHT

Hope hops out of the Mustang—without using the door—to flurries of good-byes from Danny, Bernard, and Lauren.

DANNY: I really wish you'd come skinny-dipping with us, Mrs. Steadman.

HOPE *(laughing):* Maybe next time.

INT. STEADMAN HOUSE—NIGHT

The Mustang roars away. Hope bursts through the front door, laughing, as Michael comes into the living room.

MICHAEL: Hope?

HOPE: Skinny-dipping! Wait 'til he sees my stretch marks—

MICHAEL: What?

HOPE: We have to call a tow truck, the car's way out near Lansdale, I think it's the starter—

MICHAEL: Lansdale! What the hell is going on?

Hope is still laughing. Michael isn't. She turns to him.

HOPE: Skinny-dipping.

INT. CUBAN RESTAURANT—NIGHT

Michael is reading the menu as Hope returns from the ladies room.

HOPE: They called from the dealer, by the way, it *is* just the starter, we can get it tomorrow—

MICHAEL: So I don't understand, she *had* to see Bernard?

HOPE: She had to see Bernard and so they're talking, and this kid, Danny, he must have been all of eighteen, starts coming on to me.

MICHAEL: Get out of here—

HOPE: Okay, it was improbable, but it wasn't *that* improbable—

MICHAEL: In Lansdale?

She takes his wrists, trying to pull him into her radiance.

HOPE: No, listen, it was almost wonderful, the backseat of a convertible again, out of control, it was—

He's not getting it. He's threatened. He can't offer her this.

HOPE: I wish you'd been with me, I wish we could get back there.

MICHAEL: Where—Lansdale?

She looks away, hurt. He knows it, but there's nothing he can do.

MICHAEL: Sorry. The bathrooms are that way?

She nods. He gets up and walks away.

AT THE STEPS

to the bathroom, Michael is momentarily held up by three men coming down. As they clear, his eye is drawn to the steps, and then back to Hope.

FLASHBACK

INT. BROWNSTONE STAIRWAY—NIGHT

It is New Year's Eve, 1982.

Michael, looking uncomfortable in a rented tuxedo with a coat draped over his arm, is climbing the stairs of an old brownstone. He consults a slip of paper, stuffs it in his pocket, and smooths down the pocket and his hair as he finds the right apartment. It's a blind date, it's New Year's Eve, and why did he ever say he'd do this? It's too late now.

INSIDE THE APARTMENT

Hope, in a skinny little black dress, is transferring her belongings from one purse to another. It's New Year's Eve. Why did she say she'd do this? There is a knock at the door. She takes a deep breath and braces herself for the inevitable horrible shock. Hope opens the door to Michael. We see both of their faces go from wary irritation to pleased incredulity, ending with silly little grins that they try to hide from each other.

MICHAEL: Hi, Hope?

HOPE: Yeah, hi—

MICHAEL: Michael Steadman—

HOPE: Hope Murdoch, hi—

They shake hands—and the flashback ends, and we're back in

THE RESTAURANT AGAIN

as a beer is put down in front of Hope. As the WAITER pours, Michael returns to the table.

MICHAEL: I'll just have a club soda.

Hope watches him . . . and we FLASHBACK to
A SMALL, CROWDED LIVING ROOM
where it is almost midnight. Hope and Michael are standing together in a crowd of people, including Ellyn, all of whom are trying to overcome their natural self-consciousness and be wild and crazy. The Times Square celebration is on the TV.

HOSTESS: Come on, we're going to do this right, everybody . . . Who doesn't have champagne? Come on, Eric, you too, it's almost time, okay! Ten—

EVERYBODY (reluctantly): Nine, eight . . . (etc.)

Hope and Michael turn to each other, somewhat embarrassed, somewhat enjoying themselves. They don't join in the countdown; they just drift, eyes locked, closer and closer together.

EVERYBODY: Two, one! Happy New Year!

Hope and Michael kiss. This is for real, not for Happy New Year. They break, look at each other, and go back in for more.

ELLYN (to the hostess): See, I told you . . .

And now we're
BACK IN THE RESTAURANT
and back in the present, as Hope watches Michael's club soda bubble over the top of the glass. When the waiter leaves, Michael holds up his drink and taps Hope's half-downed beer. They're trying.

MICHAEL: Hi.

HOPE: Hi.

INT. STEADMAN HOUSE—LIVING ROOM—NIGHT

Lauren greets Hope and Michael as they return from dinner.

LAUREN (doubtful): Hi . . . Did you have a good time?

HOPE: Yeah. Great . . .

MICHAEL: I'll be right there.

LAUREN: Bernard is picking me up.

Hope and Michael stare at her.

HOPE: But I thought he was gone?

Lauren gives her a radiant smile.

LAUREN: He decided he couldn't leave me. He's staying with Danny.

Hope and Michael share a look. Lauren moves to get her things off the couch.

LAUREN: I'll wait on the porch.

HOPE: No, don't do that, wait in here. Want me to pay you now, or—

LAUREN: No, Tuesday's fine.

HOPE: Okay, just lock the front door. See you Tuesday.

Hope goes upstairs as Michael heads toward the kitchen.

INT. MICHAEL AND HOPE'S BATHROOM—NIGHT

Hope is brushing her teeth as Michael walks in, still dressed.

MICHAEL: You're red, *I'm* blue.

Hope looks at the toothbrush she's using.

HOPE: Sorry.

Hope wipes her mouth with a towel. Michael embraces her, tries to lean her against the wall. She tenses. He doesn't notice, or chooses not to.

MICHAEL: I want you.

HOPE: Michael—

MICHAEL: Come on, what about on a cold hard bathroom floor—

HOPE: That's not it, just— Please.

And it's the way she shrugs him off that does it.

MICHAEL: There's no right moment or right way with you lately.

HOPE: That's not true—

MICHAEL: So when, when is it right with you?

HOPE: When you're here, with me, in your head and not at that—place, or thinking about Miles Drentell all the time—

They continue getting ready for bed, as if the argument they're having were as normal as turning down the sheets.

MICHAEL: *You* wanted me to take that job—

HOPE: Sure I did, but that doesn't mean I wanted you to check out of our marriage—

MICHAEL: Oh, come on—

HOPE: It scares me, you didn't used to be like this—

MICHAEL: It's a new job, I have to work harder—

HOPE: I thought we weren't going to have this kind of life—

MICHAEL: It's not so different, Elliot and I used to work weekends.

HOPE: Yeah, the two of you used to shoot baskets in the driveway and sit around and talk. You used to *be* here—

MICHAEL: I'm trying to be with you—

HOPE: You're trying to be in bed with me, not *with* me—

MICHAEL: You've practically got me begging, is that what you want?

HOPE: What I want is for you to pay some attention to me, to us, to anything but that stupid job of yours, but I know I'm not going to get that.

MICHAEL: What about your attention, what about sexual attention—

HOPE *(warningly):* Meaning what?

MICHAEL: That why can't you make some effort to make something happen, to help me through this, to make me feel I want you—

HOPE *(dangerous):* You're saying you don't want me anymore?

Michael is caught and stumbling badly.

MICHAEL: No, it's just not—it's not automatic anymore, I want you, of course I want you, but you, couldn't you— Never mind . . .

Michael shakes his head in exasperation and disgust. It's a horrible stalemate.

LATER—IN BED—

They are both restless, but it appears that Michael is asleep. Hope is exhausted, but sleepless as she stares mournfully into the dark. Suddenly she sits up, listening. Nothing. She starts to sink back into the covers when she hears something again, someone's voice. She gets up, putting on her robe, and goes down the hall to

THE STAIRS

She stops, listens—

HOPE: Lauren?

There's a soft moan. Hope creeps down the stairs to see into the living room. Now the sounds are unmistakable; Hope peers through the railings to see Lauren and Bernard on the sofa making love. They are oblivious to Hope as they explore one another, holding nothing back in their pleasure and surprise. Hope is too stunned to move. With yearning and a kind of wonder, she looks on something she has long forgotten.

ACT FOUR

EXT. STEADMAN HOUSE—MORNING

Michael, dressed for work but without his jacket, and Gary, dressed for whatever it is he does, carry a dismantled crib down the front steps.

GARY: You sure Hope wants to do this?

MICHAEL: She thinks if she hangs on to the crib she'll never get pregnant.

GARY: Makes perfect sense.

MICHAEL: Wait—something dropped.

They put down the crib. Gary sits on the steps. Michael retrieves a little spring and sits down beside him.

MICHAEL: How's Susannah?

GARY: She's great. Nervous, but doing great.

MICHAEL: No, I mean *you* and Susannah.

Gary considers this.

GARY: I'd say we're doing extraordinarily well for a couple who decided to have a baby together before they knew each other's birthdays or middle names. How about you guys, any news from the reproductive front?

MICHAEL: Nothing. Probably just as well, right now.

GARY: I thought you were the one who couldn't wait to have another kid.

MICHAEL: Well . . .

GARY: Uh-oh . . .

MICHAEL: No, it's just little things. A lot of little things. *(thinks about that)* Like marriage. Sex. Love. Little things like that. I mean—what do women want?

GARY: "Lord, what do they want?"

Michael gets up and attacks the crib again. Gary follows.

MICHAEL: I was thinking about how we spent our entire adolescence going crazy over women, trying to find women, trying to meet women, trying to sleep with women, and then you'd find one and you would make her the complete center of your universe, and what would happen? She'd have contempt for you 'cause you weren't cool.

GARY: Please . . . it's too painful—

MICHAEL: I remember I made a fool, a complete fool of myself over this girl from Easton—

GARY: Who?

MICHAEL: Linda Koban. She was before your time . . . And I swore I'd never let any woman subject me to that humiliation again.

GARY: Janet Halifax.

MICHAEL: Who?

GARY: She's the one who did it to *me*.

MICHAEL: Right, so you learned to keep everything under control, not to risk letting them see how much they mattered—

GARY: Right—

MICHAEL: We got the act down. I'm cool . . .

GARY: God knows we tried . . .

MICHAEL: What was that great stupid line of yours? "Life is possibility, not predictability." That got you laid a lot as I recall.

GARY *(can't help smiling):* Yeah . . .

MICHAEL: So here I am now, and Hope thinks I don't even . . . *(looks at Gary)* When did the act become reality?

INT. STEADMAN HOUSE—LIVING ROOM—MORNING

Hope comes down in her robe to find Michael at the door, ready for work.

MICHAEL *(very formal):* Janey's in the kitchen. She's had breakfast. I've got to go.

HOPE: Okay. See you later.

Michael leaves without another word. Hope stands all alone by the door for a moment, then walks into the living room and sees that the pillows are put back all wrong on the couch. She begins to rearrange them.

INT. DAA—DAY

Elliot and Michael stand outside a conference room. Michael is very well dressed and looks very calm.

ELLIOT: Think we'll still have jobs after this little soiree?

MICHAEL: How do I look?

ELLIOT: Like someone who works for DAA. They should call it DOA.

More people crowd past them to go into the conference room. Michael watches them, lost in thought. He sees Drentell with the client, claps him on the back. Drentell grabs his arm in a big phony gesture of support. Elliot smiles, goes in. Just before they join the throng, Michael pulls Drentell back into the hall.

MICHAEL: Listen, I want you to know that we've tried to work with your concept, but it's not working. I'm willing to bust my ass for you, but I have to be able to believe in the campaign. So we're going to try it my way.

Elliot closes his eyes in silent prayer. The client turns expectantly to Drentell across the conference room. Drentell smiles.

DRENTELL: Be right in—

Drentell knows there is nothing he can do. The client is waiting; they can't argue this now.

DRENTELL: Michael, you surprise me. I knew you were principled. It's one of the quaint, old-world things that I halfway like about you. But I didn't know you liked to take stupid risks.

MICHAEL: I don't think it's stupid this time.

DRENTELL: You love these little scenes with me, don't you?

Michael just stares him down.

DRENTELL: Do it your way. I suggest that your way had better be good.

They start to join the group. Drentell stops Michael.

DRENTELL: Of course, if you pull a stunt like this again—you're out of here.

Michael just smiles.

INT. STEADMAN HOUSE—LIVING ROOM—DAY

We circle around Hope, who is very still as she talks to Lauren.

HOPE: And I can't let you continue to work here if you're going to deceive us. What you did was very—irresponsible. Do you even know about birth control, and AIDS—

LAUREN: We used a condom.

HOPE: Well, that's one good thing. Lauren, I don't know how

to say this, but your first boyfriend is—just the beginning. He's not going to be the one that you spend your whole life with—*(catches herself)* You probably don't want to hear that right now.

A look from Lauren confirms that she is right.

LAUREN: It may seem like—just the beginning, and not important, to you—

HOPE: I didn't say that—

LAUREN: But, I mean, how much time do you really get? You get married, you have kids, no offense, I'm sure you're happy but it doesn't always look that great to me—

Hope is shocked to get such a sage comment from a child. She laughs.

HOPE: Are you afraid to lose him?

LAUREN: No. Because I know that no one could love him the way I do.

This hits home.

HOPE: It may seem incredible to you, but I was fifteen, I haven't completely forgotten what it's like . . . The silly truth is, I'm a parent, I wish I could spare you some of the stuff you're going to have to go through.

Lauren knows she's not in trouble anymore.

LAUREN: How did you know when you were in love with Michael—when you knew you wanted to marry him?

HOPE: That's a question. *(thinks, smiles)* But I remember . . . It was a very cold foggy day. Michael and I had just come out of this awful movie and we were walking, we couldn't find the car. It was just starting to get dark and we were laughing about it, but we were getting tired. All of a sudden I—leaned on this car and looked at him and I didn't see him, I just—*heard* him, like a pressure and a sound inside of me, in a place so deep I didn't think anyone could ever reach . . . And I knew I could listen to that sound for the rest of my life . . .

She has started out talking to Lauren, and ended up talking to herself.

INT. STEADMAN HOUSE—LIVING ROOM—NIGHT

Hope has just put Janey to bed. She comes down the stairs, sees Michael curled up on the sofa asleep, his briefcase on the floor beside him. She doesn't want to wake him. She sits on the other end of the couch and leans back, still looking at him. After a while she closes her eyes. A few moments pass this way. Michael opens his eyes.

MICHAEL: Should we talk?

HOPE: Do we know how?

They sit for a moment, then Hope finally turns to him.

HOPE: Are you having an affair?

Michael laughs, then realizes she is very serious.

MICHAEL: I don't have time to have an affair.

HOPE: What's that supposed to mean?

MICHAEL: I don't want to have an affair. I love you.

It hangs in the air, almost like a question. Hope doesn't move.

HOPE: If you love me, you'll—be with me.

MICHAEL: Sometimes I forget that I can do that—

HOPE: Why?

MICHAEL: Because—I don't know if I can cut it with this agency, and I can't talk to you about that. When I need help or—consolation, I think that's the part of me you don't like, and I'm afraid of you. And I—close up.

HOPE: But it's not true—

MICHAEL: I think it is true.

HOPE: Only when that's all I get from you. That's when it gets bad.

MICHAEL: It's weird . . . All I wanted to do today when I was in there sweating out this stupid campaign, all I wanted to do was come home to you, to see your face—

HOPE: But what's all this about not wanting me?

MICHAEL: It's not exactly the same anymore, is it?

HOPE *(sadly):* No, it isn't.

MICHAEL: I haven't figured out how to handle that yet. It's so easy, when I'm mad or I think you're not interested in me, to stop wanting you. Boy, is that scary.

HOPE: I want you to make me laugh. Like you used to.

Michael reaches out and touches her arm.

HOPE: Sometimes it seems like we should . . . introduce ourselves.

They look at one another.

MICHAEL *(softly and gently):* Hi. I'm Michael Steadman. And you know what?

HOPE: What?

MICHAEL *(still soft and gentle):* I've got to work tonight.

She laughs, a little. From upstairs we hear Janey start to cry. Hope starts to get up.

MICHAEL: No, I'll get her. I want to see her.

INT. STEADMAN LIVING ROOM—NIGHT

Michael is working on the couch. We hear the water being turned off in the kitchen and a cabinet door closing. Hope comes in, to do the final desultory straightening up before bed, loading her arms with junk—toys, clothes, a hairbrush—to take upstairs. She picks up one of Lauren's sock-puppets as Michael looks up.

MICHAEL: That's cute. Did Lauren make it?

Hope sits down beside him on the couch.

HOPE: Yeah. She gets some things right.

She deliberately reaches out and touches Michael's chest as she says this, though she does not look at him.

She stands up again. Michael watches her for a moment, then stands up.

He brushes back the hair that has fallen forward on her face. She reaches back and pulls out her ponytail, shaking out her hair. He takes the stack of junk from her and tosses it down, except for the brush. He begins brushing her hair, slowly, methodically, erotically, pulling the hair back from her face and up from her neck, almost with controlled violence. They do not speak or touch each other, but they shift positions ever so slightly so they can watch themselves in the mirror. Hope closes her eyes for a moment, then opens them, meeting his look in the mirror. She begins slowly and seriously to unbutton her shirt as he watches.

STRANGERS

BY

RICHARD KRAMER

Two guys went to bed together and talked of the deaths of friends.

Big deal.

But it was enough to cause advertisers to withdraw from that night's episode and to inspire the writing of endless letters. We split them into two piles, the positive and the not-so-positive. The hate mail, for some reason, was always handwritten, and usually listed the names and ages of our correspondent's children. The phones rang, too, for days and days. Molly, our receptionist, bravely took the calls. I could see her from my office; she would turn to me, and, after hanging up, call out "Good!" or "*Really* bad!" The papers, of course, told only the ugly half of the story. When it was time to schedule reruns at the end of our third season, advertisers once more threatened ABC with a $1.6 million loss in revenues if the show was aired again. Well— it didn't air again, and that is why I've chosen "Strangers" for this book.

It will probably always be known as our "Gay Show." I'm sorry for that, because when I wrote "Strangers" I never thought of it in that way. That would have been to go against our rule to never do shows on Subjects. Subject comes from character, and only from character; that was our group mantra. There was a downside, of course, to our insistence on breathing this clear aesthetic air. The box loves a good Subject, and not to make a subject instantly clear is to risk being viewed—in the words of one of our detractors—as "just a lot of stories about skinny white people from Hell." We were willing to take that risk. We all had plenty of statements to make, but we tried to make them only to each other, and to let these characters who were both projections of ourselves and fictional creations live their lives in their own way.

Now, this is supposed to be *my* introduction to *my* script, and I keep using the pronoun "we." I will be using it again, and I should tell you why. It is because I can't help thinking "we" when I try to summon up what went into the writing of this script. Its framework, as was the case with my other scripts, was hammered out by Ed, Marshall, and myself. "Strangers" was my tenth show; the three of us had all learned to work together. They were there at the halfway point, to encourage me to stick with it when I thought all I had was twenty-seven pages going nowhere. They were there to raise an eyebrow when I told them my idea for the wonderful fantasy sequence I hadn't, fortunately, written yet. And they were there, as they had been all the times preceding, to both push me from the top of the building and be the arms down below to catch me. Now that I've told you that, it's probably worth looking back to what we all agreed upon before those two bastards banished me to my creative dungeon.

I had written bits of "Strangers" the season before, but had never been able to make them come together. Russell had made two appearances that year—in "Trust Me," in which Melissa and Gary decide they might like to have a child together, and in "Success," in which he steered Melissa to some work for Carly Simon. Melanie Mayron and David Marshall Grant played beautifully together; we knew we wanted to do more with them, but didn't know quite what. I think it was Ed who said, "What if they both got so involved with each other that it prevented them from having other, realer relationships?" Maybe it was Marshall. Maybe it was me. Whoever it was, I sat down and wrote a batch of pages. Looking at them now isn't easy; they obey the rule that whatever was *not* filmed is embarrassing, and whatever *was* filmed seems, somehow, just right. When I wrote those early pages, Lee did not yet exist. Melanie Mayron had not yet come to see us with the idea that Melissa might have a younger boyfriend, and Jill Gordon had not yet spanked such vivid life into him in "Mr. Right" (which you will find in this book). But back to the pages themselves . . . In scene one, we learned that Melissa had eaten a questionable clam at a seafood restaurant. She had gone to register a complaint at the Board of Health, where she met a guy who, when not investigating bivalve violations, was working on a screenplay that was "sort of like *Sophie's Choice* in space." Everything was swell between them, but it turned out Russell kept calling at midnight, and Melissa kept talking to him, and it was getting terribly sophisticated and I hated it all. I also had a five-page scene in which we met the gallery owner who had discovered Russell. That scene was rich with fantasies, which, as we've all learned on the show, take three lines on the page and ten hours on the stage. As the gallery owner tried to pinpoint the influences she detected in Russell's work, we went on a little trip into his head. There he was as Toulouse-Lautrec, walking on his knees, while Melissa, dressed as Jane Avril, cancanned around him. She was a Polynesian princess to his Gauguin, a sunflower to his Van Gogh. Oh, well . . . Those five pages yielded half a line of usable material, words that would wind up coming from Peter when he spots in Russell's work the "sense of a stranger in the world." The scene where Michael plays Cupid to Russell was there, word for word, from the start. I had bits of Russell and Peter's post-sex chat, a few fragrant one-liners about the meaning of art, and no idea where to take it all. I called this non-script "Down to You," after the Joni Mitchell song I played each day before I sat down to write.

Why didn't "Strangers" happen the second season? Maybe it just needed a long time to gestate. Whatever the reason, by the time the second-year hiatus rolled around, it had jumped to the head of the line. I sat down with Ed and Marshall. We looked at my pages, at each other, at our lives and the people we knew. And we made a decision. It seems to me now that what eventually so upset people about the episode might have had its genesis in those early meetings. For we all agreed, at the time, that the radical approach to material like this was *not* to sensationalize it. "Strangers" was going to be just another *thirtysomething* story. I remember Marshall saying, "Let's go into Russell's bedroom just like we go into Hope and Michael's"; I also remember Ed saying, "Just make sure Russell's not there at the time." Then we laid out our agenda, "what we wanted to say," and what that was—I have it on my computer—was only this: "The ghosts who haunt the lonely don't divide their victims into gay and straight." I always needed a line like this to guide me through my writing. That line would never hop from a character's mouth, but it would be underneath all that happened, and it only had to make enough sense for me to be able to extract from it a psychological line, which was, for "Strangers," "The power of internalized self-judgment to fuck up your life."

Those two phrases, scrawled on Post-its, stared at me through the writing of the script, and try as I will I can't find in either of them a clear and present danger to the state. But to go back to then—my job now was to dramatize those phrases so that the audience could discover these ideas for themselves.

The notion of self-judgment was one we had wanted to play with from the start of the series. It just presented itself, early on, as one of the things *thirtysomething* was about. Somehow, the chemical mix of our writers, directors, and actors had led to the creation of a group of characters who seemed to simultaneously live their lives and *watch* themselves living them. "Strangers" could just as easily have been about Ellyn or Gary or Nancy or even Ethan. Melissa, Russell, Peter, and Lee were in the right place at the right time to magnetize those particular filings to themselves.

Maybe what was upsetting about "Strangers" was not that it showed gay characters but that it was a show about sex. There's a moment when Melissa tries to convey to Hope a sense of her relationship with Lee. The two women sit on the edge of a bed, and all the ever-articulate Melissa is able to provide for the ever-understanding Hope is this: "And when I'm with him? And he's inside me . . . ?" The words just float, as Melanie and Mel show us that Melissa couldn't have said it better and Hope couldn't have understood it more. Well, *this* made the watchdogs bark. Some helpful little person at the network suggested substituting the phrase "When he's inside my apartment. . . ." When we shot the scene, we did it in two versions. Melanie did one take as written, and one in which she said "When he's inside my heart . . ." We won, eventually, and I bring this up because this line crystallized the whole episode for me. I've listed a lot of things "Strangers" was about; I'll add one more, and hope that puts an end to it. "Strangers" is about how physical love, for two people, can be both a window and a wall. I tried to apply this to everyone in the story, knowing that if Melissa and Lee were going to spend so much time in bed, then Russell and Peter, who were their mirror, could not just be capons in sweaters. Some people felt the speed with which Russell and Peter got together was politically incorrect. That may be; I was trying to write people and not role models. But look at the circumstances. It was late. There they were. Peter had understood something about Russell that no one had ever seen before. And, as Peter says to Melissa, "these things happen . . . ," and she says, "I know what you mean." I hope some people in the audience did, too.

There's one more thing before you read this for yourself, which is to let you know how I felt when I was writing it. My best friend had, a few months before, died of complications arising from AIDS. I see now that in writing about Melissa, I had found a way to write about him. Like her, he struggled in his own ring with his own self-judgment, and it is because I feel he won that fight that I dedicate my script to the memory of David Bombyk.

RICHARD KRAMER

ACT ONE

INT. MELISSA'S LOFT—NIGHT

Strings play; moonbeams fall; Melissa and Lee make love, each a new world to the other's Columbus. They come together for a kiss, then— Click. Silence.

LEE: Tape.

MELISSA: Right.

He angles his body over hers, reaching for the cassette player to turn over the tape. She joins him.

MELISSA: What is this—"Music to Make Love to Older Women By"?

LEE *(simply):* It doesn't have a name. It's just music I like. That I thought *you* might like . . .

MELISSA: Lee?

LEE: Yeah?

MELISSA: I do. Like it. So thanks . . .

They kiss again; the phone rings; the machine picks up.

ELLYN'S VOICE: Melissa . . . ? It's Ellyn . . . I know you're there. Are you there? Call me . . .

Ellyn hangs up. Melissa and Lee settle onto the pillows. They are silent for a moment, then:

LEE: What's your middle name?

MELISSA: Jo. Like in *Little Women*. My mother let me pick it. What's yours?

He whispers his answer into her ear—a secret to us, but not to her.

MELISSA: I like that.

LEE: Don't tell anyone.

As they move into another kiss, the phone rings again and we hear Russell's voice.

RUSSELL: Melissa—it's me . . . You're eating fried pork rinds, I can hear it through the machine . . .

Her hand reaches in to kill the volume, and we go to:

INT. RUSSELL'S LOFT—NIGHT

Where we find him on the phone as he works on a large canvas.

RUSSELL: Anyway—I've got big news, I'll try you tomorrow . . .

He hangs up, steps back to consider his work, then steps forward with a brush, as—

INT. MELISSA'S LOFT—DAY

Melissa brushes makeup onto her face. Lee can be heard, offscreen, singing in the shower. There's a knock at the door.

MELISSA (*frustrated*): Wonderful . . . Coming!

She goes to get the door. Russell stands there, holding a bag.

RUSSELL: Hello. There are bagels in my bag.

MELISSA: Thanks . . . I'm sort of crazy, I've got to meet Michael and I'm late . . .

RUSSELL: You get my messages? I called you a couple of times . . .

MELISSA: I was going to call you back—

RUSSELL: I've got a little news. It's nothing important.

MELISSA: What? What's not important?

RUSSELL *(casual):* I'm going to have a show . . .

MELISSA: A show? Where?

RUSSELL: The Brisson Gallery. Just me . . .

MELISSA *(it hits her; excited):* Really? Russell—

RUSSELL: Really. With white wine and cheese puffs and a catalog—

MELISSA: Russell, that's incredible—

RUSSELL: —which I need pictures for, and Annie Leibovitz is busy. Are you?

Lee appears, wrapped in a towel, drying his hair.

RUSSELL: Lee! How are you?

LEE: Excellent. I'm in a towel.

RUSSELL *(looks around):* It came out great. The paint job . . .

LEE: Thanks. And thanks for the reference. And maybe now I'll just get dressed . . . See ya . . .

He goes back into the bathroom. Russell slyly considers Melissa.

MELISSA: What?

RUSSELL: Nothing, it's just I always pictured you, you know, schlepping around in mules and a housecoat—

MELISSA: Russell—

RUSSELL: Curled up with *Pride and Prejudice* and a quart of Häagen-Dazs—

MELISSA: *Russell*—

RUSSELL *(teasing her, laughing):* But I was wr-o-o-o-o-n-g! And the Final Jeopardy Answer is: "She gets it Regular . . ."

MELISSA: Yes. She does. Now can you drop me at DAA?

RUSSELL: I'll get the car.

MELISSA: Great. And congratulations . . .

RUSSELL *(points to bathroom):* You too.

He's off, and she's ready to go, as Lee reemerges from the bathroom.

MELISSA: Wish me luck, okay?

LEE: Luck.

She's magnetized by him right now, and falls into a kiss. And even as this is happening:

MELISSA: And when you leave—

LEE: I know, I know, make sure to push the button on the knob—

MELISSA: Right—

LEE: And slam the door tight.

MELISSA: Right. *(searches around)* Okay. Keys, keys, keys . . .

Lee finds her keys and jingles them in the air for her.

LEE: What time will you be back? In case I wanted to see you later—which I'll probably want to . . .

MELISSA: I don't know, it's a crazy day, I'll be in and out—

LEE: Oh. Okay . . .

MELISSA: What?

LEE: Nothing.

He tosses the keys to her, and, with the aid of slow motion, they hang in the air like the question she knows he's about to ask.

MELISSA: I'll have a set made. If I have time.

She blows him a kiss—and she's gone.

INT. DAA—CORRIDOR—DAY

Michael steps out of his office, looking significantly at his watch as Melissa and Russell hurry down the corridor.

MELISSA: Are you mad? You're mad. Don't be mad—

MICHAEL: How could I be mad? You're in pain.

MELISSA: I am? What kind of pain?

MICHAEL: Your neck. You've got one of the biggest hickeys I've ever seen . . .

MELISSA: Ha ha. Very funny . . .

MICHAEL: And Drentell rescheduled. So you're early . . . Hey, Russell—

RUSSELL: Michael . . . how ya doing . . .

MELISSA: Is Peter here?

MICHAEL: He's here . . .

Michael and Russell go into the office; Melissa lingers to quickly check her neck in a compact mirror.

INT. MICHAEL AND ELLIOT'S OFFICE—DAA—DAY

Elliot looks through layouts with Peter Montefiore, a fellow DAA grunt, as Melissa, Michael, and Russell enter.

PETER: Melissa . . . Hi . . .

ELLIOT: Hey, Russell . . .

MELISSA (making introductions): Okay. Russell—Peter. Peter—

RUSSELL (a handshake): Hi. Russell Weller—

PETER (a handshake): Peter Montefiore—

MICHAEL: Peter's just like us—

ELLIOT: Only respected and successful.

RUSSELL (to Peter): Melissa told me about you—

PETER (mock-aghast): Oh no—

RUSSELL: Oh yes, you do the catalogs—

PETER: Sometimes. For a couple galleries, some painter friends . . .

RUSSELL: So who do you like? You know. Who's working now . . .

PETER: Not Schnabel.

RUSSELL *(laughs):* **Me neither . . .**

We shift our attention to Michael, Melissa, and Elliot. Melissa opens her portfolio.

MICHAEL: **So what'd you bring?**

MELISSA: **Stuff. Examples of everything. I'm not going to em-barrass you . . .**

Her attention shifts to Russell and Peter, who are in flowing mid-conversation.

PETER: **But I do like Clemente . . .**

RUSSELL: **Me too.**

PETER: **I know. I've seen your work, in that group show at P.S. 1, right?**

MELISSA *(chimes in):* **Tell him about the *new* show—**

MICHAEL *(packing up):* **We'll be in the conference room . . .**

PETER: **Two minutes, okay?**

Michael, Elliot, and Melissa go out into the hallway, Melissa once more "casually" clocking what's going on between Russell and Peter, neither of whom are aware of her.

PETER: **Look, what I said about the Clemente thing? It's not an insult . . .**

RUSSELL: **I didn't take it as one.**

INT. DAA—MICHAEL'S OFFICE—DAY

Melissa gets her things ready to leave. Russell and Peter, looking through slides, are seen through the window.

MELISSA: **You really think he liked me? Drentell?**

MICHAEL: **Yeah. I think he liked you . . . Who knows? You may wind up on a retainer . . .**

MELISSA: **I hate that word. I always think of a night brace . . . And he didn't really like me. He just pretended to be-cause I'm your cousin and you gave him five dollars.**

MICHAEL: **Fine. He hated you. What did *you* think of *him?***

MELISSA: He's so—I don't know—*tense* . . . You ever notice how the tassels on his loafers are all clenched up? *(indicates Peter) He's* nice . . . They're cute together. They seemed to really hit it off.

MICHAEL: But Russell's gay.

MELISSA: So's Peter.

MICHAEL: He is? How do *you* know?

MELISSA: I thought he might be a Possible for Ellyn. So I told him about her, and he said he was gay.

MICHAEL: Melissa—if someone told *me* about Ellyn *I'd* say I was gay . . .

MELISSA: Come on! Don't you guys ever talk about your personal lives?

MICHAEL: I'm married. I don't have a personal life.

MELISSA: Michael—say something to Russell. About Peter.

MICHAEL: Say something? Like what?

MELISSA: Look. It's all the same. Just come up with a variation on "Get a load of those knockers . . ." Now can I have the ladies-room key?

He holds the key over her head, tormenting her.

MICHAEL: Hold it. Speaking of personal lives—when do we meet Lee?

MELISSA *(waffling):* I don't know. You know. Soon.

MICHAEL *(pins her down):* Tuesday. You're invited. We'll have supper and then watch *Harold and Maude.*

MELISSA: Tuesday, huh?

MICHAEL *(gives her key):* Tuesday.

MELISSA *(indicates Russell):* Talk to him.

She goes. Through the window Michael sees Russell and Peter shake hands. Peter goes back to work. As Russell is on his way out he passes Michael's office.

RUSSELL: You seen Melissa?

MICHAEL: She'll be back in a second. Come on in . . .

RUSSELL: Okay . . .

MICHAEL: So . . .

RUSSELL: Yeah.

MICHAEL *(super-casual)*: Great guy. Peter, I mean.

RUSSELL *(surprised, but—)*: Yeah. He is . . .

MICHAEL: So—

This is uncharted territory for Michael, so he gets very guylike and gives Russell a butch shot on the arm.

MICHAEL: Hey . . .

RUSSELL *(whatever)*: Hey.

MICHAEL *(a brief pause)*: He's nice-looking, too. Peter, I mean—

RUSSELL: You think so?

MICHAEL: Oh, yes. I do.

RUSSELL: Have you talked to Hope about this?

MICHAEL *(drops the pretense)*: This is totally weird for me, am I, like, completely embarrassing you here?

RUSSELL: No. I'm just surprised. I thought Melissa was the yenta.

And she returns.

MELISSA: What?

MICHAEL AND RUSSELL: Nothing . . .

INT.—MICHAEL AND HOPE'S BEDROOM—DAY

Melissa entertains Janey as Hope strips the bed.

HOPE: So can you come Tuesday?

MELISSA: Don't make a big fuss, Hope—

HOPE: I'm not. It's just us . . .

Melissa passes Hope a pillowcase.

HOPE: Thanks . . . So how is it? *(on Melissa's look)* You know . . . Lee.

MELISSA: Good. Lee is good. It's—I don't know. It's hard to talk about . . .

Hope sits with a stack of pillowcases and pillows. For a moment the two women are silent. Then:

MELISSA: He's twenty-three. Lee is.

HOPE: I know . . .

MELISSA: And I'm not. Obviously. I've been through more. You know. And some of it . . . Experience, it's supposed to teach you, and make you wise. And with him—it melts away, everything I've learned . . . And when I'm with him? And he's inside me? It's like—

Well, she doesn't know what it's like, really, but she *does,* and Hope does, too. And, for a moment, these two articulate women revel in the sharing of something for which they can't—and don't want to—find words. Hope is the first to break the spell.

HOPE: Does he have a friend?

Hope expects a laugh; instead, the mood changes, as Melissa projects onto Hope her own doubts and self-judgment.

HOPE: But he's much too young. What's wrong with you? There has to be something *seriously* wrong with you . . .

It's over. We realize that, for Hope, there has been a gap since she asked "Does he have a friend?"

HOPE: Melissa?

MELISSA *(quick):* I haven't met his friends . . .

HOPE: Whatever. It sounds great.

MELISSA: I know.

INT. MELISSA'S LOFT—NIGHT

Melissa and Lee have just made love. She reaches out to stroke his hair. He takes her hand, kisses it, then sits up and starts to dress.

MELISSA: What are you doing?

LEE: Putting my clothes on.

MELISSA: I know you're putting your clothes on. It's just—oh, you know—

LEE: Just what?

MELISSA: It's just you usually *stay* is what. You know. After. And then after we usually—

LEE: What?

MELISSA: There's another after. Lee, come on, what do you want me to say here?

LEE: That you don't want to sleep without me. That you want me here tonight.

MELISSA: You know I feel that—

LEE: *How* do I know? How can I know if you don't tell me? Am I supposed to be, like, really perceptive? Read between the lines all the time?

MELISSA: Lee? Forget the lines. There *are* no lines. I want you here tonight. Okay?

The phone rings. Melissa makes no move to get it.

LEE: You gonna get that?

MELISSA: No. It's probably work.

LEE: What if it's a friend? You never talk to your friends when I'm here.

MELISSA: I happen to like being with you.

LEE: Great. *I* like being with *you.*

MELISSA: Great—

LEE: But I also like my friends—

MELISSA (*trying to keep up*): Me too. I mean, I like mine—

LEE: And they know about you. My friends. They saw your picture, they think you're really pretty.

MELISSA (*worried*): Which picture?

LEE: The one you gave me—

MELISSA: Oh my God . . . you mean the one in the turtleneck?

LEE: Do your friends know about me?

MELISSA: Of course they do!

LEE *(not so sure):* Oh. Okay.

MELISSA: You don't believe me, do you?

LEE: Melissa—I believe you—

MELISSA: Because it just so happens that Tuesday night—*(dives in)* Tuesday night—I'm invited to my friends' house for supper. On Tuesday. And I want you to come. If you want to. You have any plans Tuesday night?

LEE: I'll check my book.

MELISSA: Great. Okay.

There's a pause.

LEE: Melissa?

MELISSA: Yes?

LEE: I don't have a book.

MELISSA: I know. So are you busy?

LEE: Tuesday?

MELISSA: Yeah.

LEE: What time?

MELISSA: Seven. *(a brief pause)*—ish.

LEE: You sure you want to do this?

MELISSA: Why wouldn't I?

LEE: It's just—Tuesdays. We've never seen each other on a Tuesday. It's Friday, Saturday, Sunday, period. Your rules. And what if we like it? What if the occasional Wednesday slipped in there? Would that be okay?

MELISSA: Why not? I mean I should maybe *think* about it, but—

LEE *(cuts her off):* Try not to. Then maybe it might happen. Just don't think . . . Can you try that for me?

A pause.

MELISSA: I can try.

ACT TWO

INT. RUSSELL'S LOFT—DAY

Melissa circles Russell with her camera as he works on a large canvas.

RUSSELL: Just don't show that I paint by numbers, okay?

MELISSA: Okay . . . Now hold it . . . don't move . . . and look spontaneous . . .

RUSSELL (*as he obeys*): How's Lee?

MELISSA: He's fine . . . This is great light, it's Vermeer light, just tilt your head a little this way . . .

RUSSELL *(notices her hesitation):* But . . . ?

MELISSA: But what?

RUSSELL: Come on! You didn't leave a little "but" dangling in the air?

MELISSA: No. Lee's fine. Maybe we could splatter some paint on your face . . . would that look stupid?

RUSSELL: Melissa—

MELISSA *(sighs, lowers her camera):* Okay. We're having dinner with Hope and Michael. And he's never met any of my friends. Except Gary. Who doesn't count. Because I don't care about the opinion of someone I've slept with. *(on his look)* Don't probe that.

RUSSELL: When's it happening?

MELISSA: Tonight.

RUSSELL: You nervous?

MELISSA: Of course. They're my best friends . . .

RUSSELL: And *nobody* judges you like your best friends. You know what I'm doing tonight? Peter Montefiore's coming here for dinner . . .

MELISSA *(nonchalant):* He is?

RUSSELL: We're going to look at my stuff, talk about the catalog . . .

MELISSA: Great. He's really nice . . .

RUSSELL: Yeah. I guess . . .

MELISSA: You're out of the light . . .

RUSSELL *(steps in; casual):* You don't think he's attractive or anything, do you?

MELISSA: Who—Peter? Very.

RUSSELL: Don't you think he's sort of queeny?

MELISSA: Queeny? Not at all.

RUSSELL: Secretly he is. I can tell. He's going to show up with a tape of *Sweeney Todd* probably. And anyway he's not my type. **Maybe we should both have headaches tonight. You won't have to humiliate yourself at Hope and Michael's, I won't have to suffer through an evening with Peter. What do you say?**

A pause. Russell's self-deprecation has set off an identical chemical response in Melissa.

MELISSA: I'm out of film.

EXT. LOCKSMITH SHOP—DAY

Melissa stands outside the locksmith shop, her keys in her hand. She looks in the window, and we look in with her, ending on a close-up of a key being ground. Melissa tosses the keys in the air, catches them, and walks on.

EXT. STEADMAN HOUSE—NIGHT

Melissa and Lee drive up to the house. Lee is excited, clearly pleased to be part of this evening. Melissa checks her makeup in the rearview mirror.

MELISSA: I look okay?

LEE: You *always* do. I love how you look—

MELISSA: You're prejudiced. Try to imagine a cold, harsh, judgmental light . . .

Lee goes on praising her, but his voice fades as a radio voice rises, seemingly addressing a horrified Melissa.

RADIO VOICE: Tonight's subject is Older Women and Younger Men. If you're a pathetic old crone who's robbed the cradle recently, we'd like to hear from you—

She quickly turns off the radio, snapping the spine of her own internalized fantasy, as—

LEE: It's me. Right?

MELISSA: You?

LEE: Yeah, it's scary, I know that, the first time the "partner" meets the "friends" . . .

MELISSA *(lying):* It's not that at all—

LEE: I swear—I won't shoot off any caps, or make fart sounds, or steal any really valuable stuff. Cub Scout's Honor.

MELISSA: I was really liking it till you threw in those Cub Scouts. Come on . . .

They make their way to the front door. Melissa rings the bell. Hope answers it, and kisses and hellos are exchanged.

HOPE *(friendly):* I'm Hope . . . and I'm assuming you're—

LEE: You're assuming correctly. It's nice to meet you . . .

HOPE: You too. Come on in . . .

Hope and Lee go inside. Michael lingers on the porch with Melissa to savor the embarrassment he knows she's feeling.

MICHAEL: So that's Lee.

MELISSA: Yes. That is. That's Lee.

MICHAEL: He's really, *really* great.

MELISSA: Thank you. I'm going home now.

But he pulls her inside with him . . .

INT. STEADMAN HOUSE—LIVING ROOM—NIGHT

Hope takes Lee's coat as Melissa floats briefly away to consider the scene in the Steadman living room. We don't yet see what she does.

LEE: Great house . . .

HOPE: It was until *we* got it. Can I get you something to drink?

LEE: Great . . . It's really nice of you, to have us over—

HOPE: Well, we've been really wanting to meet you . . .

And now we see what Melissa sees. This is quite a gathering. In the living room are Michael, Ellyn, Nancy, Elliot, and Gary. They all wave hellos at Melissa. She ducks back.

MELISSA: Hope, can I ask you a quick question? *(to Lee)* I'll be right back . . .

She pulls Hope into the dining room.

MELISSA: You said it would just be us! Your living room is filled with every registered Democrat in the tristate area!

HOPE: I know, but Nancy called, and Ellyn wasn't busy, so I thought I might as well call Gary and Susannah, only the baby has a little cold so Susannah couldn't come—

MELISSA: Give me some food. I'll drive it over to her—

HOPE *(teasing her)*: You're nervous. It's so cute to be nervous. I was *incredibly* nervous when Michael met my parents—

MELISSA: Hope? You are not my parents. You are my friends. Which is much, much worse!

HOPE: Oh come on, he's completely adorable—

MELISSA: Adorable. Great. Couldn't you have used an adjective like "imposing"? Or "statesmanlike"?

HOPE *(soothing her)*: Have a drink and calm down. I'll be out in a minute . . .

As Hope goes into the kitchen Melissa quickly downs both glasses of wine.

INT. STEADMAN HOUSE—LIVING ROOM—NIGHT

We are now about to dive into a Parallel Universe, in which Melissa's internalized self-judgment transforms reality. The following interactions are fractured; we don't sense them arising from real time. Melissa's growing discomfort and embarrassment impose their own temporal rules.

A) Lee chats with Michael. He sees Melissa looking at him and smiles at her. She smiles back—and then zeroes in on what she thinks they might be saying. Lee lights a match.

LEE *(to Michael)*: Have you ever seen a match burn twice?

MICHAEL: No, Lee.

Lee blows out the match, then touches Michael's arm with it.

LEE: Now you have!

MICHAEL: That's really funny, Lee.

LEE: And your epidermis is showing.

MICHAEL: Yes. I know.

LEE: Excuse me—did you just cut one?

Ellyn slides in next to Melissa, breaking her free from her vision.

ELLYN: You look so great . . .

MELISSA: Thanks . . .

ELLYN: I haven't seen you for ages . . . You want another drink?

MELISSA: Great . . .

B) Moments later. As Melissa spots Lee and Elliot in conversation on the stairs, Hope passes on her way into the kitchen.

HOPE: See? This isn't so bad, everyone really likes him . . .

As Hope passes off, Melissa zeroes in on Lee and Gary.

GARY: How's the cellulite? She's probably got a lot of it by now . . . (*shows on his own body*) Kind of bunched up here? Sorta cottage-cheesy?

LEE: Yeah. But give her a break. She's almost thirty—

GARY: Excuse me—almost thirty?

Nancy brushes by Melissa and reality returns.

NANCY (*re Lee*): You've got great taste . . .

MELISSA: Oh! Thanks.

And now the moments start to fly past . . .

C) LEE and ELLYN
As she writes out her address for him . . .

ELLYN: I'll be in a black negligee with a riding crop, and *you'll* come in dressed as the phone man. Got it?

D) LEE talking to NANCY AND HOPE . . .

HOPE (*trying to get it right*): Okay . . . She says, "Now baby, do it to me now"?

NANCY (*confused*): Wait . . . is it "Now, baby, baby, do it to me now"? Are there two "baby's" in there?

HOPE (*corrects her*): No, see, what she says is "Baby, do it to me now, baby . . ." So there's a baby at the beginning and at the end . . .

Hope and Nancy give it a whirl.

HOPE AND NANCY: "Baby, do it to me now, baby!"

They are thrilled with their rain-in-Spain success.

LEE: You got it! She does it every time—like a cuckoo clock.

HOPE: Well—I guess we should eat!

Melissa comes to. Lee gets up, passes her, and hugs her.

MELISSA: We won't stay late . . .

LEE: Why not? I'm having a great time!

INT. STEADMAN HOUSE—DINING ROOM—NIGHT

Everyone is seated. Platters of food go from Hope to Michael to Gary to Elliot to Ellyn to Nancy—and at last to Melissa. She gets down to business: cutting Lee's dinner into little pieces and serving it to him in his high chair.

HOPE: Pitiful . . .

ELLYN: So inappropriate . . .

INT. RUSSELL'S LOFT—NIGHT

Peter surveys the paintings Russell has arranged around the loft.

PETER: You know what might be interesting? To maybe organize the whole thing, you know, not chronologically but emotionally . . .

RUSSELL: I'm not sure what you mean . . .

PETER: Like these here . . . They sort of feel like they were painted by a stranger. You know. In the world . . . They're not sentimental, they're more—melancholy, I guess. Not much color. The figures are isolated . . .

RUSSELL: I've never thought of that.

PETER: Good. You're not supposed to think. Just paint . . . And I should go. Can I give you something for the pizza?

RUSSELL: No way. You're my guest . . .

PETER: Then I owe you one. Without anchovies next time . . .

Russell considers his work as Peter gets ready to go.

RUSSELL: You know what?

PETER: What?

RUSSELL: What you said . . . I see it, these ones—they *are* different—

PETER: Right, your work changes, it develops—

RUSSELL: Right, and when I did these . . . I was in love when I did these. So there's that. So you're perceptive. *(a brief pause)* Look—you want some ice cream or something? Or some wine? As a Perceptivity Prize?

PETER: Okay.

As Russell takes a bottle of wine from the refrigerator, Peter checks out some drawings Russell's hung in the kitchen.

PETER: I like these . . .

RUSSELL: Thanks . . .

PETER: When did you do them?

RUSSELL: About a year ago . . . You gonna keep your coat on?

Peter takes his coat off and hands it to Russell. They are, by now, very close to each other. Russell kisses him.

RUSSELL: Is this okay?

PETER: It's okay.

EXT. STEADMAN HOUSE—FRONT PORCH—NIGHT

Rain falls, and it's time for good-byes, and everyone seems to be huddled together on the porch waiting to make a run for their car.

GARY *(to Lee):* 'Night . . . *(a whisper just for him)* Treat her right. She deserves it . . .

Gary dashes out into the night.

HOPE *(to Lee):* So we finally did it . . .

LEE: Thanks. This was really nice, I had a really good time . . .

MICHAEL: Maybe next week—we could all go to a movie or something?

HOPE *(to Melissa):* **Call us. We'll pick a night.**

MELISSA: **Okay . . .** *(kisses Hope and Michael)* **Thanks . . . I'll talk to you . . .**

Michael and Hope go into the house. Melissa and Lee remain for a final moment on the dry porch.

LEE: **You have a nice time?**

MELISSA *(a shade too enthusiastic):* **Oh yeah . . . I always do here . . .**

She runs out into the rain, leaving him briefly by himself.

LEE: **Good. Good . . .**

INT. RUSSELL'S LOFT—NIGHT

Russell and Peter are in bed together, having just made love. They're in mid-conversational pause, lying back on the pillows.

PETER: **So when did *you* know?**

RUSSELL: **Always, probably. I went through all the standard denial stuff, you know, the requisite Oriental flutist girlfriend—**

PETER: **Mine played the clarinet. She was good, too . . .** *(lights a cigarette)* **Don't say anything, I'm stopping tomorrow—**

RUSSELL: **And then—when I was twenty? I met this guy. And that was it. You know . . . "Two roads diverged in a wood, and I—"**

PETER: **"I took the one less traveled by . . ."**

RUSSELL: **And thank God I'm alive to tell about it.**

PETER: **You can say that again.**

RUSSELL: **So what's it like at work?**

PETER: **Not bad. Most people know, the others just assume from the picture on my desk that I'm married to Bernadette Peters—**

RUSSELL: **Come on—**

PETER: **I just mean I don't believe in making people uncomfortable but I also don't believe in lying, like whenever I**

have to go to a funeral or a memorial service I always say
why . . .

RUSSELL: You lost a lot of friends?

PETER: One very good one, one pretty good one, one friend of
a friend. And I have one who's sick right now—

RUSSELL: Me too. I've lost three, too. And I know one who's
sick . . . You read the obituaries first every day?

PETER: Of course. Then I check out the Sixers, do the
crossword, and greet the day with a smile . . .

RUSSELL: Somebody's got to.

PETER: Right.

Another pause.

RUSSELL: If you had a choice to do it over again, would you be,
you know, boring question, straight?

PETER: Well sure, it'd be easier . . . I mean being gay, you
know, sometimes it's like walking into this huge party
where you don't know anyone and you can't find the
person who invited you. You know what I mean?

Another pause. Russell looks at Peter now.

PETER: What?

RUSSELL: You.

PETER: What about me?

RUSSELL: You know what I like about you?

PETER: Tell me.

RUSSELL: Your last name.

PETER (*full Italian pronunciation*): Montefiore . . .

RUSSELL (*repeats it perfectly*): Montefiore . . .

PETER: It means "mountain of flowers" . . .

RUSSELL (*gently*): Hey. I've been to Italy . . . I know what it
means . . .

They move closer, into each other's arms . . .

EXT. MELISSA'S ALLEY—NIGHT

And Melissa and Lee move apart. They are sitting in his truck. There's one silent moment, then she says something she doesn't mean.

MELISSA: Want to come in?

LEE: You want me to?

MELISSA: Sure . . .

LEE: Really?

MELISSA: Well, I'm sort of tired, but—

LEE: Me too. I'm tired, too . . . So—*(kisses her)* I'll call you tomorrow. We'll both get a good night's sleep. 'Night.

MELISSA: 'Night.

She gets out of the truck. As she turns back to look at him, he's still there. He waves, then drives away, leaving her alone in the alley.

ACT THREE

INT. MELISSA'S DARKROOM

Melissa shows Russell prints of the pictures she did of him.

MELISSA: What do you think? *(on his nonresponse, as he turns to her)* You're nauseous from them.

RUSSELL: No! It's just pictures of me, they always make me think, "I *know* that guy, but do I *want* to know that guy?"

MELISSA: I would. I think they really capture you—

RUSSELL: Yeah. A big fag with a paintbrush.

MELISSA: Russell—

RUSSELL *(looks in the mirror):* It's this haircut, right? *(grabs her, passionately)* Tell me! You think it's the haircut?

MELISSA: I think you're insane.

RUSSELL: Please take another roll? Oh please oh please oh please . . .

INT. MELISSA'S LOFT—DAY

Russell poses as Melissa circles him with her camera.

RUSSELL: See, the thing is that people stereotype you . . .

MELISSA: Look. If you're so worried just stick a shot of Sean Connery in the catalog.

RUSSELL: Yeah. In *Dr. No.* He was really sexy in *Dr. No* . . .

MELISSA: I never saw that. I always thought it was about a therapist . . .

She's out of film. As she reloads . . .

MELISSA: So how was last night? You haven't said anything. How'd it go?

RUSSELL: It went.

MELISSA: That's very revealing. I'm touched by your openness.

RUSSELL: He—you know. He stayed sort of late.

MELISSA: How late?

RUSSELL: The night. He spent it.

He would like to clam up here, but she wants the hot stuff.

MELISSA: And . . . ?

RUSSELL: We slept together.

MELISSA: Really?

RUSSELL: Don't worry. We were safe. We were in different rooms at the time . . . Could we take the pictures?

MELISSA: Russell—that's wonderful. I'm really happy for you—

RUSSELL: Contain yourself. He has love handles.

MELISSA: So? You have a faggy haircut. When are you seeing him again?

RUSSELL: I don't know. Soon . . .

MELISSA: Did you call him?

RUSSELL: Melissa—it's no big deal.

MELISSA: You should call him—

RUSSELL: Fine. Now how was dinner with Ozzie and Harriet?

A brief pause.

MELISSA: Delicious.

RUSSELL: That bad, huh?

MELISSA: Get over here. I don't want to lose the light . . .

INT. MELISSA'S LOFT—DARKROOM

Melissa scans images on a contact sheet— Melissa and Lee together; Lee alone; an accidentally double-exposed frame, like a Duane Michals photograph, in which Melissa is alone while the "ghost" of Lee walks away. Distant saxophone music is heard but she doesn't quite tune in to it and just works on.

INT. MELISSA'S LOFT—NIGHT

Melissa emerges from the darkroom. The saxophone music is louder in here but she still doesn't relate it to herself. She may even unconsciously hum along as she goes to dump the garbage, opening the front door to find Lee. She closes the door. He plays a note or two more, and she once again opens the door.

LEE: Hi. I'm here to annoy you.

MELISSA: Do you have any idea how many guys have stood out in this alley playing sax for me?

LEE: How many?

MELISSA: You're the first . . .

She has no choice right now but to lean forward and give him a kiss.

MELISSA: Hi . . .

LEE: I came out of pity. You said you had to work, I thought some Chinese food might cheer you up . . .

Okay. Does she ask him to come in and share it with her?

MELISSA: I ate . . .

LEE: Oh . . .

MELISSA: But it's really sweet of you . . . *(a brief pause)* You want to come in or something?

LEE: You know what'll happen. It's been a few days, I haven't seen you, and there's all those hormones and stuff . . . How's it going?

MELISSA: Slow. You know.

LEE: You think you might be done tomorrow?

MELISSA: Maybe—

LEE: Because Hope and Michael said maybe we could all go to a movie—

MELISSA: That might be nice—

LEE: I just thought you might need a break—

MELISSA: I do, but there's Russell's show, and some stuff I'm doing for Michael—

He doesn't need to hear her words anymore, and neither do we. What he *sees* is his version of her Duane Michals moment. As she's talking her ghost leaves her body and goes into the loft. Her voice returns . . .

MELISSA: And we'll go to the movies next week. Just pick a night . . .

A pause.

LEE: I'll do that.

He starts to leave when she calls after him.

MELISSA: Thanks for the dinner!

LEE: I got you spring rolls . . .

MELISSA: Great. They're my favorite.

LEE: Yeah. I know.

INT. GALLERY—DAY

Where Russell is to have his show; a scan of the space ends with Melissa, who sees two gallery assistants moving in a canvas.

MELISSA: Excuse me—is Russell Weller around? I was supposed to meet him here . . .

FIRST ASSISTANT: He had to go out. He'll be back soon . . .

MELISSA: Thanks. Thank you . . .

She examines the painting they've just put down.

MAN'S VOICE: Melissa?

And turns to discover Peter Montefiore.

MELISSA: Peter. Hi . . . How are you?

PETER (*feels need to explain*): It was lunchtime, so I thought I'd
stick my head in. You know—

MELISSA: I know. I'm waiting for him, too.

PETER: Right . . .

She senses that it hasn't been easy for Peter to come here and put
himself out like this. Peter quickly shifts gears.

PETER: I was going to call you . . . those pictures you did for
the campaign? They were great.

MELISSA: Thanks . . . Want to see something? I've got the
studio shots I did of Russell . . .

PETER (*casual, as he looks*): How is he?

MELISSA (*tests the water*): He had a really nice time with you . . .

PETER *(surprised):* Really? I mean that's nice . . . These are good, Melissa—

MELISSA: You think?

PETER: Well—they're maybe a little posed, maybe. I kind of like stuff—you know. Messier. Which isn't an insult—

MELLISSA: I'm not insulted. I agree.

PETER: And if he's not here I should go, I've got a meeting. Nice to see you . . .

MELISSA: Thanks. You too . . .

He's on his way out when—

MELISSA: Peter? This is totally none of my business, but—has he called you? Russell, I mean?

PETER: I've been impossible to reach, *he's* been trying to get stuff done for the show—

MELISSA: Okay. I was just curious. Or nosy. Or whatever.

PETER: Melissa? Things like this—they cool out sometimes. It's nobody's fault. You know what I mean?

MELISSA *(she does):* I know what you mean.

INT. ELLYN'S APARTMENT—DAY

As Ellyn watches, Lee checks out her apartment. He opens the blinds, letting in light as he consults paint samples.

ELLYN: What do you think? It's hopeless, right?

LEE: Well, it's a condo . . .

ELLYN *(what's he getting at?):* Of course it is. You're absolutely right—

LEE: And condo is like a synonym—is that the right word?

ELLYN: What? Synonym? It depends. A synonym has the same meaning as—

LEE: Right, it's like a synonym for bland—condo—no offense—so you probably want some color.

ELLYN: Either that or move. I'm just kidding. Yes. I'd like some color.

LEE: Were you thinking of doing something soon?

ELLYN: When are you available?

LEE: Tomorrow—or in a month.

ELLYN: How about tomorrow?

LEE (*offers her color chips*): Then you should look at these. You could do the moldings one color, and the walls another. Like I like—this is just an example—I like how these two go together. They're really different but they sort of make sense if you don't think about it too hard . . .

ELLYN: It's sort of like what you did with Melissa's place. Which I love . . .

LEE: Well, sometimes, you get a feeling about someone. So that tells you . . . you know . . . how to go.

ELLYN (*casual*): You must have a great feeling about her.

LEE: Yeah, well . . . So what I should do is leave this here with you, and you can do some thinking.

ELLYN: Okay . . .

LEE: You're really good friends with her, right?

ELLYN: Right. I am. I love Melissa.

LEE: That's good. You should.

ELLYN (*laughs*): Okay . . .

LEE: That came out wrong. All I mean is—see, the thing about her is—

But what's in his eyes right now says all that needs to be said. He shows Ellyn a color.

LEE: Here. Think about this one. I've got a feeling about this one . . .

INT. MELISSA'S LOFT—NIGHT

Dinner cooks on the stove; the table sparkles with Melissa's best efforts; all is in order as she sits alone, examining a fingernail. We take a look at her desired projections of what the coming evening will bring.

A) INT. MELISSA'S LOFT—NIGHT (FANTASY)

Melissa and Lee face each other over the candlelit table.

MELISSA: Then we'll end this as friends. I know that's what *I* want . . .

B) INT. MELISSA'S LOFT—NIGHT (FANTASY)

Moving closer . . .

MELISSA: This isn't your fault, Lee. It's mine. I know myself too well . . .

C) INT. MELISSA'S LOFT—NIGHT (FANTASY)

And closer still . . .

MELISSA: Call me. I'm always here for you . . .

A knock on the door shatters this last idealization. She goes to answer it, and—of course—it's Lee.

MELISSA: Hi . . .

LEE: How are you?

MELISSA: I'm great—and a pot's boiling over . . . *(as she goes to the stove)* Will you put some music on?

She attends to her cooking responsibilities, assuming he'll pick a tape. He just stands there, watching her. As, with a social smile, she turns to him:

MELISSA: Anything you want . . .

LEE: *You* choose.

MELISSA: Okay . . . Have some wine . . .

As she puts on a tape he checks out the table and the food. She notices this.

MELISSA: It must seem weird . . .

LEE: I guess. We usually order out . . .

MELISSA: I'll put it all in a pizza box, you can tip me two bucks. Would that be better?

LEE *(shrugs)*: I don't know.

Her little joke has fallen flat. A brief pause, then she takes a bowl of salad from the refrigerator.

MELISSA *(making chitchat)*: Ellyn says you're painting her place . . .

LEE: Maybe.

MELISSA: That's really great—

LEE: What's going on, Melissa?

MELISSA: We're going to have dinner is what's going on, so—

LEE: What's going on?

MELISSA: Maybe I'm not so hungry after all. I guess I could freeze these lamb chops—

He rips off a sheet of wax paper, startling her.

LEE: Here.

MELISSA: Thanks. Maybe just the salad?

He doesn't answer. He just looks at her, waiting for her to answer his original question. She knows this—

MELISSA: Okay. "What's Going On." Okay . . .

—and prepares herself to be the portrait of Reason.

MELISSA: What's going on—is a problem, not with *you*, it's with *me*—which I want to handle right because I never do. Handle it right. Because the way I am—

LEE *(stopping her)*: Okay. I get it—

MELISSA: You don't even know what I'm going to say—

LEE: I can guess!

MELISSA: Lee, give me a little credit, I've thought a lot about this—

LEE: Right—and you want to be nice, you don't want to hurt me, but if this is it for us—

MELISSA: I didn't say that—

LEE: —If this is it, it's sloppy, it's not candles and little lamb chops . . . And it's not "nice," I don't feel really "nice" right now. How about you?

MELISSA: I don't know how I feel . . .

LEE: Then I think we should call it quits.

MELISSA: Quits? How did we get to quits? I buy a few lamb chops and we're calling it quits? Wait a second! What are you doing?

LEE: Making it easy for you—

MELISSA: Making it *easy?*

LEE: Yeah! Just end it now! So starting tomorrow you can look for a guy your friends will "approve" of—

MELISSA: My friends have nothing to do with this!

LEE: They *do!* They see me, they think I'll hurt you, right? I'll dump you, because you're old! That's what you *think* they think, right?

MELISSA: Okay! Right! You want to be right? You are! Yes, they were all judging me that night, and *they* were right. And I know just what they were thinking—

LEE: Yeah. That you've really got to hate yourself—to be with a guy like me.

He's right. She knows it. The air goes out of the balloon. A brief pause, then:

MELISSA: You don't know what you're talking about, Lee . . .

LEE: All I know—I just know that nobody's watching, Melissa. And nobody cares.

As she takes this in, we fade out.

ACT FOUR

INT. MELISSA'S LOFT—NIGHT

Right where we left off: Lee shuts the door, and the keys shake as they dangle from the lock. Melissa blows out the candles on her beautifully set table . . .

And now, to the sound of distant cheers, we swing around to discover a sign on the wall. It's a list of fights, and a spotlight picks out the one we're most interested in: MELISSA "THE JUDGE" STEADMAN *VS.* "KID MELISSA" as we dissolve to:

INT. BOXING RING—BLACK AND WHITE

Michael's the announcer for tonight's fight.

MICHAEL: Ladies and gentlemen . . . In our main event title bout—the purse bein' the domination of Melissa's soul—the contenders are . . .

We swing with his pointed finger to a corner of the ring to find Melissa in a white sequinned robe. Her trainer, Ellyn, rubs her down.

MICHAEL: Introducing—in white trunks! Weighing in at a hundred and four thanks to her aerobics class this morning—the challenger—Melissa "The Kid" Steadman!

This Melissa (hereafter referred to as The Kid) timidly advances to the center of the ring. She raises her gloved hand for the wimpiest of waves, then retreats to her corner.

MICHAEL: Introducing—in black trunks and a halter top, weighing one hundred and six and a half—the world champion—Melissa "The Judge" Steadman!

Michael points to the other side of the ring. *This* Melissa (hereafter referred to as The Judge) wears a black sequinned robe. Hope is her trainer. The Judge struts out and the crowd explodes. The Judge taunts the Kid.

THE JUDGE: Hey! Girlie! Where's your little boyfriend? *(for the crowd's amusement)* Oh Lee! Kiss me, baby! *(direct to the crowd)* She's right! He is a baby! Right?

CROWD: Yeah! Kill her!

THE KID *(small):* He makes me happy . . .

THE JUDGE *(to the crowd):* He makes her happy! Awwwwww . . . Baby want a bottle? Ha? Cootchie-cootchie-coo?

THE KID: It just so happens that Lee has many positive qualities!

THE JUDGE: He's half your age, why shouldn't he? *(to the crowd)* Right?

CROWD: Right!

IN THE PRESS SECTION

Elliot is tonight's radio commentator.

ELLIOT: And the hostilities are about to start, ladies and gentlemen, as it is— *(DING!)* Round one . . .

And now—The Kid and The Judge go at it. And it's ugly, and it's painful, and it's bloody, and—

ELLIOT: A left to the jaw from The Judge! And a right to the jaw! And a left and a—

CROWD: Kill her! Maul her!

Russell leaps up from the crowd.

RUSSELL: Kid! I tried to warn ya!

In the ring, The Judge moves in.

THE JUDGE: And you shoulda listened! 'Cause wherever you go, whatever you do—I'll be there to judge you! There's not nothin' you can pull over on me—and no way to shut me up!

ELLIOT: And The Judge is in there! She's flattening The Kid!

The Kid's dazed attention wanders to the crowd, where she picks out Lee. Ellyn, in a lather, jumps out from the corner.

ELLYN: What are you lookin' out there for? Fight who's in the ring, for Chrissake!

ELLIOT: And a right to the head! And a left to the head! And a right and a left and a right and a left—

DING!

ELLIOT: And that is the end of round one—as the bloody Kid retreats to her corner.

The Judge struts proudly around her corner of the ring, signing autographs, posing for pictures. The Kid slumps down exhausted as Ellyn rubs her down.

THE KID: I'm not gonna win this one. I know it . . .

ELLYN *(fevered)*: You lose *this* fight, Kid—and all you got is a ten-cent token to Palookaville! Ya hear me? *(DING!)* Now get out there and *fight*!!

The two Melissas go back into the ring and the fight starts again.

ELLYN: Remember what I tole ya!

THE KID: What's that!

ELLYN: He made you happy! Say it!!

THE KID: He made me happy!

ELLYN: And what else?

THE KID: I forget!

ELLYN: He made ya feel loved! Say it!

THE KID: He made me feel—

THE JUDGE (*sneers*): You're up against The Judge now, pal! "Loved" and "happy" ain't enough!!

And over in the Press Section:

ELLIOT: Ladies and gentlemen! What you are seeing tonight is the longest fight in history! Thirty-three years, ladies and gentlemen! And no end in sight! All bets are off and—

DING!

IN THE CROWD

we pick out Melissa for the first time, watching her own battle against herself. Suddenly the crowd around her gets up to go.

MELISSA: Hey! Who won? Will somebody tell me who won? I got a lot of money riding on this fight!

But no one tells her, for no one can.

INT. RUSSELL'S LOFT—DAY

Russell takes a break from wrapping canvases to check the results of his second sitting with Melissa. He holds up a photograph.

RUSSELL: This one.

MELISSA (*not so sure*): Well—it's your show.

RUSSELL: What's wrong with it?

MELISSA: It's *posed*. Maybe I like the faggy ones better.

RUSSELL: But I don't.

MELISSA: Great. Then this is it.

RUSSELL: I'll get it to the gallery, they want it for the printer's. I just want to wrap a few more of these . . .

MELISSA: I was there the other day. It's a great space . . .

RUSSELL: Could you help me with this?

MELISSA *(as she helps him):* I saw Peter there. He was looking for you . . .

He moves another painting out for wrapping.

MELISSA: He ever actually do any work on the catalog?

RUSSELL: He had some ideas . . .

MELISSA: So that's it?

RUSSELL *(preoccupied):* What?

MELISSA: For him. You were going to "see what happened." So I guess nothing did? Happen?

RUSSELL *(looks at her):* Melissa . . . I appreciate it, your being interested, but I can look after myself . . .

MELISSA: Oh. Okay.

RUSSELL *(nettled now):* I mean I don't get into your stuff, you don't get into mine . . .

MELISSA *(bold):* But you do.

RUSSELL: Come on! I never give advice! I mean, look at me—

MELISSA: I *do*. And I think *I* like what *I* see, more than you do. Like what you see. Oh, I don't know what I mean—

RUSSELL: I think you do—

MELISSA: Well, I think you like Peter Montefiore—

RUSSELL: Melissa—

MELISSA: And I think that's scary for you, and you don't know what to do about it so you don't do anything—

RUSSELL: Yeah? Well maybe I don't know what to do, but *you* don't know what you're talking about! You just don't know what it's like—

MELISSA: What? To be gay? In a lousy time?

RUSSELL: This isn't the time to make attachments, Melissa! I mean, look at what's going on out there!

MELISSA: I know. People are dying. It must be incredibly scary . . .

RUSSELL: You're right! It is!

MELISSA: But I don't think that's what this is about. *(chooses a picture)* This one—*this* is you. It's lumpy, and it's goofy, and it's real—and I don't think you like it much. I don't know, maybe you never have . . . You think if he really saw this, if Peter did, if *anybody* did, then that would be it, right? I don't know . . . I just think that there's *never* been a right time to "make attachments . . ."

Somehow, through this, they have moved closer together. He looks at her, then looks away, then she holds up the picture she likes.

MELISSA *(gently)*: Trust me. This one. It's you.

INT. MELISSA'S LOFT—DAY

The golden hour, just before night falls. Melissa puts on a record, and we let the music take us to—

INT. ELLYN'S APARTMENT—DAY

Where Lee paints a wall. And as, with the music, we move off from him—

INT. DAA—NIGHT

We find Peter, working late. He picks up a slide and holds it to the light. The slide shows one of Russell's paintings, and from this we go to—

INT. GALLERY—DAY

where the actual painting hangs on the wall. Russell hands his photograph to the gallery assistant. It's the one Melissa liked.

RUSSELL: This one . . .

ASSISTANT: Nice. Nice haircut . . .

RUSSELL *(smiles)*: Thanks . . .

EXT. KEY SHOP—DAY

Melissa lingers outside the key shop, deciding whether or not to go in. She throws her keys up in the air, catches them—and goes inside.

INT. DAA—PETER'S OFFICE—DAY

A catalog lands on a desk. On its cover is a familiar painting and the name "Russell Weller." Peter looks up to see Russell standing in the doorway to his office.

RUSSELL: Hot off the press . . .

PETER: Looks nice.

RUSSELL: Yeah. It came out pretty good, didn't it? They used a lot of your ideas.

PETER: Great—

RUSSELL: So, I just wanted to thank you . . .

PETER: Anytime—

RUSSELL: And also—*(hands him a card)* The opening's Thursday . . . you're probably busy—

PETER: I am—

RUSSELL: Well, it's going to be there for six weeks—

PETER: But I can change it. The thing I have to do. I mean I can try. Make a few calls.

RUSSELL: Then maybe I'll see you there.

PETER: You nervous?

RUSSELL: I don't know. Yes. Totally . . .

PETER: Don't be. You're good.

RUSSELL: Yeah?

PETER: Yeah.

RUSSELL: Thanks.

PETER: Thanks for the invitation. *(holds up catalog)* And for this . . .

RUSSELL: Can I call you?

PETER: You can call me.

RUSSELL: It won't work out.

PETER: I know. Nothing does. But call anyway . . .

Elliot passes by in the hall.

ELLIOT: Drentell Alert, Drentell Alert . . .

PETER: You should leave, I'm going to start spouting demographics . . .

RUSSELL: See ya, Peter . . .

He starts to go when—

PETER: Russell . . . ?

Russell turns back to him.

PETER: Good luck.

INT. ELLYN'S APARTMENT—DAY

Lee does touchups on his paint job. Melissa enters, standing for a moment at the open door.

LEE *(thinking it's Ellyn)*: Hi . . . what are you doing home?

MELISSA: I'm not Ellyn.

LEE: I know.

MELISSA: I know you know. So . . . The door was open.

LEE: Fumes.

MELISSA: Right.

She takes a step inside and looks around.

MELISSA: It's weird. I've never been here when she wasn't here . . . *(sees Ellyn's datebook)* If I looked in her datebook, would you tell?

LEE: No . . .

MELISSA: She'd figure it out anyway . . . *(looks around)* It looks great here. You've done a really great job . . .

LEE: Well, sometimes, you know, you get a feeling about someone . . .

MELISSA: And what's your feeling, Lee?

A pause. He looks at her, shrugs.

LEE: Hard to say.

MELISSA: Okay.

LEE: It's just—hard to say.

MELISSA: Okay. *(a brief pause)* I know what mine is.

LEE: Yeah?

MELISSA: It's also hard to say, but—maybe I should try. You want me to?

Lee's gesture could be translated as "It's a free country."

MELISSA: I miss you. I know that . . .

She digs in her bag for the keys she's made for him and puts them on the counter.

MELISSA: These are yours. If you want them.

LEE: You're not going to make this easy, are you?

MELISSA: Lee—I don't know how to make anything easy.

LEE: No. You don't . . . I mean sometimes I would think, "How does she get through the day, anyway?"

MELISSA *(laughs)*: Yeah, well, sometimes it ain't easy . . .

LEE: I'll bet.

MELISSA: But sometimes I had *you* at the end of it. And that helped.

Lee turns the keys over in his hand.

LEE: It did? I don't seem to have made things so easy for you . . .

MELISSA: But you *did,* and we were doing great. Or I was. So you're a few years younger. We were doing great. And then—it's not what other people said, or what I *thought* they said. It's what *I* said, to myself. It's this voice I have in me, Lee . . . It may sound like it's condemning me, and it's not going to go away overnight. I'm going to have to fight it all the time. And see the thing is—with you—it was the first time I felt what it might be like not to have it there, not to have to hear it . . .

A brief pause.

MELISSA: Look. I can't make things right with a set of keys. So I guess just whatever happens—you know. Happens. With us. But whatever happens—(*jumps off the cliff*) I do love you, Lee. Whatever happens, you should know that.

LEE: Okay.

MELISSA: Okay. Then—I'll see ya . . .

LEE (*to stop her*): I love you, too, so you should know that.

MELISSA: Okay.

LEE: Okay.

MELISSA: Then—I'll see ya.

She starts to go out. He reaches for the keys on the counter. She hears this, and waits for a moment before turning.

LEE: Melissa . . . ?

She turns now. He lifts his arm, as if he's about to toss the keys to her. And indeed, he throws them up in the air. But he catches them, and puts them in his pocket.

LEE: See ya.

She smiles back at him and we fade out.

NEW BABY

BY

ANN LEWIS HAMILTON

One of the good things about being a writer is that when something terrible happens to you, at least you can write about it. I had had a miscarriage at the end of the first season of *thirtysomething*. When the decision was made to do a show in which Hope lost her baby, Ed and Marshall asked if I would write it. I didn't hesitate. Hope's miscarriage wasn't mine, of course; I had to take something that had happened to me and impose upon it the neat and orderly structure of drama. I am not Hope. I had her react as I thought her character would react. I took what I could use from my life, gave bits and pieces of it to Hope, and made up the rest, all very tidy and dramatic. Well, perhaps not so tidy—one hour after the miscarriage show aired, I went into labor, and my son Max was born the next evening.

I had arrived at *thirtysomething* midway through the first season. It was an interesting place to be. Giddy with the unexpected success of the show, Ed and Marshall were in and out of dozens of interviews. I felt like a paid observer, amazed that, in spite of all the chaos, episodes tumbled together and somehow managed to get done. It was also a little disconcerting to be the only staff writer who wasn't a wife or a best friend of Ed and Marshall. They're good writers, the friend and wives, but I felt very disengaged, out of the loop. I was unfamiliar with the show, I had no children, and my marriage was new and still reasonably idyllic. What could I possibly write about?

Things got better. I relaxed, first-season jitters ended for everybody, I learned the show. My previous writing had concentrated on action/adventure, so *thirtysomething* was a bit of an adjustment. I kept trying to write things like "Hope grabs the Uzi and wipes out the Nazi slime." I find it a bit strange, but I believe it was my miscarriage and subsequent pregnancy that helped propel me into the cadence of the show.

341

So the third season began, and because I'd just had Max, it was natural that I would write the episode where Susannah and Gary have a baby. Marshall (who would be directing the episode), Ed, and I sat down to do the outline. We resisted the standard TV childbirth approach—mom-to-be clutches her stomach, she's rushed to the hospital, pushes for a minute, and pops out a baby. We couldn't do that. In our meeting Marshall and Ed spoke of their wives' labors, I spoke of mine, and by the time the meeting was over "New Baby" had a focus; it would concentrate on the work, the process of labor, and not on the delivery.

The original outline began with Gary and Susannah in a Lamaze class. At the end of the first act, her water breaks on the hospital tour. She is sent home, her friends give her a shower anyway, and the second act ends with Melissa arriving with an unusual shower present. Susannah is in heavy labor at the end of the third act, and in the fourth act, she has the baby.

Joe Dougherty and I had been joking about doing a backward episode since the beginning of the second season of *thirtysomething*. One of our favorite plays is Harold Pinter's *Betrayal*, the story of a love triangle told backward in time. There was something very appealing about doing a show that started at the end and ended at the beginning. Joe asked how the outline was coming for "New Baby" and I told him it was okay, but a little dull. He offered a suggestion: "Why don't you do it backward?" Backward; that was pretty funny. We laughed. And then we thought about it. The show was about expectation. What will a baby mean in my life? What will it do to me? To my partner? To tell the story backward would play with the expectations of the audience. Like Gary and Susannah, the audience wouldn't know what was coming next.

Marshall agreed that the episode could be done backward, with perhaps some reservations since he had to direct it. His primary concern was that the audience understand the backward movement in time. He suggested a device to frame the show; we would open with Susannah in heavy labor, begin the backward sequence, then, in the end, close the circle with the baby's birth. To indicate the reversal of time, we talked about superimposing a digital clock at the beginning of each scene. That idea was eventually dropped in favor of using clocks that were part of the set, in Susannah's labor room, for example.

I sat down to write. The most important element of a script, I feel, is an outline. You might stray from it occasionally, but if the outline is in trouble, so are you. The "New Baby" outline was fine, but it was *backward*. Where should I start? The first scene showed Susannah in heavy labor. Nope, too hard. I wanted to get a running start at that one. How about the last scene, where the baby is born? No, I didn't want to start there either. So I began at the top of the fourth act, where Susannah is in bed and the unborn baby gets hiccups. In the next scene—we're going backward in time, remember—Melissa learns that Hope is giving Susannah a baby shower. Are you still with me? So I didn't write the script entirely backward. I wrote the fourth act first, starting with the first scene and taking it all the way through to the end. Then I wrote the third act, from the first scene to the last, and the second act next—okay, forget it, I knew I would never be able to explain this. How the hell did Harold Pinter do it? Let's just say I was able to get through a first draft.

Handing in a first draft to Ed and Marshall is a little like opening a vein. Your script is done, you're pleased with it, but nothing counts until They read it. I think their reaction to this first draft was positive, but a positive reaction doesn't mean the work is done. I took the script through five more passes; Marshall was always there, after each new draft, to remind me, "It has a ways to go . . ." Some of the changes were based on production needs, some were cuts for time, and some came from actors' notes after the full-cast read-through. I rewrote the scene where Gary and Susannah leave for the hospital many times until it achieved the level of frenzy Marshall wanted. There was one scene in the show that nearly caused Marshall and me to come to blows. Act Four, Scene One: Susannah is in bed, the baby gets hiccups. In my first draft, I had Gary suggest that a kiss might be a good way to get rid of the hiccups, the idea being that he and Susannah are going to make love. Marshall said no; he felt that the opening scene of an act needed more conflict. I said I wanted to show Gary and Susannah in love. They're terrified of the future, and this will probably be the last time they make love before the baby comes.

Oh, well. Marshall's the executive producer and he's much taller than I am; we did it *his* way. Gary suggests making love and Susannah backs off for fear of starting labor. But I put my old scene back for this book because I like it better.

Ed's notes on the script dealt mainly with the backward element. He suggested we incorporate various devices that would emphasize the backward motion of the show. For example, it was Ed's idea that Gary start a labor chart. I came up with using Pachelbel's *Canon*. When Susannah and Gary are packing to go to the hospital, she reminds him not to forget the labor tape. Once in the hospital, the tape is playing and Susannah says, "I just love Pachelbel's *Canon*." But in a later scene, when Gary turns on the tape recorder, Susannah snaps at him: "If I hear Pachelbel's *Canon* one more time, I'll jump out the window." (I use the word "later" in keeping with the backward nature of the script; it means, of course, "earlier.")

As I look through the script, I'm amazed at how it intertwines bits and pieces of the lives of other people involved with the show. Susannah's long labor is Susan Shilliday's labor. One friend told me how she and her husband did a crossword puzzle when she was in early labor; another recalled that she ate ice continuously during her pregnancy. Mary Helfrich, the *thirtysomething* writers' assistant and a close friend, left a '67 Chrysler Newport, bought for a hundred bucks, parked in front of my house for my baby shower. You may notice that, in "New Baby," Melissa does something quite similar. And if you're interested in two final ironic footnotes, how about these: A) Patricia Kalember, who played Susannah's labor so convincingly, had her son Ben on April 12, 1989, the same day I had Max. B) When I called her to let her know how the script was coming along, she was doing a play in the Berkshires: *Betrayal*.

In the middle of the show, Hope tells a nervous Susannah, "People prepare you for how *awful* it all is. The thing nobody warns you about is how much you love the baby." I agree with her and find her words apply not only to babies, but to writing, too. After the work and the process, you have a show; the process and the work no longer exist. What you see and what you hold are, in the end, all that matters.

ANN LEWIS HAMILTON

ACT ONE

INT. LABOR ROOM—NIGHT

Susannah has been pushing. She's hooked up to a monitor and an IV drip. She's just decided that she doesn't want to push anymore. Gary, wearing scrubs, is at her side. Susannah's female doctor, Dr. Silverman, a labor nurse, Isabel, and a few other technicians are nearby. The contents of a Lamaze bag are strewn across the room—a tape player and cassettes, a dirty plaid shirt of Gary's, a crossword puzzle. A magazine photo of an ocean scene is taped to the wall. A digital clock clicks as the minutes pass.

GARY: Okay, Susannah. You can do it one more time.

SUSANNAH: I'm so tired.

GARY: I know, but you're doing such a good job.

SUSANNAH: No.

DR. SILVERMAN: Susannah, the next time you push I want you to really bear down. I need you to *push* that baby out.

Susannah doesn't respond.

DR. SILVERMAN: I want you to push as hard as you can.

SUSANNAH *(she's given up):* I can't.

DR. SILVERMAN: You have to. Think of *pushing* out a tampon. Concentrate.

Susannah is silent. Dr. Silverman looks over to Isabel. Isabel shrugs. Gary notices.

GARY: What?

Dr. Silverman shakes her head. Don't worry about it.

GARY: What? You're going to do a c-section?

DR. SILVERMAN: I don't know what to tell you . . .

Gary looks at the monitor. Another contraction on the way.

GARY: Okay, Susannah. I want you to take a cleansing breath.

Susannah takes a breath and . . .

DR. SILVERMAN: Push and push . . . down towards me, can you feel where my fingers are?

The doctor is stretching Susannah's perineum. Gary watches this all, feeling somehow less and less involved.

DR. SILVERMAN: Come on, I need a big push—

Susannah gives her nothing. Time is slowing down, everything gets quiet. Susannah is still pushing, but you can't hear her. A small metal pan drops off a cabinet, no sound. Gary looks at the clock. It clicks to 11:15. And then, oddly enough, it starts to click backward.

INT. LABOR ROOM—NIGHT

The clock on the wall. 10:15. Susannah is in the middle of a terrible contraction. Gary and Isabel are there with her. The room is darker and less cluttered than how we've just seen it. The curtains are open to blackness outside.

SUSANNAH: Make them take it out, take it out.

GARY: Honey, it's almost over, breathe, can you breathe?

She is trying to breathe. Gary turns to Isabel.

GARY: You're sure this isn't too much Pitocin?

ISABEL: Dr. Silverman said twenty units.

Susannah moans. Gary looks at the monitor.

GARY: It's almost over, it's really almost over. *(to Isabel)* Can she have more Demerol?

ISABEL: I'm really sorry, she can't have more yet, it's another hour at least.

GARY: But this isn't doing anything.

ISABEL: She can still have the epidural . . .

Gary looks at Susannah, who doesn't even respond. The contraction is over. He wets a washcloth and puts it on her forehead. She takes the washcloth and presses it against her mouth.

GARY: Do you want me to shut the curtains?

SUSANNAH: I want them to stop this.

He closes the curtains. Isabel touches him on the arm.

ISABEL: You're doing great.

GARY: So this is the real thing . . .

ISABEL: This . . . is the real thing.

GARY: More ice chips?

Susannah lets out a slight moan. Gary looks at Isabel.

GARY: No.

Isabel looks at the monitor. Unbelievably, another contraction is already beginning.

GARY: Okay, I want you to breathe for me.

SUSANNAH *(not in answer to him):* No, no . . .

GARY *(to Isabel):* **She's not getting any rest between the con-tractions . . .**
    (to Susannah): **Please. Come on. Breathe.**

She takes a breath, starts her Lamaze. The pain outweighs the breathing. Does it ever.

SUSANNAH: I can't.

GARY: You can do it, you have to do it.

He watches the monitor. The contraction is huge.

GARY: Come on, Susannah.

SUSANNAH: Why did you do this to me? Why are you making me go through this?

Gary glances at Isabel, who gives him a sympathetic half-smile.

GARY: Breathe. That's right.

SUSANNAH: I hate this. Go away, just go away.

GARY *(watching the monitor):* You're at the peak and it looks like—yeah, you're coming down, breathe. It's almost over.

SUSANNAH: I can't do another one, there's no way. *(sharp)* Will you stop looking at the damn monitor?

Gary looks at Susannah.

GARY: Is that better?

SUSANNAH: No.

He does hand signals for her—four, three, two, one . . . And the contraction ends.

SUSANNAH: Oh, God . . .

ISABEL: How are you doing, Susannah?

SUSANNAH: I feel—my stomach . . .

ISABEL: Do you think you're going to be sick?

Susannah nods. Isabel gets a little pan for her.

ISABEL: Here you go. Just in case.

SUSANNAH: I feel so dizzy.

And she throws up. Gary watches for a moment, looks away. When she is finished, Isabel hands her a washcloth. Susannah wipes her mouth and looks over to Gary. Great, I didn't want this to happen and it did. He steps in close to her, a little wary.

GARY: Do you feel any better?

SUSANNAH: A little.

GARY: I'm sorry.

SUSANNAH: Yeah.

GARY: You're really doing great.

SUSANNAH: No.

GARY: Yes.

SUSANNAH: Gary—don't go away again.

GARY: I'm not going anywhere.

SUSANNAH: Promise?

GARY: Promise.

He holds her hand tight. We go up to the clock again, in time to see it start clicking backward.

INT. HOSPITAL CORRIDOR—NIGHT

Another digital clock in the hallway. Clicking backward. 9:20. Gary arrives at a pay phone. He's nervous, on edge. There's a lot of activity in the hallway. He dials.

GARY: Melissa?

But he's gotten her phone machine. He hangs up without leaving a message. Gary starts down the hall and runs into Michael. He hands Gary a camera.

MICHAEL: I put film in it.

GARY: God, I forgot film, too?

MICHAEL: How's she doing?

GARY: They want to give her Pitocin.

MICHAEL: That's rough. How are the contractions?

GARY: She's getting through them. Oh, man. Now I know why they call it labor.

MICHAEL: Has she yelled at you yet for getting her pregnant?

GARY: No.

MICHAEL: Sometimes they do that.

GARY: I just don't understand. I mean, women have been having babies for thousands of years and you'd think it would have gotten easier . . .

MICHAEL: All bets are off.

GARY: It's like here is this person that you completely care about and she's going through all this pain and I'm just standing there and I can't, there's nothing I can do and I mean, if there *was* I'm not sure she'd let me—

MICHAEL: Help her?

GARY: Yeah. I mean, this whole thing, it doesn't hurt *me* at all, does it? Not even this much . . .

Michael nods; he understands.

MICHAEL: Everybody makes this big deal about us being with them, but we're not with them—how could we be with them?

GARY: So after the kid is born—is it always gonna be like this? *Her* birth. *Her* child?

A beat.

MICHAEL *(you'll get through it)*: Yeah.

INT. LABOR ROOM—DAY

Doctor Silverman finishes examining Susannah. Gary is watching in the background. The curtains are open, it's daylight.

DR. SILVERMAN: Well, we gave it some time, but it doesn't look like much is happening down there.

Susannah can't deal with this.

SUSANNAH: Terrific.

DR. SILVERMAN: I want to get you started on Pitocin.

SUSANNAH: I don't want Pitocin.

DR. SILVERMAN: The Pitocin will make your contractions more efficient.

SUSANNAH: There must be another way.

DR. SILVERMAN: There's not. Susannah, you're three centimeters dilated. That's nothing. Nowhere. Since your water broke, there's only a certain amount of time we can wait. Because of the risk of infection.

Susannah doesn't say anything.

DR. SILVERMAN: We can give you an epidural if the pain is too much.

SUSANNAH: No. I do not want a needle in my spine.

DR. SILVERMAN: Okay. But we're gonna get you started on Pitocin. And we'll get you dilated to ten and by tonight, you'll have your baby.

Susannah is still silent.

DR. SILVERMAN: I'll check back in a little while.

The doctor goes. Gary and Susannah don't look at each other.

SUSANNAH: Damn.

GARY: It's not the end of the world.

SUSANNAH: But it's not the way I wanted it either.

GARY: So they give you Pitocin. And it'll help.

SUSANNAH: How do you know?

Silence.

GARY: Are you comfortable? Do you want another pillow?

SUSANNAH: No.

Gary turns on the tape player. Pachelbel's *Canon*.

SUSANNAH: If I hear Pachelbel's *Canon* one more time, I'll jump out the window.

Gary turns off the tape player. Isabel, the new labor nurse, comes in, laughing raucously at a co-worker's joke.

ISABEL: Hi. I'm Isabel. You're gonna be stuck with me for a while. Whaddaya say we check your temperature and all that fun stuff?

She looks at Gary.

ISABEL: Hey, your husband looks like that tennis player.

SUSANNAH: He's not my husband.

Isabel doesn't comment. She looks at the monitor printout.

ISABEL: You shouldn't be flat on your back. Let's get you in another position.

Gary and Susannah share a look. Who is this woman?

SUSANNAH: This position's fine.

GARY: It might make you feel better.

SUSANNAH: I can handle this, Gary. I can do it by myself.

A beat. Isabel assesses the situation.

ISABEL (to Gary): Why don't you go out and grab a cup of coffee?

GARY: I can't leave.

ISABEL: We'll be okay here.

GARY: But—

SUSANNAH: Why don't you go?

He doesn't want to leave her. This is not going the way he planned.

GARY: If you're sure.

Another contraction begins.

ISABEL: Go on. *(to Susannah)* Come on. Out of bed. Let's try this my way.

She starts to help Susannah up. Susannah does not look at Gary as he walks out.

EXT. HOSPITAL—DAY

Gary pushes his way slowly out the main doors of the hospital, drinking in the real air and the real light. He leans against the glass and closes his eyes.

ACT TWO

INT. LABOR ROOM—DAY

Susannah is standing beside her bed, it's the end of a contraction.
She is hooked up to the monitors. Gary is right beside her, helping
her to breathe through it. They're both in a good mood. It's going to
be a positive birth experience. Pachelbel's *Canon* floats soothingly
through the room. When the contraction is over:

GARY: How was that one?

SUSANNAH: Okay. Not great—okay. So go on.

GARY: Does the music help?

SUSANNAH: I just love Pachelbel's *Canon*. Go on.

GARY: Do you want anything before we start?

SUSANNAH: Ice chips.

Gary hands Susannah a cup. She takes out several ice chips and sucks
on them. He picks up *The New York Times* crossword.

GARY: "South American lemur."

SUSANNAH: How many letters?

GARY: Five. The second letter's an E.

SUSANNAH: Don't know. Go on.

GARY: "Melancholy."

SUSANNAH: Dane.

GARY: Very funny.

SUSANNAH: Lugubrious.

GARY: Seven letters.

SUSANNAH: Too hard.

GARY: Okay. "Expression."

SUSANNAH: Excruciating.

GARY: What?

SUSANNAH: Agonizing. Torturous.

GARY: I thought you said the contractions weren't that bad.

SUSANNAH: Stabbing.

GARY *(re the crossword)*: Do you want to stop?

SUSANNAH *(a little smile)*: No.

GARY: "Terra—"

SUSANNAH: Haute.

Another labor nurse, Clara, younger than Isabel, comes in.

CLARA: It sounds like you're having too much fun in here. How's it going?

Clara checks Susannah's blood pressure.

SUSANNAH: Fine. Except, you know, these belts are really un-comfortable.

CLARA: Yeah, you don't see me wearing 'em. How's the pain?

SUSANNAH: Awful.

CLARA: You want me to get you something?

SUSANNAH: No.

CLARA: Maybe a little Demerol?

SUSANNAH: Really, nothing.

CLARA: You're probably a lot more dilated now. I bet this baby makes an appearance before the end of my shift.

Clara checks the monitor printout.

SUSANNAH: *(she hopes so)*: Really?

CLARA: I get a feeling about these things. *(to Gary)* Your wife is really pretty.

Gary and Susannah tacitly agree not to correct the inaccuracy about their marital status. Gary starts rooting through the Lamaze bag.

CLARA: You haven't finished with that crossword yet?

GARY: Nope.

CLARA: I'll help you out. I'm good at crosswords.

SUSANNAH *(after Clara goes):* What are you looking for?

GARY: Nothing.

SUSANNAH: What did you forget?

GARY: Nothing. *(returns to the crossword)* "Testy."

SUSANNAH: Ex-academic.

INT. HOSPITAL CORRIDOR—DAY

Gary stands at a pay phone. He dials.

GARY: Hi, Melissa—

He stops. He's gotten the phone machine. He waits for the beep and then:

GARY: Hi, it's me . . . um, I'm at the hospital. No baby yet. I'm sorry about today. I don't know, things are a little crazy . . . God, I'm supposed to be this pillar of strength . . . I guess you're right, here I am calling you about something that's happening to me and I guess it *is* selfish, wanting to tell you about all this, and—yeah, this must be hard for you, but I really wish you were here. I need you here. *(after a beat)* I'm so scared . . .

He stops talking and just holds the phone.

INT. MELISSA'S DARKROOM

Melissa is sitting there. She makes no move to pick up the phone. The sound of Gary hanging up. The light on the phone machine blinks.

INT. HOSPITAL CORRIDOR—DAY

Gary is at a vending machine, purchasing some lukewarm soup. Michael comes up behind him.

MICHAEL: This is where we're going to eat?

GARY: Cafeteria's closed, go get me food.

MICHAEL: This food is wonderful, it's nutritious. How's she doing?

GARY: It's really slow . . .

MICHAEL: I remember slow.

GARY: You mean this happens to other people? All they told us in Lamaze was how great it was going to be—then we get here and the ABC room is gone, and she's "not progressing," I mean—God.

MICHAEL: How dilated is she?

GARY: Barely. Two. Almost two.

MICHAEL: And the contractions?

GARY: They're slowing down again.

MICHAEL: Are they talking about Pitocin?

GARY: It's their favorite subject.

MICHAEL: I guess it would speed things up . . . Susannah's not into all the natural stuff anyway, is she?

GARY: No, she's into fear of doctors, and medicine, and all the intervention. You know Susannah. She wants to do it by herself.

MICHAEL: That's a surprise.

GARY: I should check on her.

MICHAEL (*nods at the soup*): That's the last hot food you'll have for the next six months.

GARY: It's not hot—

MICHAEL: Did you talk to Melissa?

GARY: She doesn't want anything to do with me.

MICHAEL: Do you believe that?

GARY (*after a beat*): We don't even talk anymore. We sort of make jokes and then it all goes to hell. Damn, I really wanted to get all this sorted out before the baby comes.

MICHAEL: Why?

GARY: Because, I don't know, it just seems like there's this new phase of my life starting and I want everything to be clean and clear.

MICHAEL: But Melissa doesn't think she's going to be involved in your new life. This baby, I think she sees it as something that's been taken away from her. A piece of you. (*after a beat*) What piece, I don't know.

GARY: I love her.

MICHAEL: Not exclusively.

GARY: No, not exclusively . . .

MICHAEL: You could call her.

Gary thinks it over.

INT. LABOR ROOM—DAY

Susannah and Gary walk in, followed by Clara. Susannah is wearing street clothes. She watches as Clara organizes the room.

GARY: Are you sure about the ABC room?

CLARA: You didn't really think you were gonna get the ABC room, did you? This place is a zoo tonight. We've already had to double up a couple labor rooms.

GARY: But why, I mean, they kept raving about it on the hospital tour—how can you advertise it if it's not available?

SUSANNAH *(calm down):* Gary—

CLARA: Seems pretty stupid to me. Your doctor will be here in a little bit to check you out.

SUSANNAH: So that's the monitor.

CLARA: Yep. See here? This'll show your contractions and down here is the fetal heartbeat.

GARY: Wow. That's pretty amazing.

CLARA: You'll notice when you have a contraction that the baby's heartbeat will pick up a little. That's good. And here's your gown.

SUSANNAH: That's okay. I brought something to wear.

Gary holds the shirt out to Clara.

CLARA: This nice shirt? Oh, you don't want it to get all messed up.

GARY: But—

Clara takes the shirt from him and drapes it over a chair.

CLARA: I'll put it right here where you can see it. How's that?

Susannah looks at Gary. Okay, we'll make this *one* little concession . . .

SUSANNAH: Fine.

CLARA: How are the contractions?

SUSANNAH: Okay.

CLARA: Try to rest between them while you can.

SUSANNAH: It's sort of impossible.

CLARA: You should try anyway. Is there anything you need?

SUSANNAH: How about some sushi?

CLARA: Nice try. *(turns to Gary)* You ought to eat something. It's gonna be a while.

She goes. Gary sits on the edge of the bed.

SUSANNAH: I wonder how long "a while" is?

GARY: Beats me. I'm new at this.

He kisses her.

GARY: How are you doing?

SUSANNAH: I don't know. I'm new at this too.

A silence.

GARY: I guess it'll be what, another six hours? Eight hours?

SUSANNAH: Eight hours. And then . . .

She trails off.

SUSANNAH: You should get something to eat.

GARY: I don't want to leave you.

SUSANNAH: I'm fine. Really. Please? Eat something. And tell
    me what it's like.

GARY: If you're sure.

SUSANNAH: I'm sure. I'll listen to music.

He is reluctant to leave. He takes the photo of the ocean view from
the Lamaze bag and tapes it on the wall.

SUSANNAH: Thank you.

Gary kisses Susannah and puts his hand on her belly. Talks to the
baby.

GARY: Hurry up, the meter's running.

He goes.

INT. GARY'S BEDROOM—DAY

Susannah, a little frenzied, is looking through her closet. Gary, also
frenzied, enters. He's holding the labor chart.

GARY: What time was the last one?

SUSANNAH: I don't know. I thought you wrote it down.

GARY: You didn't tell me when it ended. What are you looking
    for?

SUSANNAH: Your plaid shirt.

GARY: It's in the hamper.

SUSANNAH: The hamper? Why'd you put it in the hamper?

GARY: Because it was dirty.

SUSANNAH: Dirty? Why is it dirty?

GARY: Because I wore it. Are you sure you can't remember when you had your last contraction?

She goes into the bathroom, comes out with the hamper. Turns it over, continues looking for the shirt.

SUSANNAH: Less than five minutes ago, I remember that. Because if we don't get to the hospital soon I'm gonna have the baby right here on this pile of dirty clothes.

She finds the shirt.

SUSANNAH: Put this in the Lamaze bag.

GARY: What?

SUSANNAH: I'm not going to wear one of those hospital gowns.

GARY: But—it's dirty.

SUSANNAH: The baby won't know it's dirty.

GARY: The baby would notice a hospital gown?

She hands him the shirt. He puts it in the already overstuffed Lamaze bag.

SUSANNAH: I don't think I should have eaten all those deviled eggs. Did you pack the tape player?

GARY: Yes.

SUSANNAH: Tapes?

GARY: The soundtrack to *A Room with a View,* Vivaldi's Greatest Hits.

SUSANNAH: Pachelbel's *Canon?*

GARY: Yep, right here on top.

SUSANNAH: The camera?

GARY: Yes. Don't you trust me?

She would protest, but she's hit with another contraction. Gary looks at his watch. They look at each other. It's time to go.

EXT. GARY'S APARTMENT—DAY

Gary walks toward his apartment. He's carrying a bag of ice. Stops to look at an incredibly beat-to-shit old American car. God, it looks awful. He moves off. Melissa appears, leaning against the side of the car.

MELISSA: Hi.

Gary stops.

MELISSA: So how's the shower? The baby make a surprise appearance?

GARY: Not yet. I got sent out for ice. Susannah goes through a bag a day. Thirsty.

MELISSA: Well, I wanted to drop off my shower present.

GARY: That's nice of you. Really.

But she's not holding a package.

MELISSA: So what do you think?

Gary grins a little, not getting it.

GARY: Think about what?

MELISSA: The gift.

He still doesn't see anything.

GARY: Okay. What gift?

Melissa gestures to the car, à la Carol Merrill.

MELISSA: I couldn't make up my mind. Booties or a car.

Gary looks shocked.

MELISSA: I get it. You wanted booties.

GARY: You bought a car? How much did you—this is a *car.*

MELISSA: I got to thinking, what does every kid need to start off in life? And a car just seemed to be the logical thing. *(off his look)* Oh, I get it. You already got him or her a car.

GARY *(really moved):* No. This is the first.

His instinct is to touch her, to thank her. But something in her tells him not to.

GARY: I hope you didn't have to take out a loan or anything.

MELISSA: Between you and me—a hundred bucks. Look, it's even got painted-on whitewalls.

GARY: Thank you. A car?

Gary does touch her. She pulls away a little.

MELISSA: Well, I was thinking, somebody's got to teach your kid how to drive since you're such a rotten driver and I don't know about Susannah—I just thought it was important for me to teach it something. You know, moral ambiguity, knock-knock jokes, some of the other things you and Susannah might not think of. Not that you're going to be bad parents . . .

GARY: But we'll need all the help we can get.

He takes her hand.

GARY: Why don't you come upstairs?

MELISSA: No, somebody's got to keep an eye out for car thieves.

GARY: Seriously. Hope's there. And Ellyn.

MELISSA: Really, I'll pass.

GARY: Come upstairs. Just for a cup of ice?

MELISSA: Gary, can't you be happy with the car?

GARY: I just want—

MELISSA: For everybody to be best friends again, right.

GARY: Yes. And what's that going to take?

MELISSA: I don't know.

She looks away. He starts to shake his head, exasperated.

GARY: So now I'm supposed to read your mind . . .

MELISSA: No, I'm just tired of me trying to explain to you how I feel.

GARY: Yeah, I'm a little tired of it, too. You always talking about how you feel.

MELISSA: How I feel? You have no idea how I feel . . . where were you when I was trying to sort this all out? I'm supposed to be steadfast and your good buddy and you didn't even think about me, how hard this was for me.

GARY: Melissa, that was nine months ago.

MELISSA: Yes, and for nine months you've been all wrapped up in your baby and your new life, and that's a great thing, that's a wonderful thing. Except I was still there, Gary— but I was upset and you couldn't accept that. Well I'm not upset about the baby anymore. I'm upset about you.

She hands him the car keys and walks off. He's left holding his melting bag of ice.

ACT THREE

INT. GARY'S KITCHEN—DAY

Ellyn and Nancy are unwrapping vast amounts of food. Ethan and Brittany are helping.

ELLYN: Okay, so I forgot she was a vegetarian and I went out and got this whole honey-baked ham.

NANCY: That's okay. I made enough deviled eggs to last two or three years.

Brittany puts her fingers into a deviled egg.

NANCY: Don't do that, sweetie.

Gary comes in, he heads straight for the food.

GARY: Wow. We ought to do this baby thing more often.

NANCY: How's Susannah?

GARY: Cranky. *(off their looks)* Crankier.

ELLYN: Are you sure this is okay, us coming over?

GARY: Why not? We're just sitting around waiting for contractions anyway. These are good.

He eats another egg. Ellyn and Nancy and the kids pick up the food and walk into the living room where Rosie and Hope are arranging a pyramid of presents on the sofa. There are a few other women there, Susannah's friends. Susannah appears from the bedroom. She looks tired, but she's willing to give it her best shot.

SUSANNAH: Hi.

NANCY: You look great.

SUSANNAH: Right. I haven't seen my feet in a month. I have to put my shoes on with butter.

ELLYN: You should use margarine. Less caloric.

ROSIE: How do you feel?

SUSANNAH *(sits):* The contractions kind of come and go. But I'm okay.

ELLYN: We shouldn't be here. We should let you hide in the bushes till the baby comes.

SUSANNAH: At this rate, that'll be nineteen ninety-two.

ELLYN: Well, maybe we should open the presents right away. Just in case.

Gary pokes his head in from the kitchen.

GARY: 'Bye, girls . . .

Everyone says good-bye, with a certain amount of teasing thrown in. Gary gives Susannah a direct and loving look. The one he gets back is more like that from a drowning person. Nancy hands Susannah a strangely wrapped package.

BRITTANY: I wrapped it.

NANCY: Ethan hid the Scotch tape. You'll know soon enough.

Susannah smiles and opens the package. It's a black-and-white mobile for the crib. Ooohs and ahhs from the women.

NANCY: It's black and white, see, because newborns can't really distinguish colors yet.

HOPE: Yes, they can—

A discussion ensues among the mothers concerning recent studies into infant vision abilities.

SUSANNAH *(looking at the mobile)*: This is really wonderful.

But there's a zombielike sense to her, like she's not really part of the proceedings. Ellyn hands Susannah a package.

ELLYN: Baby stores make me a little nervous. All those sizes and they go up to twelve and then they start at one again. What's that all about?

NANCY: I love baby clothes. They're so tiny. Like doll clothes.

HOPE: Only they cost about ten times as much. At least you have two, so you can reuse them.

NANCY: Are you kidding? Brittany won't go near Ethan's clothes . . .

The women are eating the food, playing with the presents. Susannah ignores them and starts to eat the deviled eggs. Rosie pushes her big box towards Susannah.

ROSIE: Here.

Susannah pulls away the paper to reveal a baby swing. Unassembled. The women squeal.

HOPE: They're great. They save your life, they really do.

NANCY: Brittany practically lived in hers, it knocked her right out. Didn't it, honey?

ELLYN: I'd like to have one of those for me.

HOPE *(to Nancy)*: Did you try one with Ethan?

NANCY: Once. We borrowed one or something. Of course it did nothing. Nothing worked on Ethan.

HOPE: Nancy basically got a total of four hours of sleep during the first six months of Ethan's life—

And all the mothers chime in, in unison, assuring Susannah that her baby will sleep fine. The only problem being that Susannah is no longer listening.

The discussion of sleep continues for a moment until someone realizes Susannah is having a contraction.

EXT. OUTSIDE GARY'S APARTMENT—DAY

Susannah is watching as Hope unloads shower fixings from her car.

SUSANNAH: I suppose your labor was a piece of cake.

HOPE: Yeah. I rolled over in my sleep and looked down and there was Janey.

Susannah smiles.

SUSANNAH: And you're willing to go through it again. I think that's noble.

HOPE: You know, they say the brain can't really remember pain.

SUSANNAH: Do you remember the pain?

HOPE: Yes.

They walk.

SUSANNAH: Episiotomies. And throwing up.

HOPE: I didn't throw up.

SUSANNAH: But you had an episiotomy.

HOPE: It's really not so—

SUSANNAH: I mean, why do they have to do it?

HOPE: Well, you could tear.

SUSANNAH: Yeah, the only reason it's done is because it's easier for the doctors. Liability and all that.

HOPE: But I think if that were true we'd all be having c-sections . . .

SUSANNAH: Aren't we?

HOPE (smiles): You know what? I don't even remember the episiotomy. You feel it afterwards, but there's so much other stuff going on—I wouldn't worry about it.

A silence.

HOPE: Have you talked to anybody, I mean, you probably have friends who've had babies.

SUSANNAH: Lots of fifteen-year-old unwed mothers from Race Street, they're really good for advice . . . Never mind.

HOPE: No, no—it's okay . . .

SUSANNAH: I just—what do you do, Hope?

HOPE: You do your breathing, and then you give up and ask for major drugs.

SUSANNAH: No, I mean after. When they bring you the baby.

HOPE: You just—hold her. And make her warm. And smell her head.

SUSANNAH: But I don't know anything. I mean, breast feeding. Will I be able to do it? Will I have enough milk? Comforting a baby—how do I do that? Oh, God. (a beat) And how do you get anything done? How do you work and read the paper and take a shower?

Hope has been there.

HOPE: Basically you don't.

SUSANNAH (smiles): Thank you for clearing that up.

HOPE: You will figure it all out. And the best part is, you enjoy figuring it out. I mean, not all the time. But there's this moment when your baby cries and you pick her up and suddenly she's all smiles and making these sounds and— it's like magic.

SUSANNAH (wants to believe this): Really?

HOPE: People prepare you for how awful it all is. The thing nobody warns you about is how much you love the baby.

Another contraction begins.

SUSANNAH: Uh-oh. Maybe I should keep walking.

They walk.

INT. GARY'S APARTMENT, THE BABY'S ROOM—DAY

It's really more like a big closet. Michael is helping Gary assemble Janey's old crib. It's not going well.

GARY: It's not supposed to happen like this, is it?

MICHAEL: It'll be okay.

GARY: She hasn't had a contraction in at least two hours.

MICHAEL: She'll have another one. And another one and the next thing you know you'll be teaching him how to shave.

GARY: Him?

MICHAEL: Teaching *her* how to shave? You knew there was going to be a sex involved here.

GARY: Sure. It's just—wow. When somebody else says it. "Him." It's like—I can't think about this now. (*overwhelmed*) Oh, man.

MICHAEL: What?

GARY: There's just—I don't know anything.

MICHAEL: Join the club.

GARY: What time do you wake 'em up in the morning?

Michael grins.

GARY: How do you know when to change a diaper?

MICHAEL: You don't have to change diapers now. They're so absorbent they wear the same one till they're ten.

GARY: Shut up. And vomiting? I read about projectile vomiting. And reading—am I supposed to read all these books? Do I have enough books?

Michael looks around at all the books.

MICHAEL: Gary, nobody reads these books. They leaf through them to see how advanced their kid is.

GARY: Our parents had Dr. Spock.

MICHAEL: And we had *Mr.* Spock—

GARY: And suppose in the middle of the night he wakes up and he's crying and he won't stop—

MICHAEL: He'll stop.

GARY: And suppose he doesn't like me.

Bingo.

MICHAEL: They love you. That's what's so amazing. Unconditional love. They're too little to judge you. And too stupid. That's why they get screwed up later.

Silence.

GARY: That sounds a lot like the way my father raised me.

MICHAEL: Hey, you're the new generation. Erase the slate. You get to start all over.

GARY: Yeah?

Michael nods.

GARY: Suppose he can't play basketball?

MICHAEL: Suppose she's the first girl to play in the NBA?

Gary has to think that one over.

GARY: She'd be tall.

INT. GARY'S APARTMENT—NIGHT

The sound of a key in the lock, the door opens. Susannah enters and Gary turns on the lights.

SUSANNAH: I can't believe this.

GARY: Did you want to stay at the hospital?

SUSANNAH: Of course not.

GARY: Some doctors would make you stay.

SUSANNAH: It's just so stupid. I mean, we were right there on the maternity ward and everybody was looking—God.

GARY: Why don't you try to sleep? Both of us, we should try to rest up.

SUSANNAH: How can I possibly sleep? Maybe if I took a handful of sleeping pills . . .

A beat.

GARY: The doctor said a little wine. Why don't you put your feet up?

Susannah does as she's told. A small contraction. Susannah breathes through it. Gary returns, notices.

GARY: Are you—

She nods, I'm okay. He checks his watch.

GARY: I think I'll start the chart.

He rushes to get a pad and a pen.

SUSANNAH: The what?

GARY: A labor chart. You know, I'll time the contractions, I'll write everything down. It'll make things easier.

SUSANNAH: For who?

GARY: We're supposed to do it. She said so at Lamaze.

SUSANNAH: Fine, you want busywork?

GARY: What's that supposed to mean?

SUSANNAH: Gary. Excuse me, but I have a little more to deal with here than a labor chart.

GARY: And I'm only trying to *help* you deal with it.

SUSANNAH: Do you want to have my contractions for me?

GARY: Yes, if that's what it takes for you to let me in a little bit—

A silence. They're both aware they've gone too far.

SUSANNAH: Sorry—

GARY: No, I'm sorry. I'm really sorry.

Silence.

GARY: This is hard.

SUSANNAH: This is *very* hard.

GARY: It's harder for me. You're just having a baby.

They sit there, overwhelmed.

INT. ABC ROOM, HOSPITAL—NIGHT

The Alternative Birthing Center. A large room, wallpapered, cheery prints on the wall. Eight couples, the women all at least eight months pregnant, take the hospital tour. Gary and Susannah among them. The tour leader is Mrs. Smith, an enthusiastic hospital volunteer in her sixties.

MRS. SMITH: You'll notice that the birthing bed is the same as in the rest of our labor rooms. But the atmosphere here is much more relaxed. It's—soothing. So you'll feel comfortable, like you're at home.

A MOTHER-TO-BE: Is there any way you can reserve the ABC room in advance?

MRS. SMITH: I'm afraid that since there's only one, it's availability is pretty much first come, first served.

ANOTHER MOTHER-TO-BE: But where are the monitors and all the equipment?

MRS. SMITH: They're here in the cupboards. You can deliver your baby and spend your recovery time in here as well. Unless, of course, there are complications.

Susannah and Gary are trailing behind the others.

SUSANNAH: I hate this.

GARY: What? The tour guide? Yeah, she's driving me nuts.

SUSANNAH: No. All this. Hiding the monitors, pretending like you're at home. Who do you think they're fooling?

Mrs. Smith turns back to them.

MRS. SMITH: Did you have a question back here?

GARY: No, we're fine. Thanks.

A FATHER-TO-BE: What about parking?

The group moves out of the room. Susannah lingers, examines the birthing bed.

OUTSIDE THE ABC ROOM

a rack of windows and the nursery. Here are the babies. The touring couples stop to ooh and ahh. Gary rushes right to a window. Susannah hangs back.

MRS. SMITH: Visiting hours for nonfamily members are from one to two in the afternoon and seven to eight at night. But the baby will have to go back to the nursery then. That's to protect the baby from infection.

GARY: Wow. Look at that. All these babies born on the same day. Pretty amazing.

He turns to Susannah.

GARY: Susannah?

She isn't saying anything.

GARY: Look at that one there. He looks like Larry "Bud" Melman.

The rest of the group has moved off to another set of windows. Gary follows them a little way, looks back to Susannah.

GARY: Susannah?

She is leaning against the wall. Gary comes over to her. The front of her dress is wet. She has a strange look on her face.

SUSANNAH: My water broke.

ACT FOUR

INT. GARY'S BEDROOM—NIGHT

Susannah in bed, a bowl of ice cubes on her lap. She's sucking on an ice cube and talking to the baby in her stomach.

SUSANNAH: So, what's going on in there? Have you decided to stop kicking my ribs? Thanks, I appreciate that.

Gary appears in the doorway. Susannah doesn't see him.

SUSANNAH: You're keeping a big secret from me, you know? Are you a boy or a girl? Or maybe—did you see *The Fly*? Forget it, I can't think about that. Can you give me a hint? If you kick right now, you're a boy.

She waits for the kick. Gary walks over to her.

GARY: Well?

Susannah is a little embarrassed at being overheard.

SUSANNAH: I couldn't tell.

Gary gets into bed with her.

GARY *(re the ice cubes):* That can't be good for your teeth.

She ignores him. He picks up the book beside his bed, Sheila Kitzinger's *Complete Book of Pregnancy and Childbirth.*

GARY: "In many cultures, the placenta is saved and used as a decorative wall hanging . . ."

Susannah looks at him. You've got to be kidding. He is. She takes the book.

GARY: We should practice.

SUSANNAH: Hee-hee-hee.

GARY: We need to practice.

SUSANNAH: I know.

GARY: So the mean old doctors won't yell at you.

SUSANNAH: Stop it.

GARY: So they won't use their torture instruments and come at you with big tongs that—

SUSANNAH: Leave me alone, everybody's allowed to have their own paranoia. I know they have secret c-section quotas and enema devices . . .

GARY: Why are you so afraid of doctors? Karen Silverman's just a kid like us. Younger . . .

SUSANNAH: I just am.

She draws her breath in quickly.

GARY: What? Braxton Hicks?

SUSANNAH: Hiccups.

GARY: Oh. Do you want some water?

SUSANNAH: Not me.

He puts his hand on her stomach. They smile.

GARY: Maybe if you hold your breath.

SUSANNAH: I don't think so.

Gary leans down close to her stomach.

GARY: Boo!

SUSANNAH: Gary.

GARY: I read that babies who have hiccups in the womb are more likely to have hiccups after they're born.

SUSANNAH: Really?

Another hiccup. Gary leans in close to Susannah.

GARY: Maybe if we try . . .

SUSANNAH: What?

He kisses her.

GARY: Of course, this might take a little work.

As he maneuvers around her nine-month belly.

SUSANNAH (*lovingly*): Shut up.

EXT. STEADMAN PORCH—DAY

Ellyn and Janey are coloring in a coloring book as Hope addresses shower invitations.

HOPE: I can't believe I waited until the last minute.

ELLYN: I can't believe you're giving her a shower. (*to Janey*) Oooh, purple hair. Do you want purple hair?

HOPE: Rosie said her place was too small.

ELLYN: What an excuse. (*turns to Hope*) I'm sorry. God. Isn't the consensus now that Susannah's not that bad? That she's actually a human being?

HOPE: And more evolved than Gary.

ELLYN: So she's having a baby. So she needs a shower.

HOPE: Right.

ELLYN: And your house probably isn't big enough to hold all her friends.

She laughs.

HOPE: Ellyn—

ELLYN: Sorry. Where's the gold crayon, Janey? That's always the first one you lose. *(to Hope)* Are you gonna have games and stuff?

Melissa appears. She spots the coloring book.

MELISSA: Oh, that's nice, Ellyn. You could get a showing.

ELLYN: Yes, I am rather proud of it . . .

Melissa slumps down beside Hope.

MELISSA: What's going on?

Melissa picks up one of the invitations.

MELISSA: A baby shower. Let me guess.

A silence.

HOPE: I didn't know if I should send you one.

MELISSA: Go ahead.

ELLYN: Oh, so will you come?

MELISSA: No.

Another silence.

MELISSA: Maybe. I don't know.

HOPE: It's probably weird for you.

MELISSA: No, it's not weird.

They don't believe her. She knows they don't believe her.

MELISSA: It's just . . . waiting for this baby to be born, it's like—Pebbles or Little Ricky or something. Who needs it? You're probably getting nice gifts . . .

HOPE: I was going to spend at least two thousand dollars.

ELLYN: I thought I'd give the baby a college education.

Melissa grins. A silence. Hope is aware that this is all very hard for Melissa.

HOPE *(gentle):* You're going to have to see the baby sometime.

MELISSA: When he's all grown up maybe I can date him. Or Janey can date him.

HOPE: Over my dead body.

ELLYN: Maybe you could swing by the shower and just throw a gift at the door.

MELISSA: Yeah, maybe.

Melissa sits on the floor between Janey and Ellyn.

MELISSA: Move over, girls. Let Aunt Melissa show you how to color. Where's that gold crayon?

She colors.

INT. SUPERMARKET—DAY

Susannah has stopped in front of the frozen dessert section. Gary rolls the grocery cart up behind her.

GARY: Protein.

Susannah holds up a box of some rich disgusting dessert.

SUSANNAH: There's protein in here.

GARY: There is not.

SUSANNAH (*reading the box*): Right here. Protein, one gram.

GARY: One gram. What's the point of being a vegetarian if you're going to eat all this junk?

SUSANNAH: This makes up for tofu.

GARY: Meet you in the produce.

Gary takes the cart and wheels off to the produce section where he examines a cantaloupe. Melissa is nearby sorting through broccoli. She sees Gary. A moment where she could run away without him seeing her. But before she can go, he turns. Spots her.

GARY: Hey.

MELISSA: Hi, I was—I had this shoot down this way and I had a craving for broccoli. I guess you know about cravings.

GARY: Yeah.

A silence.

MELISSA (*re the melon*): That looks like a good one.

GARY: It's got a little green spot on this side.

MELISSA: Oh. Mold probably.

He puts it back.

MELISSA: So, how's the baby thing coming along? Ready to pop?

GARY: Almost. Two weeks. How are you doing?

MELISSA: I'm great.

ARY: Did you—get your invitation?

MELISSA: Invitation?

GARY: Hope's throwing a shower, she'd better have sent out those invitations . . .

MELISSA: Oh, well, I didn't check my mailbox today.

GARY: You'll be there, won't you?

MELISSA: What, you think I'm gonna stiff you on the gift?

GARY: I don't care about the gift.

Melissa doesn't say anything.

GARY: There'll be games. Food. Pony rides . . .

MELISSA: Gary, I really don't think—

GARY: What?

MELISSA: Never mind. I really have to go home.

GARY: Why?

MELISSA: You tell me.

GARY: Melissa. God.

The truth is, he's annoyed at her recalcitrance—but he can't show it.

GARY: Can't we just—go back? Start over? Tell me, what can I do?

MELISSA: I can't tell you.

GARY: Why? I'm asking you—I mean, anything you want, anything you want me to say, just tell me.

Melissa wants him to figure it out for himself.

GARY: Help me out here, Melissa.

She can't.

SUSANNAH *(V.O.)*: Well, this has a lot of calcium—

Susannah appears, carrying two gallons of ice cream. She sees Melissa.

SUSANNAH: Hi, Melissa, how are you?

MELISSA *(totally uncomfortable)*: Fine, actually. Just looking for broccoli.

And they stand there, frozen in their separate awkward postures.

INT. LAMAZE CLASS—NIGHT

A poster shows the stages of labor. We linger on the graph that shows the jagged curve illustrating the dreaded "transition."

ELAINE *(V.O.)*: I could tell you it's not as bad as it looks. Really, I could tell you that, but I'd be lying.

A few nervous laughs. Six couples, including Gary and Susannah, are sprawled with their pillows on the floor of a clinic room. Elaine, the Lamaze teacher, sits by her labor poster.

ELAINE: I mean, in transition your cervix is opening those last few centimeters and it's definitely the most painful time, but it also means you're in the home stretch.

The women don't look convinced.

ELAINE: Really. The population would have died out years ago if it was that bad. Let's try the transition breathing technique again, okay?

The couples adjust themselves on the floor.

ELAINE: Remember, this is just a simulation so you can get an idea of how you'll have to breathe. Are you ready? Coaches?

She holds up a large clock with a minute hand. When the hand reaches twelve:

ELAINE: Deep cleansing breath, relax, and focus.

The couples begin their breathing technique.

ELAINE: Fifteen seconds . . . thirty seconds.

As she counts, Susannah breathes in and out. Gary is doing effleurage.

ELAINE: We're at the peak of the contraction now . . . blow, blow, blow . . .

SUSANNAH: Wait, I'm behind.

GARY: You're fine. Breathe, breathe.

SUSANNAH: No, I can't—

GARY: Shhh. Breathe.

SUSANNAH: Let me do it at my own speed.

ELAINE: Sixty seconds.

GARY: Slow down, you're fine. Shorter breaths, right. You're doing great. That's it. Good.

ELAINE: Ninety seconds. Take a deep cleansing breath, relax. Okay. Anybody pass out?

No one looks very confident.

MOTHER-TO-BE: It's really hard to concentrate.

ELAINE: Don't forget your visualization. And be sure to bring along a picture or something you can use as a focal point. It'll really help.

MOTHER-TO-BE: But it's still so hard.

ELAINE: That's why you have to rely on your coach.

Susannah looks at Gary, a little doubtful. He grins at her.

ELAINE: And you have to practice. It takes a while to get the hang of it. How about a five-minute bathroom break and we'll try it again.

Several pregnant women race for the door. Gary and Susannah remain on the floor.

GARY: We could practice again, right now, if you want.

SUSANNAH: That's okay.

GARY: Really. I've got my watch. Do you want to try?

SUSANNAH (light): No, I don't.

GARY: Come on. You heard what she said. You've got to rely on me. I'm your coach.

SUSANNAH: Yeah, and I'm the one who's having the baby.

She didn't mean it to come out that way. She senses that she's hurt him.

SUSANNAH: I'm sorry—you know what I mean.

GARY: Sure.

SUSANNAH: It's just—there's too much to absorb. I mean, suppose I *can't* do the breathing?

GARY: You'll be able to do it.

SUSANNAH: No, it'll go right out of my head. Everything. And they'll try to give me all kinds of drugs—

GARY: You don't have to have anything you don't want.

SUSANNAH: And I'll probably throw up. Oh, God. Suppose I throw up?

GARY: I'll be there.

SUSANNAH: Oh, right. Laughing.

GARY: No. Not laughing.

Silence. Susannah looks at the labor chart.

SUSANNAH: Gary—

GARY: What?

SUSANNAH: Suppose . . . suppose it doesn't all work? And, I don't know, I can't believe I'm here in a Lamaze class, I can't believe I look like all these other fat women. What are we doing?

Gary kisses her head.

SUSANNAH: I just don't know . . .

GARY: What?

SUSANNAH: I don't know if I can do it.

He puts his hand on her stomach. He doesn't say anything. They sit there, waiting for the baby to kick.

INT. LABOR ROOM—DAY

We've been here before. The clock is where it was at the top of the show.

GARY: Okay, Susannah. I want you to take a cleansing breath—

Susannah takes a breath and . . .

DR. SILVERMAN: Push and push . . . down towards me, can you feel where my fingers are?

The doctor is stretching Susannah's perineum. Gary watches this all, feeling somehow less and less involved.

DR. SILVERMAN: You're going to have to help us, Susannah.

But Susannah's heart isn't in it.

DR. SILVERMAN: Come on, I need a big push—

Susannah isn't responding. A metal pan clatters to the floor.

GARY: Come on, Susannah—you're almost there—

SUSANNAH: I can't.

GARY: Don't quit now.

DR. SILVERMAN (with force): Push. Push.

GARY: If you don't push this baby out, who's gonna read all those crazy Dr. Seuss books we bought?

Susannah's pushing, but not hard enough.

DR. SILVERMAN: Come on, Susannah.

GARY: That's what he's saying, this baby. I want to read Dr. Seuss. (as the baby) I want to watch MTV. I want to meet my dad.

SUSANNAH: No.

GARY: I want to meet my mom.

A silence.

GARY: I want to meet my mom.

Susannah starts to cry.

SUSANNAH: I can't . . .

Dr. Silverman looks at Isabel.

DR. SILVERMAN: Let's get her ready and go down the hall.

ISABEL: Poor thing, she's completely exhausted—

And Susannah realizes that she's got to fight because all this, what she's going through, is going to result in something spectacular.

SUSANNAH: No.

Another contraction is coming . . . Gary glances at the monitor, looks back to Susannah.

GARY: Here we go, it looks like the Himalayas of contractions here, but I've got my money on this one.

Susannah starts to breathe and to push.

DOCTOR SILVERMAN: That's right, come on, Susannah.

GARY: Push, yeah. It's the Himalayas, yikes, it's Mt. Everest, no, I think it's the Matterhorn, I see the bobsled—

DR. SILVERMAN: Here we go.

And the baby arrives . . .

THE LABOR ROOM

afterward. Quiet. Most of the technicians have cleared out. The baby in Susannah's arms. Small and perfect. Gary and Susannah almost holding their breath, unable to believe it.

OUTSIDE THE LABOR ROOM

Gary steps outside, starts down the hallway, stops. Melissa is standing in front of the nursery, looking through the window. Gary walks over to her.

GARY: Not one of those in there is mine.

A silence.

GARY: Do you want to see her?

MELISSA: What, now?

GARY: Yeah.

MELISSA: I don't know . . .

Gary takes Melissa's arm. They start down the hallway.

HOSPITAL ROOM

Gary and Melissa walk in. Susannah is in bed with the new baby. No one says anything. Melissa steps in close to the bed and Susannah hands her the baby.

SUSANNAH: **Be careful with her head.**

And Melissa is very careful.

I'M NOBODY! WHO ARE YOU?

BY
WINNIE HOLZMAN

In September of 1989, my life took an unexpected turn for the more interesting. I'd written a spec script for *thirtysomething* in my spare time (which described nearly *all* my time, at the time) and the impossible occurred. They'd liked it. I remember my first meeting with them (Marshall Herskovitz, Ed Zwick, Richard Kramer) because it wasn't like any first meeting I'd ever had. It wasn't like any conversation I'd ever had. It started in the middle. It was already in progress. It was like coming in on the middle of a very involved anecdote that somebody had been telling for three years. I remember Ed saying to me in his pretending-to-pick-a-fight tone: "What do you *want?*" "I want to work here," I said. (I was playing hard to get.)

I loved them, right off. I loved listening to them talk. I even understood most of what they were talking *about*. Which was amazing, because they're old friends, and they speak "Old-Friend." Fluently. But I understood, and when I didn't, I smiled and smoked cigarettes. I got my first script assignment that day.

The story of how I came to write that spec script and how it actually landed me a job became my favorite story. You've probably heard it, I probably told it to you. I told everybody. I told waitresses, shopkeepers; I told it so I could hear it, so I could believe it. You see, I hadn't spent the last ten years waking up in the morning and saying, "Please God, let today be the day I join the staff of a well-respected prime time television show." I was too busy wondering if I really was a writer. I'd written and not written. I'd had people ask me, in hushed tones, as though someone were in the hospital, "Are you still writing?" And I'd had other people encourage me. But at parties, and on bank applications, where it said "Occupation," I'd never been absolutely certain what to say. Until this job.

"I'm Nobody, Who Are You?" explores (in part) what it means to feel like a failure. I wrote it at a time when I'd never experienced more of what the world calls success. Success and failure are very similar: Both are frightening and oddly freeing— opposite sides of the same illusion. Success pays better. Both put your friendships to the test. This was one of the many themes I planned to explore, just as soon as I got miserable enough to begin writing.

It didn't take long. Sure, I had my brand-new, great-conversation-piece of a job, but luckily I remained my deeply disturbed self. I say luckily, because if landing this job had actually given me confidence, I don't know how I would have written anything. I write out of fear. Fear is my copilot; it gets the script off the ground. I don't start writing until I feel my life is at stake.

But I had nothing to worry about; I was still afraid. I feared the script was boring. It featured Gary, and I feared that Gary, in my anxious hands, would sound suspiciously like a Jewish girl from Long Island. I would lie there at night, whispering to my unbelievably patient husband: "You don't understand! Nothing happens! The baby coughs, Gary doesn't meet Charles Barkley and Susannah takes a bath. Nothing happens." "But you wrote that other one," my husband would say. "And it came out great. What's the problem?" My first assigned script (an Ellyn show, which Polly Draper performed to perfection) had, in fact, turned out fine. I knew what that meant: this one was destined to fail.

I was afraid of the basketball stuff. In the story meetings with Marshall and Ed, we had discussed a scene (it was later, mercifully, cut) where Gary would play basketball with the DAA team. I attempted to explain to Marshall just how little firsthand (or any hand) knowledge I could bring to such a scene. Marshall smiled his Young Abe Lincoln smile and said, "It's easy, make it up." Now, that happens to be great advice. But I just couldn't picture myself, a person who flinches when you throw a beach ball at her, making something like basketball "up." I forced myself to write the scene and it was pretty wretched; lots of desperate sounding "manliness," like an Irish Spring commercial on steroids. You won't find it in the script, and I'll never show it to you.

I'd like to say a word about those story meetings. To start work on a given script, you first have to sit for a while in either Marshall's or Ed's office and wait for them to get off the phone. I happen to like this part. You're not writing yet, and they're both so good at outlining stories that they make it seem easy. The conversation becomes immediately, and insanely, personal. They become two mad scientists in lab coats, pouncing on some detail from your past so they can smear it on a slide and examine it under a microscope. Their dedication to making the scripts personal just slays me. Not autobiographical—personal. They want you to ransack your psyche for buried treasure (or ransack *theirs,* if yours is at the cleaners) and use that buried treasure in whatever way you choose, as long as you deliver the emotional goods. The emotional goods should be about fifty-five pages long, without too many outside locations.

This script started with a series of images. Some were tiny; I wanted them to simply accumulate, to gather power. Gary and Susannah had to feel and seem deprived, so I made sure they never had quite enough of anything. The camera can't be found. They run out of hot water. Gary never gets to eat lunch at DAA, and he can't find the book he needs. Wherever I could, I took things away from them: Even memo pads elude them. Susannah keeps making lists of what they need, and finally both of them end up on "the waiting list." That's the way my mind works, and that's the kind of stuff I love to write.

As soon as we'd determined that Gary would be teaching again, I knew his subject would be Emily Dickinson. I wanted him on shaky ground, teaching something he didn't feel secure with, to feed the sense of failure. Emily Dickinson is shaky ground. She kind of dares you to understand her. And, of course, she's one of the few people I can think of who's famous for being a nobody.

It was Richard who suggested I actually make her a character. My first and favorite version of the Emily scene took place in a Laundromat. Gary's doing his laundry late at night, going over his poetry notes as the dryer spins. Emily appears, they have a conversation, and right after Emma is mentioned, Emily vanishes. The dryer buzzes, Gary opens the dryer door, and a tiny white T-shirt falls out. I just go nuts for stuff like that. But we couldn't afford a Laundromat.

Richard ended up directing the episode. We talked a lot, and argued a lot, and then there was that ghastly stretch when we both became polite. Handing a script to a director is one of the hardest challenges I ever face. People say writing is like giving birth. If it is, then handing your script to the director is like pulling the newborn off your breast and sending her to military school. Maybe it's not like this for other people. Maybe there are writers who thrust their finished scripts into the directors' and actors' hands saying cheerfully, "I've done my part. It's all yours. Go nuts." If you are one of those people, don't ever call me. Because, no matter how I try to prepare myself, or how wonderful and talented the actors are, when I get to that moment, I'm never ready. I'm never ready for the shock of letting other people in on this impassioned conversation I've been having with myself. Because I'm not hearing it for the first time when the actors get there, I've been hearing it for weeks, listening to it instead of answering my daughter's questions; instead of laughing at my husband's puns. For weeks I've taken my life in my hands just getting in the car; I start thinking about a particular line and about which would be funnier, a "but" or a "yet"—and I forget to notice things like oncoming traffic.

Now, sometimes "yet" is funnier, and sometimes it isn't, and often I have to have that particular Ping-Pong match in my head for a day and a half before I know for sure. My house will be a mess, my dishes will be growing moss in the sink, I won't be able to find my glasses (or my husband's glasses, or my husband, for that matter) and I'll be sitting there, fretting about "but" and "yet."

Most people (many of them actors and directors) don't want to know from "but" and "yet." And as heart breaking as it is for us "but/yet" people (and I know you're out there, I can hear you muttering to yourselves), we have to accept it. Because you have to keep going, or your dishes (and your life) got mossy for nothing. You have to let go. It's not easy, because, yes, I'm writing the script for other people to interpret, and yet (or *but*), when the moment comes, and they're ignoring my stage directions, those people appear to be getting in the way. I keep forgetting that they *are* the way. That things like rewrites and self-expression are not supposed to go smoothly. A coma goes smoothly. Watching *The Love Connection* tends to go smoothly. The worthwhile stuff—writing, child-rearing, and falling in love—never does. And yes, I can tell someone I barely know a smooth story about how I landed this wonderful job, but it's only the cleaned-up, Disney version of what happened. I'll never be able to describe to anyone the circuitous route I took to get here, or why it was worth the trip.

Right after the episode aired, my brother called me. "I loved it," he said. "It was *sad*." He sounded surprised; I was surprised back. I'd been so caught up with "buts" and "yets" and various other ego problems that I'd forgotten it was sad. I'd forgotten it was anything. But he thought it was sad—which made me happy. I was happy for at least ten minutes. And then I wanted to start another one.

WINNIE HOLZMAN

ACT ONE

Gary . . . close up. We don't know where he is yet.

GARY: What I'm trying to say is—I've been offered this job. It's not a great job. The money's not—what I was earning before. Of course, it's still money. It's just that I'd have to teach a semester of Modern American Poetry, which is practically an oxymoron. And I'm probably just oxymoronic enough to teach it. Anyway, I could use some feedback . . .

We now find that we are in

INT. GARY'S LIVING ROOM

and that Gary's confidante is Emma, seated across from him in a baby seat as he spoons cottage cheese into her. He reaches to catch a mouthful.

GARY: Hey—not food back, *feed*back.

Susannah enters, in the middle of getting dressed.

SUSANNAH: Did you say something?

GARY: It's a first—it's a breakthrough! Like in *The Miracle Worker* when Patty Duke discovers water? Only it's cottage cheese and Emma's cuter.

SUSANNAH: Let me do some. Is there any coffee?

GARY: We're out.

SUSANNAH *(as she takes over feeding the baby . . .):* Did you call them?

GARY: Not yet. You taking her to work today?

SUSANNAH: Today's her checkup. And she's a mess, where are the Wet Wipes . . . ?

GARY: Is this incredible? Baby's first curd.

SUSANNAH: Are you going to call them today?

GARY: We're not doing this right! When she does something for the first time we're supposed to take a picture of it . . . where's that camera?

SUSANNAH: Gary . . . ?

GARY: It's around here somewhere—

SUSANNAH: Gary—

GARY: Did I see it in the bedroom?

SUSANNAH: I thought you were going to tell them yes today.

GARY: Yeah, I know, but—what happens to her? What do we do about her?

SUSANNAH: If you want to take this job, why can't you just say so?

GARY *(after a pause):* I want to take this job.

She looks up at him.

GARY: I made a decision.

SUSANNAH *(with a trace of a smile):* Another first.

GARY: Too bad we don't have the camera.

INT. DAA—ELLIOT'S OFFICE—DAY

Michael and Elliot are seated, the desk strewn with work.

MICHAEL: Just listen. Miles puts in a hundred, he wants five partners at ten each, there's a monthly income, when they sell there's a huge return, *plus* the tax break—

ELLIOT: What did you do, buy a phrase book? Conversational Republican?

MICHAEL: Elliot—Miles is offering this as a *friend*. That's all this is. Friends.

ELLIOT: And money.

MICHAEL: Just think about it.

ELLIOT: I don't want to think about it.

MICHAEL: You don't?

ELLIOT: No. I'll just do it.

Gary enters, dressed like his idea of an adult.

GARY: I'll just do it, too. What is it? Where's my lunch? I thought I was invited to lunch—

Catherine, Michael's secretary, enters with lunch.

CATHERINE: Lunch!

MICHAEL: So how's everything, how's Emma?

GARY: Still unemployed—but her dad just got a job. I'm teaching again.

MICHAEL: Great! Gary—

ELLIOT: That's great—

MICHAEL: Listen. Gary.

ELLIOT: You want to play some basketball?

GARY: Can I have lunch first?

ELLIOT: Seriously.

MICHAEL: Advertising League.

ELLIOT: Uniforms.

MICHAEL: Lost a player.

ELLIOT: Tendonitis.

MICHAEL: Big game Wednesday.

ELLIOT: Have a dumpling.

MICHAEL: So we're thinking—

ELLIOT: Then it hits us—

Michael and Elliot look at each other, and then look at Gary.

GARY: No.

MICHAEL AND ELLIOT *(in unison):* Oh come on . . . Please? Please? Please?

GARY: Why should I play for DAA? I don't work here—

ELLIOT: You think *we* do?

MICHAEL: You'll be a ringer—

ELLIOT: We'll say you work in the mail room.

GARY: I have a *job*! I have to teach Emily Dickinson!

ELLIOT: Teach her what?

GARY: Look, things are really—Susannah needs me at home.

ELLIOT: Forget it. He's person-whipped.

Michael and Elliot take Gary's lunch out of his hand and toss it.

GARY: Wait a second—

Catherine appears in the doorway.

CATHERINE: Excuse me—Charles Barkley's people are here.

MICHAEL: They're early.

ELLIOT: We'd better go.

As Michael and Elliot go out, Gary follows behind.

GARY *(brought up short):* Charles Barkley's people?

DAA—HALLWAY—DAY

As we move with the three of them down the hall.

MICHAEL: I told you about that, didn't I?

ELLIOT: We're doing a spot with him!

GARY *(trying to absorb it):* You're doing a commercial with Charles Barkley.

MICHAEL: I thought I told you—

GARY: Oh yeah, like I might have *forgotten.*

MICHAEL: Yeah, well, we were gonna introduce you—

ELLIOT: Seeing how you're such a good friend and all—

MICHAEL: *Plus* throw in courtside seats to the next Sixers' game—

ELLIOT: But if you're not gonna play ball—

A tense silence. Then:

GARY: Does it have to be the mail room?

INT. GARY'S LIVING ROOM—NIGHT

Early evening chaos. Gary, on the floor, sits at the coffee table, books and papers scattered around him.

GARY: I can't believe they're making me start off with Emily Dickinson. What a bitch.

Susannah enters from the kitchen.

SUSANNAH: Okay. I'm making a list of everything we need . . .

GARY: She's incomprehensible. There was *one* guy in grad school who actually understood her. He dropped out. Now he dips candles.

SUSANNAH *(reading from list):* Paper towels. Bananas. Day care.

GARY: What'll I wear tomorrow? What do you wear to teach Emily Dickinson?

SUSANNAH *(not listening):* I don't know . . .

GARY: Michael's doing a commercial with Charles Barkley.

SUSANNAH *(mind elsewhere):* Charles Barkley? Oh, that—basketball person?

GARY *(frustrated):* Yeah. That basketball person.

SUSANNAH: Okay, we need Wet Wipes, we need to talk to the super, the heat's still not coming up . . . We really need to sit down and figure out a schedule, I mean we need to figure out—Gary!

GARY: What? I'm listening. Wet Wipes.

SUSANNAH: Every morning it's like—oh, she's still *here.* We need some kind of *routine*—

GARY *(re his paperwork):* Let me just finish this . . .

SUSANNAH: That light in the refrigerator went out. *(writing again)* "Tiny light bulb."

This reminds Gary of Emma. He looks up from his work to the spill of light coming from Emma's room.

GARY: She's never this quiet. Probably wondering when the *real* parents get here.

SUSANNAH: She's *fine.* If she weren't fine she'd be screaming.

INT. GARY'S LIVING ROOM—NIGHT

It's now 1 A.M. and we hear one bloodcurdling baby scream. Gary turns a light on and we see

Susannah, petrified, holding Emma. We hear choking and gasping from the baby. Gary emerges from the bathroom.

SUSANNAH: Oh my God . . . What do I do?

GARY: Give her this, take her temperature—

SUSANNAH: Just feel her! She's burning up! They said she was fine at the clinic, that was this *morning,* how could this happen?

GARY: I'll call the clinic. What's the number?

SUSANNAH: The clinic is closed!

GARY *(desperately trying to stay calm):* Okay, so—so we—what? Where's that baby book?

SUSANNAH: Forget that book! I *hate* Penelope Leach! I hate *all* British people—oh my God, Gary, what's that sound she's making?

GARY *(helpless):* I don't know—

SUSANNAH: Gary—

GARY: Should I call nine-one-one? I'm calling nine-one-one . . .

INT. STEADMAN BEDROOM—NIGHT

Michael, in bed, picks up the ringing phone; we now intercut between Hope and Michael in their bedroom and Gary and Susannah.

MICHAEL *(groggy):* Uh-huh? No, that's okay—*(to Hope)* Gary. The baby's sick . . .

A half-asleep Hope instinctively takes the receiver.

HOPE: Gary . . . ? Uh-huh. Does it sound like barking? Because it could be croup—

GARY *(not in good shape):* It sounds like—

SUSANNAH: The worst sound I've ever heard—

GARY: The worst sound I've ever heard—

HOPE: If it *is* croup, you need a humidifier . . .

GARY *(whispers, to Susannah):* We might need a humidifier!

SUSANNAH: Do we have a humidifier?

GARY *(back to Hope):* We don't have a humidifier—

HOPE: You need a cool air humidifier. Gary? You want me to call my pediatrician?

GARY *(to Susannah):* Do we want her to call her pediatrician?

SUSANNAH *(way out there):* I don't know!

HOPE: Because—hello? She would probably just tell you to take her to the emergency room—

GARY *(to Susannah):* She says take her to the emergency room—

SUSANNAH *(horrified):* The emergency room!

HOPE: Hello? Gary? Gary—is the baby blue?

GARY *(to Susannah):* Is she blue?

SUSANNAH *(alarmed):* No, she's not blue, why . . . ?

HOPE: Because, Gary . . . ? You should probably take her to the emergency room, just to be safe. Gary?

A COMPUTER SCREEN—VERY CLOSE UP

Cool, impersonal letters spill out and become words: "Name of patient: Hart-Shepherd, Emma . . ."

INT. HOSPITAL EXAMINING ROOM—NIGHT

Gary and Susannah watch anxiously as a young intern wraps up his examination of Emma. Susannah is in her nightgown with a coat over it. The intern looks up at them.

INTERN: **Croup.**

Gary and Susannah look at each other.

GARY AND SUSANNAH: **Croup.**

ON THE COMPUTER SCREEN

"Diagnosis: Croup. Charges—" And we go back to

INT. HOSPITAL EXAMINING ROOM—NIGHT

The intern is gone now.

GARY *(to Emma):* **It's all right, sweetie . . .**

SUSANNAH: **Everything's all right . . .**

Gary looks at Susannah.

GARY: **How much you think this'll cost?**

SUSANNAH: **I don't know . . .**

And we briefly revisit

THE COMPUTER SCREEN

as the charges add up, culminating in the words "Insurance: Not Covered." Which sends us back to

INT. HOSPITAL EXAMINING ROOM—NIGHT

GARY: **So you'll be okay with her while I do this?**

SUSANNAH: **We'll be okay . . .**

GARY: **They just did—a few tests. I mean how much could it *be?***

SUSANNAH: **I don't know. I don't know anything.**

GARY: **Me neither.**

ACT TWO

INT. GARY'S BEDROOM—DAY

As Gary gets dressed, Susannah enters with Emma. She's still wearing her nightgown.

SUSANNAH: No more hot water. Now we're out of steam . . .

GARY: Hope says we need a humidifier.

SUSANNAH (*mimicking him*): "Hope says, Hope says—" If Hope told you to jump off a bridge would you do it?

GARY: Today I would. Look—I better go get a humidifier.

SUSANNAH: And be late, your first day? Even you know that's crazy!

GARY: Well you can't take her out, she's sick, what are you gonna do?

SUSANNAH *(fed up):* Why are you always asking me what I'm gonna *do?* I don't *know* what I'm gonna do, okay? I live on the edge.

GARY: Just—call somebody. Call Hope.

SUSANNAH: No! Gary! I mean, pardon me, I know she's married to your best friend, I know she's beyond reproach, I know she breast-fed *her* daughter until the kid actually *begged* her to stop—

GARY: Look, whatever you want to do is fine, send Emma to the cleaners, let *them* steam her—

SUSANNAH: Well, I'm sorry, but I think I can live my life without—

INT. GARY'S LIVING ROOM—DAY

Susannah opens the door to a serene-looking Hope, who carries a large shopping bag.

SUSANNAH: Hope! I'm really sorry.

HOPE: It's really okay.

SUSANNAH: I just hate—you know. Disturbing you like this.

HOPE: I'm not disturbed. Really.

A brief pause.

HOPE *(ever so gently):* Can I come in?

INT. GARY'S KITCHEN—DAY

Hope fills the humidifier at the sink while Susannah looks through the shopping bag Hope brought. Its contents fill her with nameless anxiety.

HOPE: Isn't croup fun? You didn't know she could imitate a cocker spaniel, did you?

SUSANNAH: Coffee . . . orange juice . . . ! And what are these?

HOPE: They're muffins. They're a popular baked good.

SUSANNAH *(thrown):* You didn't have to bring all this. Ginger ale?

HOPE: Yeah, you let it go flat, and then you give it to them instead of formula. Settles the stomach. And they don't dehydrate. That's this big thing, you can't let them dehydrate. Unless you're *really* mad at them.

Susannah stares at her with utter seriousness.

HOPE: I'm kidding. *(re the humidifier)* Where do you want this?

SUSANNAH: Oh, in Emma's room—Let me pay you for that—

HOPE: I didn't buy this, we had two.

Susannah has to accept this charity. And she will. And it kills her.

INT. EMMA'S ROOM—DAY

Minutes later. They have plugged in the humidifier, and are watching Emma sleep peacefully.

HOPE: It's scary when they're sick.

SUSANNAH: I feel—partially responsible.

HOPE: Only partially? When Janey gets sick I *know* it's directly related to the fact that I'm a bad mother and a terrible person.

SUSANNAH: Yesterday I took her to the clinic for her checkup. We waited six hours. And then, we never even saw an actual *doctor,* it was one of those—practitioners. Which, I mean, I support that wholeheartedly, the medical community *needs* that, it's just difficult when—you know—

HOPE: Right. When it's *your* baby. *(after the tiniest pause)* Would you like the number of our pediatrician?

SUSANNAH: Oh. Thanks, but—no. Really. I've disturbed you enough.

HOPE: But you wouldn't be disturbing me. You'd be disturbing my pediatrician. Who wouldn't be disturbed.

SUSANNAH: Hope, we can't afford your pediatrician, okay?

HOPE: How do you know? I mean—what about Gary's new job, they must have given him a health plan—

SUSANNAH: Oh yeah, big help—any illness under five hundred dollars? Not covered! I mean, it cost us seven hundred *dollars* last night for two hours in the emergency room! Gary and I both have jobs and we're barely getting by! I mean, what do people *do* when their kids get sick? I don't mean people like you, I mean—

She stops short, realizing she's said too much.

HOPE *(polite, but . . .)*: I know what you mean.

INT. STEADMAN HOUSE—KITCHEN—NIGHT

Hope's dishing up dinner, Ellyn's merely dishing.

ELLYN: So what happened? I mean, in what way was she weird? I mean, she's *always* weird but, in what way was she *weirder?*

HOPE: I don't know. I think they're both under a lot of strain—

ELLYN: Why? Did somebody tell Gary that Simon and Garfunkel broke up?

HOPE: I brought her this humidifier . . .

ELLYN: Hope! How—*unkind.*

HOPE: And she was—somewhat cold.

ELLYN: She *is* somewhat cold. Look, I'm your best friend. You can tell me. Is she your new best friend?

HOPE: Come on. You know what she said? She said they're barely getting by—

Michael enters from the dining room.

MICHAEL *(to Hope)*: Who's barely getting by?

HOPE: Gary and Susannah. Those were her words.

ELLYN: But Gary couldn't really be poor. Just think what he must spend on conditioner!

HOPE: Ellyn—

ELLYN: No, seriously—that *poor* image. Don't they just kind of put that on, to seem principled?

HOPE: Ellyn—could you put the potatoes out, please? Where's Janey?

MICHAEL: Upstairs. Practicing her oboe. *(as he goes out)* Janey . . . ?

INT. EMMA'S ROOM—NIGHT

Two in the morning. Gary's singing softly to the baby.

GARY: "Hush little baby don't say a word. Papa's gonna buy you a mockingbird. If that mockingbird don't sing, Papa's gonna buy you—"

Susannah enters. They whisper.

SUSANNAH: Why is it freezing, it's *April* . . .

GARY: Stupid, materialistic lullaby. Extolling the virtues of waste and greed.

SUSANNAH: Why is this room so cold?

GARY: Unfortunately, it's true, though. I *do* want to buy her things.

SUSANNAH: I talk to the super and he nods, and it's *still* cold.

GARY: You know what I've been trying to figure out . . . ?

GARY'S BEDROOM—NIGHT

As Gary and Susannah enter . . .

GARY: . . . First there's a cart and *bull*. Two incredibly useful items for an infant, right? And then later, when the dog can't bark, there's a *horse* and cart. I mean, why *two carts?*

SUSANNAH *(after a beat)*: I don't know. I just want her to be warm.

GARY: I mean, cart doesn't even *rhyme* with bark.

SUSANNAH: Maybe we should ask your mother to buy us a space heater.

GARY: I never thought about heat. Growing up.

SUSANNAH: Or maybe we should move her into our bedroom. Until this cold snap is over . . .

GARY: The house was just—warm. Then it was air-conditioned. Then it was warm again. I never gave it a thought.

SUSANNAH: I want her to have her own room. Not her own *nook*. A person should have their own place. I'm going to put another blanket on her . . .

Susannah goes out. We linger for a beat with Gary, then:

EMMA'S ROOM—NIGHT

The only light is the night-light from the hall. Susannah smooths the blanket over Emma and looks down at her for a moment. She looks up. Gary is in the doorway.

GARY: I have to figure out a way to make some money. I mean—*real* money. (*another beat, he looks at her*) You're not arguing with me.

SUSANNAH: No. I'm not.

INT. STEADMAN BEDROOM—NIGHT

Hope sits on the edge of the bed, half-watching TV. Michael emerges from the bathroom.

MICHAEL: We actually have money now. That's all I'm saying.

HOPE: I know.

MICHAEL: Which is why this real estate thing's a good idea. You know?

He waits for her response; it doesn't come.

MICHAEL: I just can't get used to it. Having money. (*after a beat*) Suannah said they were barely making it?

HOPE: She pretty much did, yeah.

MICHAEL: You know, it might even be possible—I mean, I'd have to figure out if I could even do this, but—I could invest ten thousand for me and another ten thousand for him. For Gary. I might be able to handle that . . .

HOPE: Michael, you can't do favors like that for people.

MICHAEL: Why not?

HOPE: Because they never forgive you.

MICHAEL: But this isn't people. This is *Gary*. *(a beat, quietly . . .)* So it's different.

INT. LOCKER ROOM—SHOWERS—DAY

Michael and Gary take a post-basketball shower. Gary's high on how well he played.

MICHAEL: So how's the baby, Hope was right, it was croup?

GARY: Hope was right. She's better—

Elliot passes by on his way out.

ELLIOT: Hey, nice going, Gary! You were great—

GARY: Thanks! *(back to Michael)* You know, speaking of Emma? Last night I had this kind of incredible idea—

He waits; is Michael listening? Michael turns to him.

GARY *(excited, intense)*: It's really kind of a *business* idea—

MICHAEL *(mildly surprised)*: Oh, yeah . . . ?

GARY: Yeah, I was thinking, you know what there's probably a real *demand* for, these days?

INT. LOCKER ROOM—DAY

They are getting dressed.

MICHAEL *(wary)*: Lullabies?

GARY: Yeah! I mean, think about it—there are *no decent lullabies!* They're all about babies falling out of cradles and blackbirds biting off noses, it's like a Brian De Palma movie! So I thought, rewrite the lyrics, make 'em reflect people's *lives,* like, I don't know—

Totally caught up in this, he sings, to the tune of *Rockabye Baby* . . .

GARY: "Rockabye, baby, here on my chest/Too bad your dad is post-natally depressed . . ."

MICHAEL: You're depressed?

GARY: No! That's just an example! Of course, I'd need a recording studio. I thought maybe you could help me with that part—

MICHAEL: You mean like—for fun.

GARY: No! I'm talking about a real business thing!

Michael looks at Gary, and impulsively steps across an invisible line into a place he wasn't even sure he was ready to explore.

MICHAEL: Look, there's this thing I've been offered. And I was thinking—

Suddenly Michael stops, losing his nerve. Only there's no turning back.

GARY: What?

MICHAEL (*uncomfortable now*): Nothing.

GARY (*really curious*): *What?* You were thinking *what?*

MICHAEL (*not looking at him*): That—see, I'm going in on this investment deal at work, it's a commercial building on City Line? You invest, and you get a monthly income? And I was thinking maybe—we could go in on it together, that I could invest ten thousand for myself, and—ten for you. And then in a few years, when the building sells—I get my ten thousand back and you keep the increase.

Gary is silent. Michael waits, then continues.

MICHAEL: I'm saying—it's a very sound investment.

GARY (*impossible to read*): Uh-huh.

Did they make a wrong turn somewhere? Because now they're truly in uncharted territory. Michael plows on.

MICHAEL: It's just something you should think about. It has nothing to do with your idea—which, you know, you could still *do*—

GARY: Oh. Right.

MICHAEL: I mean, I hope it didn't come out sounding—strange.

GARY (*eerily polite*): Uh-huh. Strange in what way?

MICHAEL: Because, I mean, I wouldn't do this with just anyone.

GARY: No. Of course.

MICHAEL: But, you know, you say you're interested in something real? Well this is real.

GARY: It sounds real.

Michael edges to the door.

MICHAEL: I gotta get moving.

Michael hesitates. He senses on some level that he has taken
something from his friend, and now has to give something back.

MICHAEL: You played great today.

GARY: I know.

Michael leaves. Gary watches him go. A beat. Then he kicks a
locker door, hard.

ACT THREE

INT. GARY'S LIVING ROOM—DAY

Morning. Susannah buckles Emma into her stroller as Gary looks with increasing frustration through his bookcase.

GARY: **Have you seen a really beat-up copy of Emily Dickinson . . . ?**

SUSANNAH *(pointing to his school stuff):* **It's right there—**

GARY *(continuing to search):* **No, my *other* copy. From college. I took notes in the margins. God, I wonder if it could be in with the cookbooks . . . ?**

Susannah follows Gary as he heads for the kitchen.

INT. GARY'S KITCHEN—DAY

SUSANNAH: **Look, I'm taking her to work, okay? I mean, what else can I do—she's not barking anymore.**

Susannah prepares a bottle for Emma. Gary is distracted from his search for Emily Dickinson by a ragged piece of paper towel that he finds on the counter.

GARY: **What's this . . . ?** *(reading the towel)* **103 Broom?**

SUSANNAH: The address of that day-care center, the one with the vacancy—

GARY: We've got to start using memo pads . . .

SUSANNAH: Yeah. That'll fix everything. I went there.

GARY: And . . . ?

SUSANNAH: It sucked.

GARY: Could you elaborate?

SUSANNAH: It sucked eggs. It was overcrowded, it was disorganized—

GARY: So she'd feel right at home. What about that place I saw advertised? I wrote their number on a napkin . . .

He picks through the trash for said napkin, can't find it, then picks up a tissue box with something scrawled on it.

GARY *(reading off the tissue box)*: What's this, "dinner, thurs"?

SUSANNAH: Hope called yesterday, I said yes.

GARY: Without asking me first?

SUSANNAH: I checked your paper towel. You were free.

She heads back for the living room, Gary follows her.

INT. GARY'S LIVING ROOM—DAY

Susannah gives Emma her bottle as

GARY: Well, how come Michael didn't mention it?

SUSANNAH: Isn't that the custom in your tribe? The men hunt and play basketball, the women gather kindling and dinner dates?

GARY: Call her back. Say we couldn't get a sitter.

SUSANNAH: No way! She probably thinks I dislike her as it is—

GARY: Why would she think that?

SUSANNAH: Because I sort of—almost—do. Sometimes.

GARY: Why? She's been incredibly—helpful, hasn't she?

SUSANNAH: Exactly!

GARY: Look, fine! You almost sometimes don't like her? Then call her back and tell her we couldn't get a sitter.

Susannah looks up and studies him.

SUSANNAH: Why don't you want to go?

Gary turns away from her, puts his coat on.

GARY: I don't know. Look, the truth is we shouldn't be going out to dinner this week, we shouldn't be spending money on *sitters*!

SUSANNAH *(gently):* Rosie volunteered. I think she's kind of looking *forward* to it.

She waits, but there's no reply, so . . .

SUSANNAH: I'm sorry, I should have asked you first.

GARY: No. Look, you want to go, we'll go. I just don't—I don't know. I don't understand people anymore.

SUSANNAH *(wanting to help):* Who don't you understand?

GARY: I don't know. Emily Dickinson.

He picks up his briefcase and kisses her good-bye. The kiss answers none of her questions; she watches him leave.

INT. COLLEGE CLASSROOM—DAY

A room of freshmen stare up at Gary as he reads to them from Emily Dickinson.

GARY: "I'm Nobody! Who are you?/ Are you Nobody, too?/ Then there's a pair of us!—don't tell!/ They'd banish us, you know!" *(he looks up, pauses)* So . . . what do we have here? We have somebody who's admitting she's "nobody." Well, not just admitting it, *enjoying* it, right? In a kind of . . .

He looks out at the class, sensing that he's not reaching them. Then, to cover this insecurity—he drags out the Ivy League Lingo.

GARY: . . . In what could almost be described as a kind of— existential exploration. Of ego-less-ness. If you will. Questions?

Several students raise their hands.

GARY: Yes . . . ?

STUDENT 1: Yeah, in employing such phrases as "existential exploration" and "if you will," aren't you attempting to boost your *own* ego? I'm referring to your lack of tenure, lack of ambition, and of course the fact that you've never met Charles Barkley—

GARY: What?

More hands go up, and . . .

STUDENT 2 *(to student 1):* But isn't his lack of ambition a smoke screen, to mask his deep hunger for approval? We see this behavior in Dickinson, who kept her poems locked in a drawer, while yearning for recognition.

STUDENT 3 *(to student 2):* Yes, but Emily Dickinson was a genius. He's just an assistant professor at a second-rate city college—

GARY: Uh, let's not let this degenerate into—I mean I think we're losing track of—yes?

STUDENT 4: Yeah, this is kind of a two-part question: When you first encountered Dickinson's poetry as an undergraduate, did you ever imagine that Michael Steadman would end up earning so much more money than you? And second: regarding those sneakers, do you wear them because you can't afford new ones, or are they some kind of—metaphor?

Gary, bewildered, looks out at the sea of faces. The fantasy fades. The students stare blankly back at him. No hands in the air. Dead silence.

GARY: Well, if nobody has any questions . . . we'll break a little early.

Gary watches the students go, then looks down self-consciously at his sneakers.

INT. CHIC RESTAURANT—NIGHT

Hope, Michael, Elliot, Nancy, Susannah, and Gary share a crowded table. Susannah and Gary glance anxiously at the menu as the conversation percolates around them.

NANCY: No, listen, first they rub you all over with sea salt, or something? To remove your dead skin . . .

ELLIOT: Hey, I gave at the office—

NANCY: . . . Then they cover you with oil and wrap you in hot towels . . .

MICHAEL: And throw you from a moving car?

HOPE: But, aren't those places just—incredibly expensive?

ELLIOT: So what, you can afford it—

MICHAEL: Susannah, you look great, did you do something different, with your hair . . . ?

Everyone looks expectantly at Susannah.

SUSANNAH: Just—stopped washing it.

NANCY: Here's where we should all go together—my editor told me about this retreat, upstate New York? It's really peaceful, like basket-weaving peaceful? And it's run by Quakers . . . ?

ELLIOT: First they rub you all over with *oatmeal*—

The waitress approaches to recite tonight's vaguely unsettling specials.

WAITRESS: Good evening, tonight we have the orange roughy, it's swimming in a light tomato cream sauce, it's twenty-three ninety-five—

Hope and Michael attempt to release some of the growing pressure.

MICHAEL *(to Susannah):* The roughy is good here—

HOPE: Well, but *everything's* good here—

WAITER: We have the sea bass, it's grilled, it comes with avocado butter, it's twenty-one dollars—and finally the gnocchi, they are hand-rolled, stuffed with pumpkin and parmesan, seventeen-fifty.

A silence as they all contemplate gnocchi.

GARY: I'll have the Caesar salad.

SUSANNAH: Two.

ELLIOT: I'll have the, uh, hand-rolled . . . thing?

WAITER: Gnocchi.

ELLIOT: That. And another wine.

MICHAEL: Let's get a bottle for the table—okay?

He looks around the table for reactions, ending up at Gary, who shrugs, and looks away.

INT. CHIC RESTAURANT—NIGHT

The end of the meal. As we hear the following conversation, we see Gary, who watches the waiter bring the check, watches Michael receive the check, looks to see who else has seen Michael receive the check . . .

NANCY *(to Gary):* So you're teaching again—are you enjoying it?

SUSANNAH: Yes, I think he is—*(to Gary)* Are you?

Gary nods, but his attention remains on the check.

NANCY *(to Susannah):* So what are you gonna do about the baby, now that he's working again?

SUSANNAH: We're looking into day care.

NANCY: That's gotta be scary . . .

HOPE: Why? There's plenty of decent day care out there—

NANCY: I'm just saying—her baby's very young; we're not talking about a toddler—

HOPE: There are just as many studies that say day care has no ill effects as there are saying it's harmful.

NANCY: Look, I know it's a choice people make, I'm just saying—

SUSANNAH: It's not a choice.

They stop arguing and turn to her.

SUSANNAH: I mean, we don't really *have* a choice.

And now Michael's just taking out his credit card, when

GARY: Uh—let's split that, okay?

MICHAEL: It's fine, I got it.

Elliot gets in on this, whipping out *his* card.

ELLIOT: Okay, put the card down and reach for the sky—

MICHAEL (*as he sends the waiter off with his card*): Too late! Too little, too late!

ELLIOT: Oh, good—

INT. CHIC RESTAURANT—FOYER—NIGHT

They are parting for the evening. Michael moves over to Gary.

GARY: Well, thanks.

MICHAEL: Look . . .

He fumbles for something in his jacket pocket, finally producing two tickets.

MICHAEL: Courtside seats.

GARY: You didn't have to do that—

MICHAEL: C'mon, that was the deal!

Michael holds out the tickets, until, at last, Gary takes them.

GARY: Well, thanks. Again.

MICHAEL: So, have you given it any thought? What we were talking about?

GARY: What were we talking about?

Susannah moves from her conversation over to Gary and Michael.

MICHAEL: You know. The real estate thing.

SUSANNAH (*before Gary can speak*): What real estate thing?

INT. GARY'S BEDROOM—NIGHT

Susannah and Gary, getting ready for bed.

GARY: I never mentioned it because I knew how you'd feel about it.

He waits for some response from her. Silence.

GARY: I mean I don't know all the details but it's obviously— not something we would want to get involved in.

Again, he waits. Again, silence.

GARY: Look, if you think I'm *considering* it, forget it! Because I'm not. Considering it.

More silence.

GARY: Is that why you're angry? Because I never mentioned it?

SUSANNAH *(after a long beat):* I don't know why I'm angry.

GARY: Me neither. *(after another beat)* Do you realize how much that bottle of wine must have cost?

INT. DAA—ELLIOT'S OFFICE—DAY

Elliot works on a storyboard as Michael hovers over him, making suggestions.

MICHAEL: This is fine, this is just what we talked about . . .

ELLIOT: So you met Charles Barkley?

MICHAEL: Yeah, I met him, and I'm about to have a meeting with him . . .

Michael looks up to find Gary standing in the doorway.

MICHAEL: Hi—

GARY: Hi . . . Do you have a second?

MICHAEL: Sure—

Michael steps out to join him in the hallway. They move briskly; Michael—delighted to see Gary—has somewhere to go. . . .

MICHAEL: This is perfect timing—Charles Barkley's here! Come meet him—

GARY: I can't now, I'm not really here, I just wanted to get these tickets back to you—

Gary holds out the tickets to a surprised Michael.

MICHAEL: I don't want them. They're yours!

GARY: You don't understand. I can't use them—

Gary follows Michael into the kitchen area.

GARY: I've got all these lectures to prepare, and—

MICHAEL (*grabbing a drink from the fridge*): Okay, okay. Just meet him!

GARY: I don't want to meet him. Okay?

MICHAEL: Okay—

GARY: I'm nobody to him—

MICHAEL: Okay! Well, *I've* got to meet him, I've got a meeting with him . . .

And Michael's off again. Gary hesitates a moment, then follows.

GARY: It just makes me a little uncomfortable—

MICHAEL: What does?

GARY (*on the spot now*): Well, that—people admire him, and you're basically—you're going to exploit those emotions to sell a product.

Michael looks at Gary and decides not to get angry—yet.

MICHAEL: You don't even know what we're planning, it's going to be a very classy campaign—

GARY: Oh, right, and that justifies everything—

MICHAEL: Hey—I don't have to justify anything!

GARY: Yeah, well, maybe you do! Maybe that's why you're trying to drag me into that real estate crap!

MICHAEL: *What?*

GARY: Sure, there's safety in numbers, right? Maybe if all your friends are doing it too it won't seem so bad—

MICHAEL: What are you *talking* about?

GARY: Just tell me something: how many people are gonna be put out of *work* by that building?

MICHAEL: You're really—I don't believe this! *(on his way)* I'll see you, Gary . . .

GARY *(pursuing him):* I just can't believe you haven't considered the *consequences* of what you're doing—

MICHAEL *(cutting him off):* We'll talk later—

GARY: I mean *politically*!

MICHAEL: You have no idea—that building was *empty*! Okay? I mean, you are so far off—

GARY: Good. Fine. Tell yourself that . . .

MICHAEL: I don't believe this, I come to you, as a friend, trying to help—

GARY: Oh, right, and I'm supposed to let you help me—

Michael moves into his office area, where Catherine is at work. He turns to Gary, struggling to control his fury.

MICHAEL: I can't—I have work to do—

GARY: No, so you can *feel* better, right? I mean, that's the deal, right?

MICHAEL: What do you think . . . ? You think because you don't have money that you're *better* than me?

GARY: You're crazy!

MICHAEL: Is that what you think?

GARY: Just—leave me out of it, okay?

MICHAEL: Oh, believe me—I will! *(to Catherine)* Were there any calls?

CATHERINE: No—

Michael goes into his office and shuts the door.

GARY *(to the closed door):* Good! Thanks! Thanks a lot—

Gary, desperate to make a dignified exit, nearly collides with Catherine on his way out.

ACT FOUR

INT. MELISSA'S LOFT—DAY

Gary searches through Melissa's bookcase, Melissa tosses a salad for lunch.

GARY: I know you have it . . .

MELISSA: I don't think I do. You hungry?

GARY: You borrowed it. You were leafing through it, in my other apartment, the one where the stove exploded? And you said can I borrow this, I promise to return it.

MELISSA: I have no memory of this. I don't even *get* poetry . . .

GARY: Then why did you keep it so long?

MELISSA: Gary, I don't have it! You know, it's okay if you feel like seeing me. You don't have to pretend I kidnapped some book—

GARY *(finds it):* Ah-ha!!

MELISSA: That's it?? I've been wondering what that was.

Gary eagerly leafs through the book . . .

GARY: I knew you had it—oh thank God! All my lecture notes are in here—

MELISSA: That book's been there six years, I never knew what it was.

GARY: Wait, where are my notes . . . ? I had all these great, insightful *notes*—

MELISSA *(looking over his shoulder):* Well, here's something—what's that?

GARY: That's the address and phone number of this girl I was trying to get to sleep with me.

MELISSA *(pointing to a place in the book):* What's that . . . ?

GARY: That's—oh no. That's a list of all the reasons *why* she should sleep with me. My God, what was I doing? I wasn't even paying *attention.*

MELISSA *(trying to cheer him):* Well, you have her number now— call her up. Maybe *she* was taking notes.

GARY: You know what I haven't been doing? For so long?

He looks up at her and she just waits, for whatever he needs to say.

GARY: I haven't been paying attention.

He closes the book, and then holds it out to her.

GARY: You want this?

INT. STEADMAN HOUSE—DAY

Susannah stands in the doorway, holding the infamous humidifier, as Wendy, the sitter, lets her in.

SUSANNAH: Oh! You're the sitter!

WENDY: Yeah. Hi.

SUSANNAH: Oh good—so she's not here? I mean—

WENDY: She was going to take a bath . . . you want to just wait a second, I can check—

SUSANNAH: No! I just wanted to return this. Could I just leave it? I don't need to see her—

HOPE'S VOICE *(calling from upstairs):* Wendy? Is that somebody?

SUSANNAH *(to Wendy):* No—

INT. STEADMAN HOUSE—BATHROOM—DAY

Hope, wearing a robe, turns off the water in the tub. Susannah remains uneasily in the hallway, still clutching the humidifier.

HOPE: . . . Actually I was working on an article about that incinerator disaster. But then, my back was sort of killing me—

SUSANNAH: You really don't have to explain taking a *bath*—

HOPE: Well, I don't want you to think . . .

SUSANNAH: What?

HOPE: That I would hire a sitter just to, you know—take a bubble bath!

SUSANNAH: Well, why not? If you *can.*

HOPE *(defensive):* But I *can't.* Well, I mean, maybe I *can,* but I *don't.*

SUSANNAH: Okay, you don't. Look, I just wanted to return this. So, thanks a lot—

Hope opens the linen closet. Luxuriant terrycloth towels tumble out. Susannah helps pick them up.

HOPE: But I gave it to you! We have another one, we don't need it.

SUSANNAH: Well, we don't need it either!

A beat. Uh-oh . . .

HOPE *(tight):* Fine, give it to me—

SUSANNAH: It's not that I don't appreciate everything you've done—

HOPE: But stop doing it. Fine. I will!

Hope, bearing the humidifier, goes out of the bathroom and down the hall. Susannah follows.

SUSANNAH: Hope, wait a second—

HOPE: I was just doing what people do. For their friends. But I can stop—

Hope goes into the bedroom; she gathers up toys as Susannah remains edgily at the doorway . . .

SUSANNAH (*very nervous*): Well, but, you see, that brings up an interesting—because I'm not sure we *are.*

HOPE: We're not friends?

Susannah takes a deep breath—this is truly scary for her.

SUSANNAH: No, clearly we *are,* but, mostly in that we know a lot of the same people and therefore have to deal with each other. All the time. (*after a confused hesitation*) Here's my point—I'm an extremely independent person . . .

HOPE: Me too.

SUSANNAH: I have—my own way of doing things.

HOPE: Same here.

SUSANNAH: I really feel—I'm sorry, but I feel like you're looking down on me!

HOPE: I feel the same way!

SUSANNAH: And, consequently, I feel like—you feel the same *way?*

HOPE: Yes! Ever since I met you—like you think you're better than I am—

SUSANNAH: This is very ironic—

HOPE: It's absurd! I feel humiliated because you caught me taking a bath when I should be out—building affordable *housing* or something—

SUSANNAH: Why shouldn't you take a bath! I'd kill for a bath—we're always out of hot water—

HOPE: Oh shut up!

SUSANNAH *(stunned)*: Shut *up?*

HOPE: Well, you're always throwing it up to me about how *hard* you have it!

SUSANNAH: I *am?*

HOPE: Yes! You are! And it's not my *fault!*

SUSANNAH: Well, then stop *apologizing* for having money! Nobody's holding it against you!

HOPE: *You* are!

SUSANNAH: I *am?*

HOPE: Yes! You don't look me in the *eye,* you won't *call* me unless your baby's got *croup!*

SUSANNAH *(really loud)*: Well, maybe I'm *introverted!* Did that ever occur to you?! I'm *shy,* and you have—plenty of hot water and *two* humidifiers and *seven thousand* friends, you're *lucky!*

INT. STEADMAN BATHROOM—DAY

Susannah soaks dreamily in the tub. Hope enters the bathroom and hands Susannah a glass of wine.

SUSANNAH: You know why they had that argument, don't you? Michael and Gary? *(she takes a sip of wine)* Fear of smallness.

HOPE: Exactly.

SUSANNAH: That's the whole thing. That's why there are wars and the Empire State Building. And—NASA.

HOPE: Yeah. It explains a lot—

SUSANNAH: And the thing is—you can tell them it's just the right size, over and over. They never really believe you.

A silence, then:

HOPE *(mischievously)*: So it's just the right size . . . ?

Susannah grins, and splashes water in Hope's direction.

INT. GARY'S APARTMENT—KITCHEN—NIGHT

Gary reads his Emily Dickinson book. Tons of index cards are spread out on the table. He scribbles notes. Susannah cleans up the remains of dinner.

SUSANNAH: I found a day-care center I liked today.

GARY: You did, great!

SUSANNAH: It's really nice. Which is why there's no available space. We're on the waiting list.

GARY: That describes us, all right.

SUSANNAH (*after a hesitation*): Are you going to make up with Michael?

GARY: Make *up* with him?

SUSANNAH (*stronger*): I mean, tell him you're sorry.

GARY: Look, I said what I said as much for *you* as for me, I know how you feel about this kind of thing—

SUSANNAH: Why do you keep saying that? You don't know how I feel about it—*I* don't know how I feel about it! (*a beat, gently*) I think you're jealous.

GARY: Oh come on!

SUSANNAH (*overlapping*): I think you're jealous of your friend.

GARY: Come *on!* You'd feel comfortable, taking that money?

SUSANNAH: No—but I'll do it. I'm doing a lot of things I never thought I'd do.

Silence. Gary sits back down, attempts to get back to work, but . . .

GARY: I can't—I can't concentrate on Emily Dickinson! I have no idea what any of this *means!*

SUSANNAH: Why don't you just put it aside for now? Work on it later, we'll probably be up half the night anyway. Just— give yourself a break.

GARY (*after a beat, quietly*): I am jealous.

She gently touches his shoulder.

SUSANNAH: I know.

INT. GARY'S LIVING ROOM—NIGHT

The middle of the night. Gary sleeps on the couch, the Emily Dickinson book open on his chest. All at once he wakes, startled. There is a wildflower on his pillow. He sits up; a woman in a long white dress is standing at the window, sorting through a basket of wildflowers. She's Emily Dickinson.

GARY: Who are you?

EMILY: Nobody. Who are you?

GARY: Look, I'm in real trouble here. Will you please just— explain all this to me . . . ?

EMILY: Explain what?

GARY (*indicating poetry book*): This! All of this—I mean, you wrote it, you must understand it. God knows I don't, and I—I *have* to.

EMILY: Why?

GARY: Because! I have to be able—to explain it, to my class, I have to explain *myself,* to my friends!

EMILY: Why?

GARY: Why? *Why?* Because—if I can't explain what you wrote, then I'm not even—a teacher. And if I'm not even a *teacher,* then . . . I'm nobody.

EMILY: You? You seem so confident—

GARY: It's just an act. I feel like a total failure. Everyone I know is more successful than I am.

EMILY (*reciting by heart*): "Success is counted sweetest/By those who ne'er succeed./To comprehend a nectar/Requires sorest need." (*pointing to the book*) I wrote that—that's in the book!

GARY: Look, just—cut the crap, will you? Are you going to help me or not?

EMILY: I can't help you, I'm nobody.

GARY: Don't give me that!

EMILY: Also, I don't think I like you. You have a very poor attitude.

GARY (*stunned*): What?

EMILY: You have no sense of perspective! You've got that beautiful poem, right under your nose, and you're not even grateful.

Gary immediately begins to search feverishly through the book.

GARY: Which poem . . . ?

EMILY: Not *my* poem. Yours.

Gary suddenly comprehends something; he closes the book.

GARY: Emma.

He looks up. Emily Dickinson's gone.

INT. DAA—MICHAEL'S OFFICE—DAY

Catherine hands Michael a sheaf of papers to sign. Gary appears at the door.

GARY (*to Catherine*): Oh. Hi.

CATHERINE: Hi.

GARY (*to Michael*): Hi. Listen—

Gary stops short. He's never been in Michael's new office. Catherine exits. Michael waits for Gary to say something. Finally:

MICHAEL: Well?

GARY (*thrown*): Your office is really—big. It's really—

MICHAEL: Big.

GARY: Yeah. Listen, I'm—(*he's having trouble*) Boy, it's just so strange to see you behind that desk.

Michael's response is carefully neutral.

MICHAEL: Well, I'm sorry. This is my desk.

GARY: Right. Listen . . . (*and now it just comes out of him . . .*)

What are you *doing* there, how did all this *happen?* I'm sorry. I'll try to get to the point . . .

MICHAEL *(quite composed):* No, please. Take all the time you need.

GARY: Just—do me a favor, don't do that.

MICHAEL: Don't do what?

GARY: Be—*polite* like that, that's not—

MICHAEL: Look—

GARY: That's not us.

MICHAEL: You want to know what I'm doing here? Making a living. Making *money.*

GARY: I know, I know! It's just strange—

MICHAEL: It's not strange. It's money. You don't like that I have it? Well I'm sorry. I have it. I'm stuck with it.

Silence. Uncomfortably long. Then . . .

GARY: What I said, the other day? I shouldn't have said it. I should have just said—thank you. But, anyway. I've had a few hours sleep, and I had them—in a *row,* so I guess I was wondering . . . you know. If the offer still stands.

Michael is silent, not looking at him.

GARY: Well, c'mon. Say something.

MICHAEL: It's up to you. I'm still willing to do it.

GARY *(not easy to say)*: Thanks.

MICHAEL *(embarrassed)*: Well.

GARY: No, it's very generous.

MICHAEL: Well, I mean, I'd be getting something out of it. It would be like—having company.

GARY: As opposed to—

MICHAEL: Being all alone. *(beat)* So it's up to you. If you think you can handle it—

GARY: I just wouldn't want to do anything that could—

MICHAEL: Screw up our friendship?

GARY: Right. Like it already—

MICHAEL: Almost did?

Gary looks at his oldest friend, and he looks at the risk of losing him—and he makes a choice.

GARY: We better not do it. *(beat)* I'm sorry.

MICHAEL: Don't be sorry.

GARY: But I am.

MICHAEL: I know.

And for a moment there's nothing to say. Then . . .

GARY: I wish—

Michael looks at him.

GARY: I wish I could use those tickets, but—

MICHAEL: Next time. *(beat)* How's teaching?

GARY: It's good. I'm learning a lot.

Catherine appears in the doorway.

CATHERINE: I'm sorry, Barkley's publicist is here—

MICHAEL: Oh, no . . . *(to Gary)* I have to deal with this person.

GARY: Oh. Sure.

Michael starts to go, stops.

MICHAEL: Gary—don't leave yet, okay?

GARY: Okay.

Michael exits with Catherine. Gary glances around self-consciously. The phone rings, startling him. It won't stop ringing. He doesn't want to answer it. He answers it.

GARY: Uh, hello? No, he—he had to go meet someone.

He listens for a moment to the person on the other end, then:

GARY: Nobody. Just—a friend of his.

The person on the other end hangs up. Gary hangs up. And sits there, waiting for his friend.

List of Scripts and Directors

"Thirtysomething" was directed by Marshall Herskovitz.

"Therapy" was directed by Marshall Herskovitz.

"The Mike Van Dyke Show" was directed by Ron Lagomarsino.

"Michael Writes a Story" was directed by Tom Moore.

"Mr. Right" was directed by Scott Winant.

"Love and Sex" was directed by Marshall Herskovitz.

"Strangers" was directed by Peter O'Fallon.

"New Baby" was directed by Marshall Herskovitz.

"I'm Nobody! Who Are You?" was directed by Richard Kramer.